MW01065116

LLEWELLYN'S

2007 SUN SIGN BOOK

HOROSCOPES FOR EVERYONE!

Forecasts by
Kris Brandt Riske

Book Editing and Design: Ed Day
Cover Design: Kevin R. Brown

P.O. Box 64383 Dept. 0-7387-0326-5, St. Paul, MN 55164-0383
Astrological charts produced with Kepler software
by permission of Cosmic Patterns Software, Inc.

2006

JANUARY

S	M	T	W	T	F	S
1	2	3	4	5	6	7
8	9	10	11	12	13	14
15	16	17	18	19	20	21
22	23	24	25	26	27	28
29	30	31				

FEBRUARY

S	M	T	W	T	F	S
			1	2	3	4
5	6	7	8	9	10	11
12	13	14	15	16	17	18
19	20	21	22	23	24	25
26	27	28				

MARCH

S	M	T	W	T	F	S
			1	2	3	4
5	6	7	8	9	10	11
12	13	14	15	16	17	18
19	20	21	22	23	24	25
26	27	28	29	30	31	

APRIL

S	M	T	W	T	F	S
						1
2	3	4	5	6	7	8
9	10	11	12	13	14	15
16	17	18	19	20	21	22
23	24	25	26	27	28	29
30						

MAY

S	M	T	W	T	F	S
	1	2	3	4	5	6
7	8	9	10	11	12	13
14	15	16	17	18	19	20
21	22	23	24	25	26	27
28	29	30	31			

JUNE

S	M	T	W	T	F	S
				1	2	3
4	5	6	7	8	9	10
11	12	13	14	15	16	17
18	19	20	21	22	23	24
25	26	27	28	29	30	

JULY

S	M	T	W	T	F	S
						1
2	3	4	5	6	7	8
9	10	11	12	13	14	15
16	17	18	19	20	21	22
23	24	25	26	27	28	29
30	31					

AUGUST

S	M	T	W	T	F	S
		1	2	3	4	5
6	7	8	9	10	11	12
13	14	15	16	17	18	19
20	21	22	23	24	25	26
27	28	29	30	31		

SEPTEMBER

S	M	T	W	T	F	S
					1	2
3	4	5	6	7	8	9
10	11	12	13	14	15	16
17	18	19	20	21	22	23
24	25	26	27	28	29	30

OCTOBER

S	M	T	W	T	F	S
1	2	3	4	5	6	7
8	9	10	11	12	13	14
15	16	17	18	19	20	21
22	23	24	25	26	27	28
29	30	31				

NOVEMBER

S	M	T	W	T	F	S
			1	2	3	4
5	6	7	8	9	10	11
12	13	14	15	16	17	18
19	20	21	22	23	24	25
26	27	28	29	30		

DECEMBER

S	M	T	W	T	F	S
					1	2
3	4	5	6	7	8	9
10	11	12	13	14	15	16
17	18	19	20	21	22	23
24	25	26	27	28	29	30
31						

2007

JANUARY

S	M	T	W	T	F	S
	1	2	3	4	5	6
7	8	9	10	11	12	13
14	15	16	17	18	19	20
21	22	23	24	25	26	27
28	29	30	31			

FEBRUARY

S	M	T	W	T	F	S
				1	2	3
4	5	6	7	8	9	10
11	12	13	14	15	16	17
18	19	20	21	22	23	24
25	26	27	28			

MARCH

S	M	T	W	T	F	S
				1	2	3
4	5	6	7	8	9	10
11	12	13	14	15	16	17
18	19	20	21	22	23	24
25	26	27	28	29	30	31

APRIL

S	M	T	W	T	F	S
1	2	3	4	5	6	7
8	9	10	11	12	13	14
15	16	17	18	19	20	21
22	23	24	25	26	27	28
29	30					

MAY

S	M	T	W	T	F	S
		1	2	3	4	5
6	7	8	9	10	11	12
13	14	15	16	17	18	19
20	21	22	23	24	25	26
27	28	29	30	31		

JUNE

S	M	T	W	T	F	S
					1	2
3	4	5	6	7	8	9
10	11	12	13	14	15	16
17	18	19	20	21	22	23
24	25	26	27	28	29	30

JULY

S	M	T	W	T	F	S
1	2	3	4	5	6	7
8	9	10	11	12	13	14
15	16	17	18	19	20	21
22	23	24	25	26	27	28
29	30	31				

AUGUST

S	M	T	W	T	F	S
			1	2	3	4
5	6	7	8	9	10	11
12	13	14	15	16	17	18
19	20	21	22	23	24	25
26	27	28	29	30	31	

SEPTEMBER

S	M	T	W	T	F	S
						1
2	3	4	5	6	7	8
9	10	11	12	13	14	15
16	17	18	19	20	21	22
23	24	25	26	27	28	29
30						

OCTOBER

S	M	T	W	T	F	S
	1	2	3	4	5	6
7	8	9	10	11	12	13
14	15	16	17	18	19	20
21	22	23	24	25	26	27
28	29	30	31			

NOVEMBER

S	M	T	W	T	F	S
				1	2	3
4	5	6	7	8	9	10
11	12	13	14	15	16	17
18	19	20	21	22	23	24
25	26	27	28	29	30	

DECEMBER

S	M	T	W	T	F	S
						1
2	3	4	5	6	7	8
9	10	11	12	13	14	15
16	17	18	19	20	21	22
23	24	25	26	27	28	29
30	31					

2008

JANUARY

S	M	T	W	T	F	S
		1	2	3	4	5
6	7	8	9	10	11	12
13	14	15	16	17	18	19
20	21	22	23	24	25	26
27	28	29	30	31		

FEBRUARY

S	M	T	W	T	F	S
					1	2
3	4	5	6	7	8	9
10	11	12	13	14	15	16
17	18	19	20	21	22	23
24	25	26	27	28	29	

MARCH

S	M	T	W	T	F	S
						1
2	3	4	5	6	7	8
9	10	11	12	13	14	15
16	17	18	19	20	21	22
23	24	25	26	27	28	29
30	31					

APRIL

S	M	T	W	T	F	S
		1	2	3	4	5
6	7	8	9	10	11	12
13	14	15	16	17	18	19
20	21	22	23	24	25	26
27	28	29	30			

MAY

S	M	T	W	T	F	S
				1	2	3
4	5	6	7	8	9	10
11	12	13	14	15	16	17
18	19	20	21	22	23	24
25	26	27	28	29	30	31

JUNE

S	M	T	W	T	F	S
1	2	3	4	5	6	7
8	9	10	11	12	13	14
15	16	17	18	19	20	21
22	23	24	25	26	27	28
29	30					

JULY

S	M	T	W	T	F	S
		1	2	3	4	5
6	7	8	9	10	11	12
13	14	15	16	17	18	19
20	21	22	23	24	25	26
27	28	29	30	31		

AUGUST

S	M	T	W	T	F	S
					1	2
3	4	5	6	7	8	9
10	11	12	13	14	15	16
17	18	19	20	21	22	23
24	25	26	27	28	29	30
31						

SEPTEMBER

S	M	T	W	T	F	S
	1	2	3	4	5	6
7	8	9	10	11	12	13
14	15	16	17	18	19	20
21	22	23	24	25	26	27
28	29	30				

OCTOBER

S	M	T	W	T	F	S
			1	2	3	4
5	6	7	8	9	10	11
12	13	14	15	16	17	18
19	20	21	22	23	24	25
26	27	28	29	30	31	

NOVEMBER

S	M	T	W	T	F	S
						1
2	3	4	5	6	7	8
9	10	11	12	13	14	15
16	17	18	19	20	21	22
23	24	25	26	27	28	29
30						

DECEMBER

S	M	T	W	T	F	S
	1	2	3	4	5	6
7	8	9	10	11	12	13
14	15	16	17	18	19	20
21	22	23	24	25	26	27
28	29	30	31			

Table of Contents

2007 Sun Sign Articles

Meet Kris Brandt Riske

The horoscopes and sign descriptions for this book were written by Kris Brandt Riske, a professional astrologer certified by the American Federation of Astrologers with a master's degree in journalism. She is the author of *Mapping Your Future* and *Mapping Your Money*, and coauthor of *Mapping Your Travels and Relocation*. Her specialties are predictive astrology and astrometeorology (astrological weather forecasting), and she is the author of the 2007 weather forecasts for Llewellyn's *Moon Sign Book*. Kris also writes for other popular astrology publications and has been a speaker at various astrology conferences.

Outside of her professional life, Kris is an avid stock car racing fan, and enjoys gardening, reading, and her three black cats. She also is studying the Chinese language.

Kris believes astrology is a life tool, unmatched in its ability to help the individual map a successful course based on maximizing strengths and overcoming challenges. Astrology is an excellent route to deeper self-discovery and self-understanding, which can lead to positive personal change. Foreknowledge is power, and astrology can provide additional information about when to act, when to retreat, and when to maintain the status quo. In a fast-paced world, this information can define the difference between success and missed opportunities. Astrology, however, is not fateful. Rather, it provides another level of knowledge to use in decision-making. The planets do not predict the outcome of a situation. That is up to people and the choices they make. And lucky are those who have the additional "life ammo" provided by astrology!

New Concepts for Signs of the Zodiac

The signs of the zodiac represent characteristics and traits that indicate how energy operates within our lives. The signs tell the story of human evolution and development, and all are necessary to form the continuum of whole life experience. In fact, all twelve signs are represented within your astrological chart.

Although the traditional metaphors for the twelve signs (such as Aries, the Ram) are always functional, these alternative concepts for each of the twelve signs also describe the gradual unfolding of the human spirit.

Aries: The Initiator is the first sign of the zodiac and encompasses the primary concept of getting things started. This fiery ignition and bright beginning can prove to be the thrust necessary for new life, but the Initiator also can appear before a situation is ready for change and create disruption.

Taurus: The Maintainer sustains what Aries has begun and brings stability and focus into the picture, yet there also can be a tendency to try to maintain something in its current state without allowing for new growth.

Gemini: The Questioner seeks to determine whether alternatives are possible and offers diversity to the processes Taurus has brought into stability. Yet questioning can also lead to distraction, subsequently scattering energy and diffusing focus.

Cancer: The Nurturer provides the qualities necessary for growth and security, and encourages a deepening awareness of emotional needs. Yet this same nurturing can stifle individuation if it becomes too smothering.

Leo: The Loyalist directs and centralizes the experiences Cancer feeds. This quality is powerfully targeted toward self-awareness, but can be shortsighted. Hence, the Loyalist can hold steadfastly to viewpoints or feelings that inhibit new experiences.

Virgo: The Modifier analyzes the situations Leo brings to light and determines possibilities for change. Even though this change may be in the name of improvement, it can lead to dissatisfaction with the self if not directed in harmony with higher needs.

Libra: The Judge is constantly comparing everything to be sure that a certain level of rightness and perfection is presented. However, the Judge can also present possibilities that are harsh and seem to be cold or without feeling.

Scorpio: The Catalyst steps into the play of life to provide the quality of alchemical transformation. The Catalyst can stir the brew just enough to create a healing potion, or may get things going to such a powerful extent that they boil out of control.

Sagittarius: The Adventurer moves away from Scorpio's dimension to seek what lies beyond the horizon. The Adventurer continually looks for possibilities that answer the ultimate questions, but may forget the pathway back home.

Capricorn: The Pragmatist attempts to put everything into its rightful place and find ways to make life work out right. The Pragmatist can teach lessons of practicality and determination, but can become highly self-righteous when shortsighted.

Aquarius: The Reformer looks for ways to take what Capricorn has built and bring it up to date. Yet there is also a tendency to scrap the original in favor of a new plan that may not have the stable foundation necessary to operate effectively.

Pisces: The Visionary brings mysticism and imagination, and challenges the soul to move beyond the physical plane, into the realm of what might be. The Visionary can pierce the veil, returning enlightened to the physical world. The challenge is to avoid getting lost within the illusion of an alternate reality.

Understanding the Basics of Astrology

Astrology is an ancient and continually evolving system used to clarify your identity and your needs. An astrological chart—which is calculated using the date, time, and place of birth—contains many factors which symbolically represent the needs, expressions, and experiences that make up the whole person. A professional astrologer interprets this symbolic picture, offering you an accurate portrait of your personality.

The chart itself—the horoscope—is a portrait of an individual. Generally, a natal (or birth) horoscope is drawn on a circular wheel. The wheel is divided into twelve segments, called houses. Each of the twelve houses represents a different aspect of the individual, much like the facets of a brilliantly cut stone. The houses depict different environments, such as home, school, and work. The houses also represent roles and relationships: parents, friends, lovers, children, partners. In each environment, individuals show a different side of their personality. At home, you may represent yourself quite differently than you do on the job. Additionally, in each relationship you will project a different image of yourself. Your parents rarely see the side you show to intimate friends.

Symbols for the planets, the Sun, and the Moon are drawn inside the houses. Each planet represents a separate kind of energy. You experience and express that energy in specific ways. (For a complete list, refer to the table on the next page.) The way you use each of these energies is up to you. The planets in your chart do not make you do anything!

The twelve signs of the zodiac indicate characteristics and traits that further define your personality. Each sign can be expressed in positive and negative ways. (The basic meaning of each of the signs is explained in the corresponding sections ahead.) What's more, you have all twelve signs somewhere in your chart. Signs that are strongly emphasized by the planets have greater force. The Sun, Moon, and planets are placed on the chart according to their position at the time of birth. The qualities of a sign, combined with the

Signs of the Zodiac

Aries	♈	The Initiator
Taurus	♉	The Maintainer
Gemini	♊	The Questioner
Cancer	♋	The Nurturer
Leo	♌	The Loyalist
Virgo	♍	The Modifier
Libra	♎	The Judge
Scorpio	♏	The Catalyst
Sagittarius	♐	The Adventurer
Capricorn	♑	The Pragmatist
Aquarius	♒	The Reformer
Pisces	♓	The Visionary

energy of a planet, indicate how you might be most likely to use that energy and the best ways to develop that energy. The signs add color, emphasis, and dimension to the personality.

Signs are also placed at the cusps, or dividing lines, of each of the houses. The influence of the signs on the houses is much the same as their influence on the Sun, Moon, and planets. Each house is shaped by the sign on its cusp.

When you view a horoscope, you will notice that there appear to be four distinctive angles dividing the wheel of the chart. The line that divides the chart into a top and bottom half represents the horizon. In most cases, the left side of the horizon is called the Ascendant. The zodiac sign on the Ascendant is your rising sign. The Ascendant indicates the way others are likely to view you.

The Sun, Moon, or planet can be compared to an actor in a play. The sign shows how the energy works, like the role the actor plays in a drama. The house indicates where the energy operates, like the setting of a play. On a psychological level, the Sun represents who

The Planets

Sun	☉	The ego, self, willpower
Moon	☽	The subconscious self, habits
Mercury	☿	Communication, the intellect
Venus	♀	Emotional expression, love, appreciation, artistry
Mars	♂	Physical drive, assertiveness, anger
Jupiter	♃	Philosophy, ethics, generosity
Saturn	♄	Discipline, focus, responsibility
Uranus	♅	Individuality, rebelliousness
Neptune	♆	Imagination, sensitivity, compassion
Pluto	♇	Transformation, healing, regeneration

you think you are. The Ascendant describes who others think you are, and the Moon reflects your inner self.

Astrologers also study the geometric relationships between the Sun, Moon, and planets. These geometric angles are called aspects. Aspects further define the strengths, weaknesses, and challenges within your physical, mental, emotional, and spiritual self. Sometimes, patterns also appear in an astrological chart. These patterns have meaning.

To understand cycles for any given point in time, astrologers study several factors. Many use transits, which refer to the movement and positions of the planets. When astrologers compare those positions to the birth horoscope, the transits indicate activity in particular areas of the chart. The *Sun Sign Book* uses transits.

As you can see, your Sun sign is just one of many factors that describes who you are—but it is a powerful one! As the symbol of the ego, the Sun in your chart reflects your drive to be noticed. Most people can easily relate to the concepts associated with their Sun sign, since it is tied to their sense of personal identity.

Using this Book

This book contains what is called "Sun sign astrology," that is, astrology based on the sign that your Sun was in at the time of your birth. The technique has its foundation in ancient Greek astrology, in which the Sun was one of five points in the chart that was used as a focal point for delineation.

The most effective way to use astrology, however, is through one-on-one work with a professional astrologer, who can integrate the eight or so other astrological bodies into his or her interpretation to provide you with guidance. There are factors related to the year and time of day you were born that are highly significant in the way you approach life and vital to making wise choices. In addition, there are ways of using astrology that aren't addressed here, such as compatibility between two specific individuals, discovering family patterns, or picking a day for a wedding or grand opening.

To best use the information in the monthly forecasts, you'll want to determine your Ascendant, or rising sign. If you don't know your Ascendant, the tables following this description will help you determine your rising sign. They are most accurate for those born in the continental United States. They're only an approximation, but they can be used as a good rule of thumb. Your exact Ascendant may vary from the tables according to your time and place of birth. Once you've approximated your ascending sign using the tables or determined your Ascendant by having your chart calculated, you'll know two significant factors in your chart. Read the monthly forecast sections for both your Sun and Ascendant to gain the most useful information. In addition, you can read the section about the sign your Moon is in. The Sun is the true, inner you; the Ascendant is your shell or appearance and the person you are becoming; the Moon is the person you were—or still are—based on habits and memories.

I've also included information about the planets' retrogrades this year. Most people have heard of "Mercury retrograde." In fact, all the planets except the Sun and Moon appear to travel backward (retrograde) in their path periodically. This only appears to happen because we on the Earth are not seeing the other planets from the middle of the solar system. Rather, we are watching them from our own moving object. We are like a train that moves past cars on the freeway that are going at a slower speed. To us on the train, the cars look like they're going backward. Mercury turns retrograde about every four months for three weeks; Venus every eighteen months for six weeks; Mars every two years for two to three months. The rest of the planets each retrograde once a year for four to five months. During each retrograde, we have the opportunity to try something new, something we conceived of at the beginning of the planet's yearly cycle. The times when the planets change direction are significant, as are the beginning and midpoint (peak or culmination) of each cycle. These are noted in your forecast each month.

Your "Rewarding and Challenging Days" sections indicate times when you'll feel either more centered or more out of balance. The rewarding days are not the only times you can perform well, but the times you're likely to feel better integrated! During challenging days, take extra time to center yourself by meditating or using other techniques that help you feel more objective.

The Action Table found at the end of each sign's section offers general guidelines for the best time to take a particular action. Please note, however, that your whole chart will provide more accurate guidelines for the best time to do something. Therefore, use this table with a grain of salt, and never let it stop you from taking an action you feel compelled to take.

You can use this information for an objective awareness about the way the current cycles are affecting you. Realize that the power of astrology is even more useful when you have a complete chart and professional guidance.

2007 at a Glance

Life, people, and the universe are ever-changing, a part of the perpetual evolution reflected in—not caused by—the shifting patterns and placements of the planets.

Some years are relatively easygoing, with only minor ripples affecting daily life. Others can bring one major event after another for individuals and the world. Much of this is due to the slower moving planets—Jupiter, Saturn, Uranus, Neptune, and Pluto. Two faster moving planets—Venus and Mars—are another factor. In 2007, both are retrograde part of the year.

Venus, the universal planet of love and money is retrograde, July 27-September 8, so you can expect fewer social opportunities and possibly financial mix-ups. If possible, avoid major purchases and significant money matters. However, watch for steep discounts on luxury items, especially clothing and jewelry. Romances often cool when Venus is retrograde, making it a poor time for weddings.

With Mars, a high energy planet, retrograde from November 15 to January 30, 2008, action slows, which can cause frustration as a "wait-and-see" attitude may prevail. Indecision becomes the norm, and progress at times nearly nonexistent. Because fiery Mars will turn retrograde in emotional, watery Cancer, people will be unusually sensitive. This period is also unfavorable for making major financial deals.

This year's big planetary picture features Saturn-Neptune and Saturn-Pluto alignments, with Jupiter involved in both plus a separate contact with Uranus.

Saturn and Neptune are diverse energies, so blending the two is a challenge. Saturn is practical and tangible, where Neptune is mystical and elusive. Because this alignment is an opposition (180 degrees apart), people, personalities, and relationships will be involved in some way. Saturn can strip away the "romantic" veil of Neptune, resulting in disillusionment, but Neptune can soften Saturn's nuts-and-bolts approach to form a firm foundation on which to build realistic dreams. On an everyday level, the combined energies can result in creative, yet useful, ideas, plans, and products.

With powerful Pluto, serious Saturn forms a beneficial 120-degree angle that can provide the determination and resolve to successfully blend the energies of Saturn and Neptune. This transformation may or may not be easy, but the final outcome will be a new reality on which to build the future—personally and universally.

Jupiter in an action angle (90 degrees) with Uranus promotes change, freedom, and opportunity. But the potential downside is change for the sake of change, when Saturn and Pluto are more geared to slow and lasting evolution. Yet Jupiter also brings an element of hope and optimism that can empower people and the world-at-large to take those bold steps into the future.

Ascendant Table

	Your Time of Birth					
Your Sun Sign	**6–8 am**	**8–10 am**	**10 am–Noon**	**Noon–2 pm**	**2–4 pm**	**4–6 pm**
Aries	Taurus	Gemini	Cancer	Leo	Virgo	Libra
Taurus	Gemini	Cancer	Leo	Virgo	Libra	Scorpio
Gemini	Cancer	Leo	Virgo	Libra	Scorpio	Sagittarius
Cancer	Leo	Virgo	Libra	Scorpio	Sagittarius	Capricorn
Leo	Virgo	Libra	Scorpio	Sagittarius	Capricorn	Aquarius
Virgo	Libra	Scorpio	Sagittarius	Capricorn	Aquarius	Pisces
Libra	Scorpio	Sagittarius	Capricorn	Aquarius	Pisces	Aries
Scorpio	Sagittarius	Capricorn	Aquarius	Pisces	Aries	Taurus
Sagittarius	Capricorn	Aquarius	Pisces	Aries	Taurus	Gemini
Capricorn	Aquarius	Pisces	Aries	Taurus	Gemini	Cancer
Aquarius	Pisces	Aries	Taurus	Gemini	Cancer	Leo
Pisces	Aries	Taurus	Gemini	Cancer	Leo	Virgo

	Your Time of Birth					
Your Sun Sign	**6–8 pm**	**8–10 pm**	**10 pm–Midnight**	**Midnight–2 am**	**2–4 am**	**4–6 am**
Aries	Scorpio	Sagittarius	Capricorn	Aquarius	Pisces	Aries
Taurus	Sagittarius	Capricorn	Aquarius	Pisces	Aries	Taurus
Gemini	Capricorn	Aquarius	Pisces	Aries	Taurus	Gemini
Cancer	Aquarius	Pisces	Aries	Taurus	Gemini	Cancer
Leo	Pisces	Aries	Taurus	Gemini	Cancer	Leo
Virgo	Aries	Taurus	Gemini	Cancer	Leo	Virgo
Libra	Taurus	Gemini	Cancer	Leo	Virgo	Libra
Scorpio	Gemini	Cancer	Leo	Virgo	Libra	Scorpio
Sagittarius	Cancer	Leo	Virgo	Libra	Scorpio	Sagittarius
Capricorn	Leo	Virgo	Libra	Scorpio	Sagittarius	Capricorn
Aquarius	Virgo	Libra	Scorpio	Sagittarius	Capricorn	Aquarius
Pisces	Libra	Scorpio	Sagittarius	Capricorn	Aquarius	Pisces

How to use this table:

1. Find your Sun sign in the left column.
2. Find your approximate birth time in a vertical column.
3. Line up your Sun sign and birth time to find your Ascendant.

This table will give you an approximation of your Ascendant. If you feel that the sign listed as your Ascendant is incorrect, try the one either before or after the listed sign. It is difficult to determine your exact Ascendant without a complete natal chart.

Astrological Glossary

Air: One of the four basic elements. The air signs are Gemini, Libra, and Aquarius.

Angles: The four points of the chart that divide it into quadrants. The angles are sensitive areas that lend emphasis to planets located near them. These points are located on the cusps of the First, Fourth, Seventh, and Tenth Houses in a chart.

Ascendant: Rising sign. The degree of the zodiac on the eastern horizon at the time and place for which the horoscope is calculated. It can indicate the image or physical appearance you project to the world. The cusp of the First House.

Aspect: The angular relationship between planets, sensitive points, or house cusps in a horoscope. Lines drawn between the two points and the center of the chart, representing the Earth, form the angle of the aspect. Astrological aspects include conjunction (two points that are 0 degrees apart), opposition (two points, 180 degrees apart), square (two points, 90 degrees apart), sextile (two points, 60 degrees apart), and trine (two points, 120 degrees apart). Aspects can indicate harmony or challenge.

Cardinal Sign: One of the three qualities, or categories, that describe how a sign expresses itself. Aries, Cancer, Libra, and Capricorn are the cardinal signs, believed to initiate activity.

Chiron: Chiron is a comet traveling in orbit between Saturn and Uranus. Although research on its effect on natal charts is not yet complete, it is believed to represent a key or doorway, healing, ecology, and a bridge between traditional and modern methods.

Conjunction: An aspect or angle between two points in a chart where the two points are close enough so that the energies join. Can be considered either harmonious or challenging, depending on the planets involved and their placement.

Cusp: A dividing line between signs or houses in a chart.

Degree: Degree of arc. One of 360 divisions of a circle. The circle of the zodiac is divided into twelve astrological signs of 30 degrees each. Each degree is made up of 60 minutes, and each minute is made up of 60 seconds of zodiacal longitude.

Earth: One of the four basic elements. The earth signs are Taurus, Virgo, and Capricorn.

Eclipse: A solar eclipse is the full or partial covering of the Sun by the Moon (as viewed from Earth), and a lunar eclipse is the full or partial covering of the Moon by the Earth's own shadow.

Ecliptic: The Sun's apparent path around the Earth, which is actually the plane of the Earth's orbit extended out into space. The ecliptic forms the center of the zodiac.

Electional Astrology: A branch of astrology concerned with choosing the best time to initiate an activity.

Elements: The signs of the zodiac are divided into four groups of three zodiacal signs, each symbolized by one of the four elements of the ancients: fire, earth, air, and water. The element of a sign is said to express its essential nature.

Ephemeris: A listing of the Sun, Moon, and planets' positions and related information for astrological purposes.

Equinox: Equal night. The point in the Earth's orbit around the Sun at which the day and night are equal in length.

Feminine Signs: Each zodiac sign is either masculine or feminine. Earth signs (Taurus, Virgo, and Capricorn) and water signs (Cancer, Scorpio, and Pisces) are feminine.

Fire: One of the four basic elements. The fire signs are Aries, Leo, and Sagittarius.

Fixed Signs: Fixed is one of the three qualities, or categories, that describe how a sign expresses itself. The fixed signs are Taurus, Leo, Scorpio, and Aquarius. Fixed signs are said to be predisposed to existing patterns and somewhat resistant to change.

Hard Aspects: Hard aspects are those aspects in a chart that astrologers believe to represent difficulty or challenges. Among the hard aspects are the square, the opposition, and the conjunction (depending on which planets are conjunct).

Horizon: The word "horizon" is used in astrology in a manner similar to its common usage, except that only the eastern and western horizons are considered useful. The eastern horizon at the point of birth is the Ascendant, or First House cusp, of a natal chart, and the western horizon at the point of birth is the Descendant, or Seventh House cusp.

Houses: Division of the horoscope into twelve segments, beginning with the Ascendant. The dividing line between the houses are called house cusps. Each house corresponds to certain aspects of daily living, and is ruled by the astrological sign that governs the cusp, or dividing line between the house and the one previous.

Ingress: The point of entry of a planet into a sign.

Lagna: A term used in Hindu or Vedic astrology for Ascendant, the degree of the zodiac on the eastern horizon at the time of birth.

Masculine Signs: Each of the twelve signs of the zodiac is either "masculine" or "feminine." The fire signs (Aries, Leo, and Sagittarius) and the air signs (Gemini, Libra, and Aquarius) are masculine.

Midheaven: The highest point on the ecliptic, where it intersects the meridian that passes directly above the place for which the horoscope is cast; the southern point of the horoscope.

Midpoint: A point equally distant to two planets or house cusps. Midpoints are considered by some astrologers to be sensitive points in a person's chart.

Mundane Astrology: Mundane astrology is the branch of astrology generally concerned with political and economic events, and the nations involved in these events.

Mutable Signs: Mutable is one of the three qualities, or categories, that describe how a sign expresses itself. Mutable signs are Gemini, Virgo, Sagittarius, and Pisces. Mutable signs are said to be very adaptable and sometimes changeable.

Natal Chart: A person's birth chart. A natal chart is essentially a "snapshot" showing the placement of each of the planets at the exact time of a person's birth.

Node: The point where the planets cross the ecliptic, or the Earth's apparent path around the Sun. The North Node is the point where a planet moves northward, from the Earth's perspective, as it crosses the ecliptic; the South Node is where it moves south.

Opposition: Two points in a chart that are 180 degrees apart.

Orb: A small degree of margin used when calculating aspects in a chart. For example, although 180 degrees form an exact opposition, an astrologer might consider an aspect within 3 or 4 degrees on either side of 180 degrees to be an opposition, as the impact of the aspect can still be felt within this range. The less orb on an aspect, the stronger the aspect. Astrologers' opinions vary on how many degrees of orb to allow for each aspect.

Outer Planets: Uranus, Neptune, and Pluto are known as the outer planets. Because of their distance from the Sun, they take a long time to complete a single rotation. Everyone born within a few years on either side of a given date will have similar placements of these planets.

Planets: The planets used in astrology are Mercury, Venus, Mars, Jupiter, Saturn, Uranus, Neptune, and Pluto. For astrological purposes, the Sun and Moon are also considered planets. A natal or birth chart lists planetary placement at the moment of birth.

Planetary Rulership: The sign in which a planet is most harmoniously placed. Examples are the Sun in Leo, Jupiter in Sagittarius, and the Moon in Cancer.

Precession of Equinoxes: The gradual movement of the point of the Spring Equinox, located at 0 degrees Aries. This point marks the beginning of the tropical zodiac. The point moves slowly backward through the constellations of the zodiac, so that about every 2,000 years the equinox begins in an earlier constellation.

Qualities: In addition to categorizing the signs by element, astrologers place the twelve signs of the zodiac into three additional categories, or qualities: cardinal, mutable, or fixed. Each sign is considered to be a combination of its element and quality. Where the element of a sign describes its basic nature, the quality describes its mode of expression.

Retrograde Motion: Apparent backward motion of a planet. This is an illusion caused by the relative motion of the Earth and other planets in their elliptical orbits.

Sextile: Two points in a chart that are 60 degrees apart.

Sidereal Zodiac: Generally used by Hindu or Vedic astrologers. The sidereal zodiac is located where the constellations are actually positioned in the sky.

Soft Aspects: Soft aspects indicate good fortune or an easy relationship in the chart. Among the soft aspects are the trine, the sextile, and the conjunction (depending on which planets are conjunct each other).

Square: Two points in a chart that are 90 degrees apart.

Sun Sign: The sign of the zodiac in which the Sun is located at any given time.

Synodic Cycle: The time between conjunctions of two planets.

Trine: Two points in a chart that are 120 degrees apart.

Tropical Zodiac: The tropical zodiac begins at 0 degrees Aries, where the Sun is located during the Spring Equinox. This system is used by most Western astrologers and throughout this book.

Void-of-Course: A planet is void-of-course after it has made its last aspect within a sign, but before it has entered a new sign.

Water: One of the four basic elements. Water signs are Cancer, Scorpio, and Pisces.

Meanings of the Planets

The Sun

The Sun indicates the psychological bias that will dominate your actions. What you see, and why, is told in the reading for your Sun. The Sun also shows the basic energy patterns of your body and psyche. In many ways, the Sun is the dominant force in your horoscope and your life. Other influences, especially that of the Moon, may modify the Sun's influence, but nothing will cause you to depart very far from the basic solar pattern. Always keep in mind the basic influence of the Sun and remember all other influences must be interpreted in terms of it, especially insofar as they play a visible role in your life. You may think, dream, imagine, and hope a thousand things, according to your Moon and your other planets, but the Sun is what you are. To be your best self in terms of your Sun is to cause your energies to work along the path in which they will have maximum help from planetary vibrations.

The Moon

The Moon tells the desire of your life. When you know what you mean but can't verbalize it, it is your Moon that knows it and your Sun that can't say it. The wordless ecstasy, the mute sorrow, the secret dream, the esoteric picture of yourself that you can't get across to the world, or that the world doesn't comprehend or value—these are the products of the Moon. When you are misunderstood, it is your Moon nature, expressed imperfectly through the Sun sign, that feels betrayed. Things you know without thought—intuitions, hunches, instincts—are the products of the Moon. Modes of expression that you feel truly reflect your deepest self belong to the Moon: art, letters, creative work of any kind; sometimes love; sometimes business. Whatever you feel to be most deeply yourself is the product of your Moon and of the sign your Moon occupies at birth.

Mercury

Mercury is the sensory antenna of your horoscope. Its position by sign indicates your reactions to sights, sounds, odors, tastes, and touch impressions, affording a key to the attitude you have toward the physical world around you. Mercury is the messenger through which your physical body and brain (ruled by the Sun) and your inner nature (ruled by the Moon) are kept in contact with the outer world, which will appear to you according to the index of Mercury's position by sign in the horoscope. Mercury rules your rational mind.

Venus

Venus is the emotional antenna of your horoscope. Through Venus, impressions come to you from the outer world, to which you react emotionally. The position of Venus by sign at the time of your birth determines your attitude toward these experiences. As Mercury is the messenger linking sense impressions (sight, smell, etc.) to the basic nature of your Sun and Moon, so Venus is the messenger linking emotional impressions. If Venus is found in the same sign as the Sun, emotions gain importance in your life, and have a direct bearing on your actions. If Venus is in the same sign as the Moon, emotions bear directly on your inner nature, add self-confidence, make you sensitive to emotional impressions, and frequently indicate that you have more love in your heart than you are able to express. If Venus is in the same sign as Mercury, emotional impressions and sense impressions work together; you tend to idealize the world of the senses and sensualize the world of the emotions to interpret emotionally what you see and hear.

Mars

Mars is the energy principle in the horoscope. Its position indicates the channels into which energy will most easily be directed. It is the planet through which the activities of the Sun and the desires of the Moon express themselves in action. In the same sign as the Sun, Mars gives abundant energy, sometimes misdirected in temper, temperament, and quarrels. In the same sign as the Moon, it gives a great capacity to make use of the innermost aims, and to make the inner desires articulate and practical. In the same sign as Venus, it quickens emotional reactions and causes you to act on them, makes for ardor and passion in love, and fosters an earthly awareness of emotional realities.

Jupiter

Jupiter is the feeler for opportunity that you have out in the world. It passes along chances of a lifetime for consideration according to the basic nature of your Sun and Moon. Jupiter's sign position indicates the places where you will look for opportunity, the uses to which you wish to put it, and the capacity you have to react and profit by it. Jupiter is ordinarily, and erroneously, called the planet of luck. It is "luck" insofar as it is the index of opportunity, but your luck depends less on what comes to you than on what you do with what comes to you. In the same sign as the Sun or Moon, Jupiter gives a direct, and generally effective, response to opportunity and is likely to show forth at its "luckiest." If Jupiter is in the same sign as Mercury, sense impressions are interpreted opportunistically. If Jupiter is in the same sign as Venus, you interpret emotions in such a way as to turn them to your advantage; your feelings work harmoniously with the chances for progress that the world has to offer. If Jupiter is in the same sign as Mars, you follow opportunity with energy, dash, enthusiasm, and courage; take long chances; and play your cards wide open.

Saturn

Saturn indicates the direction that will be taken in life by the self-preservation principle that, in its highest manifestation, ceases to be purely defensive and becomes ambitious and aspiring. Your defense or attack against the world is shown by the sign position of Saturn in the horoscope of birth. If Saturn is in the same sign as the Sun or Moon, defense predominates, and there is danger of introversion. The farther Saturn is from the Sun, Moon, and Ascendant, the better for objectivity and extroversion. If Saturn is in the same sign as Mercury, there is a profound and serious reaction to sense impressions; this position generally accompanies a deep and efficient mind. If Saturn is in the same sign as Venus, a defensive attitude toward emotional experience makes for apparent coolness in love and difficulty with the emotions and human relations. If Saturn is in the same sign as Mars, confusion between defensive and aggressive urges can make an indecisive person—or, if the Sun and Moon are strong and the total personality well developed, a balanced, peaceful, and calm individual of sober judgment and moderate actions may be indicated. If Saturn is in the same sign as Jupiter, the reaction to opportunity is sober and balanced.

Uranus

Uranus in a general way relates to creativity, originality, or individuality, and its position by sign in the horoscope tells the direction in which you will seek to express yourself. In the same sign as Mercury or the Moon, Uranus suggests acute awareness, a quick reaction to sense impressions and experiences, or a hair-trigger mind. In the same sign as the Sun, it points to great nervous activity, a high-strung nature, and an original, creative, or eccentric personality. In the same sign as Mars, Uranus indicates high-speed activity, love of swift motion, and perhaps love of danger. In the same sign as Venus, it suggests an unusual reaction to emotional experience, idealism, sensuality, and original ideas about love and human relations. In the same sign as Saturn, Uranus points to good sense; this can be a practical, creative position, but, more often than not, it sets up a destructive conflict between practicality and originality that can result in a stalemate. In the same sign as Jupiter, Uranus makes opportunity, creates wealth and the means of getting it, and is conducive to the inventive, executive, and daring.

Neptune

Neptune relates to the deepest wells of the subconscious, inherited mentality, and spirituality, indicating what you take for granted in life. Neptune in the same sign as the Sun or Moon indicates that intuitions and hunches—or delusions—dominate; there is a need for rigidly holding to reality. In the same sign as Mercury, Neptune indicates sharp sensory perceptions, a sensitive and perhaps creative mind, and a quivering intensity of reaction to sensory experience. In the same sign as Venus, it reveals idealistic and romantic (or sentimental) reaction to emotional experience, as well as the danger of sensationalism and a love of strange pleasures. In the same sign as Mars, Neptune indicates energy and intuition that work together to make mastery of life—one of the signs of having angels (or devils) on your side. In the same sign as Jupiter, Neptune describes intuitive response to opportunity generally along practical and money-making lines; one of the signs of security if not indeed of wealth. In the same sign as Saturn, Neptune indicates intuitive defense and attack on the world, generally successful unless Saturn is polarized on the negative side; then there is danger of unhappiness.

Pluto

Pluto is a planet of extremes—from the lowest criminal and violent level of our society to the heights people can attain when they realize their significance in the collectivity of humanity. Pluto also rules three important mysteries of life—sex, death, and rebirth—and links them to each other. One level of death symbolized by Pluto is the physical death of an individual, which occurs so that a person can be reborn into another body to further his or her spiritual development. On another level, individuals can experience a "death" of their old self when they realize the deeper significance of life; thus they become one of the "second born." In a natal horoscope, Pluto signifies our perspective on the world, our conscious and subconscious. Since so many of Pluto's qualities are centered on the deeper mysteries of life, the house position of Pluto, and aspects to it, can show you how to attain a deeper understanding of the importance of the spiritual in your life.

2007 SUN SIGN BOOK

Forecasts

By Kris Brandt Riske

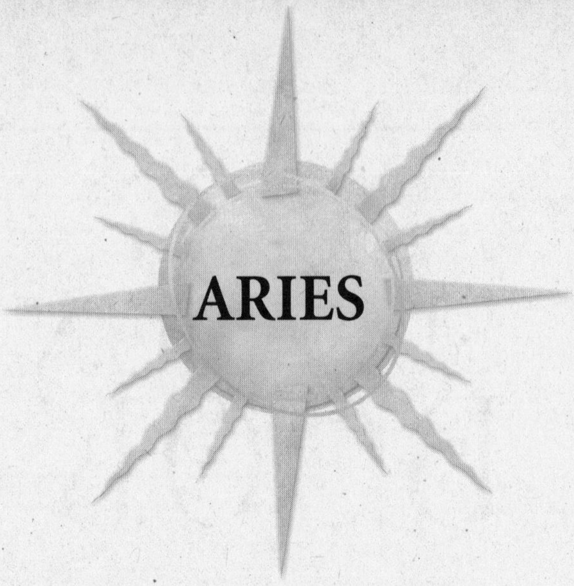

The Ram
March 19 to April 21

♈

Element:	Fire
Quality:	Cardinal
Polarity:	Yang/Masculine
Planetary Ruler:	Mars
Meditation:	I build upon my strengths
Gemstone:	Diamond
Power Stones:	Bloodstone, carnelian, ruby
Key Phrase:	I am
Glyph:	Ram's head
Anatomy:	Head, face, throat
Color:	Red, white
Animal:	Ram
Myths/Legends:	Artemis, Jason and the Golden Fleece
House:	First
Opposite Sign:	Libra
Flower:	Geranium
Key Word:	Initiative

Your Ego's Strengths and Weaknesses

Aries is the first sign of the zodiac, so it's no surprise you're a leader and a pioneer who meets every challenge with a can-do attitude. Like spring, the season of Aries, your aura is fresh and new—at times almost naive. That's not to say you're inexperienced or unsophisticated. Far from it. Rather, you are bold and daring, embracing new experiences with little thought given to limitations. To you, each day is an undiscovered opportunity to conquer new territory. Beginnings are fun; endings are boring.

Mars, your ruling planet, inspires you to go above and beyond, to excel at every activity that catches your interest. The red planet also reinforces the fiery energy of your sign, which thrives in a high-paced atmosphere.

You prefer to operate on your own, prizing individual accomplishment above all else. Where others pause and reflect, you leap over obstacles with enthusiasm and rarely look back. All this persistence and drive can benefit you in certain situations, but result in setbacks in others. Learn to look into the future to consider potential consequences before your need for excitement prompts quick action and decisions. Doing so saves you time and effort while helping build your reputation as a pacesetter, one who rejects impulsiveness in favor of dynamic action. Then your rapid response becomes a major asset that identifies you as a mover and shaker.

When a job needs to be done, you're usually the first to volunteer, and others depend upon you to get things moving fast and furiously. Few can match your talent as the spark plug of the universe, the one who makes things happen. Yet these admirable traits can cross the line into an aggressive, headstrong attitude that can defeat exactly what you're trying to accomplish. Go easy on people. A softer approach—assertive, yet caring and kind—can get you much farther in the long run. People skills are all-important, and carefully chosen words help build strong, supportive relationships.

Shining Your Love Light

Playful and romantic, you approach love with the same energetic enthusiasm that distinguishes your life, and instinctively know how to add the zest that keeps a relationship fresh, alive, and fun. Your affectionate nature eagerly embraces each new heartthrob that comes your way. But your eagerness and impatience could overwhelm a potential mate, so try to let love evolve at its own pace.

The freedom to be yourself is a key component in a long-lasting relationship. Intellectual rapport is another. When you find a partner who fulfills these needs, togetherness takes on a whole new meaning; you feel complete as never before.

You have an instant rapport with the fire signs—Leo, Sagittarius, or another Aries—and your interests parallel one other. Love and passion can sizzle with another Aries, although competitive urges can have you at odds. Leo may require more attention on a daily basis than your independent nature is willing to give, and you might discover that Sagittarius is too free-spirited even for your tastes.

Taurus may be too slow for you, but this sensual sign will delight you in other ways, and changeable, flirtatious Gemini will amuse and enchant you. Cancer's nurturing qualities soothe and calm you even though this sign's emotional and security needs are far different from your own. Practical Virgo will help you keep your feet on the ground, but may be too analytical and detail-oriented.

Your opposite sign, Libra, can be an ideal mate because you complement and learn from each other. Smoldering Scorpio's energy might be too intense, although you could experience the ultimate passion. Capricorn shares your ambitious desire for success, but love can be a challenge when you both want to be in charge. An Aquarius mate is both friend and lover, and this free spirit appreciates your need for independence. With Pisces you have a deeper, spiritual connection, although this ultrasensitive sign also requires a softer, more tender approach.

Making Your Place in the World

Your desire to be first fuels your ambitions and you're motivated to make your mark in the world. That's a snap as long as your work life includes plenty of activity, mental or physical, and the chance to let your initiative shine. A mundane eight-to-five job is not for you.

A hard worker once committed and in the right environment, you give your job your all. Although you prefer a series of quick projects, you also can dig in and devote your energy to a major undertaking—if for no other reason than because you love a challenge. But once your interest in a job begins to wane, you turn to the classifieds in search of a new quest. Do that too often and it could undermine your rise to the top. A more effective approach is to set short- and long-term goals and embrace the concept of a slower, but steadier, climb.

You could find success in the military, or as a firefighter or police officer. If the health care field appeals to you, consider surgery, acupuncture, emergency medicine, or dentistry. You could excel as a hair stylist, sculptor, welder, mason, or metalworker. In the business world, you might become a world-class entrepreneur or rise to the upper echelons of corporate life.

Whatever your career direction, be sure it offers opportunities for advancement and avenues for independent thought and action.

Putting Your Best Foot Forward

Is it new? Is it exciting? Is it an adventure? Answer yes to these three questions and you're in your element and at your finest, making the most of your energetic personality. Daily life, however, rarely meets these expectations. And therein lies your challenge.

You're a starter, not a finisher, and find follow-through less than stimulating. To your credit, you have a knack for leadership and gravitate toward situations where you can fulfill these roles. But you'll be expected to fall in step and see tasks through to completion—at least until you reach your career pinnacle. You can successfully meet this challenge by treating it as just that: another stimulating challenge that motivates you to put your best foot forward.

You're also the person that others look to, to find a way around stumbling blocks, a task at which you excel. But when faced with a single-minded mission, it's all too easy to push others as hard as you push yourself and forget the tactful words that help build supportive relationships. This challenge also has a simple solution: tune in and be aware of how your actions and words affect others.

Complement diplomacy with listening. It's to your advantage to open your mind and ears to other thoughts, ideas, and opinions because brainstorming helps you fine-tune your own thinking. So rather than view others as competition, see them as partners who can bring out the best in you. Listening is also a terrific way to satisfy your curiosity and pick up bits and pieces of information that will come in handy in the future.

Self-knowledge, one of your life quests, is a powerful force. When you learn more about yourself, you learn more about people and how the universe ebbs and flows in the perpetual cycle of action and reaction.

Tools for Change

Your energetic dash through life offers little time for contemplation and getting in touch with your inner voice. By opening yourself up to the unseen self within, you will discover another of yourself.

On a practical level, intuition can give you the edge in daily life and help you stay a step ahead of the competition. You'll also become more aware of the world around you, the people within it, and the subtle nuances that color events and decisions.

This is almost as easily said as done. You can learn the basics in a class or achieve the same result on your own through meditation. That doesn't mean you have to sit still! There are many forms of meditation, including walking meditation, which has the dual benefit of exercise. Yoga simultaneously calms your mind and strengthens your body. Once you nudge your inner voice into wakefulness, listen to it. The more you do, the stronger it will become.

On another level, accept the challenge to take on more responsibility in your professional life. Although the rewards might be slow in coming, come they will. And like your intuition, the more you expand our area of influence, the more satisfying it will become. The same is true of the many relationships in your life, both personal and professional.

Make it a priority to balance your career and family lives—for your benefit and theirs. Share yourself with those you love, recognizing that creating an emotional connection is a time-consuming endeavor. That's tough with a busy lifestyle, but doable if you set your mind to it. One way is to establish a fixed weekly time for a family activity or talk to catch up on each other's lives. It won't be long before you see the results: closer ties and more openness.

Be bold! Be brave! Be strong!

Affirmation for the Year

I embrace new opportunities for growth.

The Year Ahead for Aries

You're primed for major successes in 2007, which brings the culmination of an upward trend that began a few years ago. Many of your wishes and all you've been striving for can come true as the planets harmoniously align with your sign.

Heading the list of beneficial influences is expansive Jupiter in Sagittarius, your solar Ninth House of travel and education. This fortunate planet encourages you to experience more of the wider world in order to fulfill your quest for knowledge, adventure, and wisdom. On a practical level, what you learn now can pay off in career gains next year. People you meet and network with while traveling on business can also boost your career potential, so be sure to follow up and stay in touch. Take a class or return to school if you think it will further your aims, or study on your own. Either way, your curiosity is at a high point and you'll find yourself reading more than usual to satisfy your thirst for information. You'll also want to travel for pleasure this year—do as much as time and money allow. Consider a trip where you can tour historical sites or one that mixes fun and learning, such as a week at a gourmet cooking school or time behind the wheel of a race car.

Saturn brings rewards as it wraps up its two-year tour through Leo in positive alignment with your Sun. Continue to develop your creative talents and put them to practical use. Now might be the time to take the first—or final—steps toward turning a hobby into a second income, which you might expand into a new career next year. You may find yourself taking love and romance more seriously and evaluating the future of a dating relationship if you're single. If you're a parent, you'll take pride in your children's successes, in part, because of the time and energy you've invested in them the past few years. Continue to foster growth opportunities—music, sports, art, etc.—and learn from your children as much as they learn from you. If you're hoping to start a family, your wish may come true. Much of your social life will be centered around your career. Take advantage of these terrific times to network and to advance your status in the eyes of decision-makers. What you do from January through the summer months can pay off handsomely after Saturn enters Virgo, your solar Sixth House, September 2. This new phase focuses on work and added responsibilities, both of which will contribute to a career peak ten years from now.

Uranus continues to travel in Pisces, your solar Twelfth House. Now in its fifth year in this sign, you've become attuned to this erratic planet's sometimes surprising and almost always enlightening energy. Your intuition continues to be active, and flashes of insight become frequent. Listen closely to your inner voice this year for clues about your life, career, and personal goals and how they reflect your deepest desires. Faith in yourself and your abilities is also a strong component, and your spiritual connection can guide you in search of answers to what you value most in life. This may come partly through your involvement in a good cause with a like-minded group of people who motivate you to help others help themselves. You could find it personally rewarding to be a coach or tutor for at-risk kids or to establish a mentoring relationship with a youngster through a local organization.

Friends and groups have had an influential role in your life since Neptune entered Aquarius eight years ago. This year you will begin to experience a subtle shift in the mystical planet's energy as your focus turns more to individual relationships. Someone you meet now could inspire you in a very personal way and bring out your softer, hidden side. Be a little cautious, though, about whose advice you take; not everyone shares your ideals. Nevertheless, many situations and people offer learning experiences, even those that may disappoint you. Although tough, in some situations the better choice might be to accept reality, cut ties, and move ahead into the unknown. Neptune also can empower you to dream big, set high goals, and visualize success. Once you've set your sights on a target, don't let anyone steer you off course. Neptune is as much about believing in yourself as it is about the practical application of your skills and talents. But don't hesitate to sever the relationship with a group that no longer works for you.

Pluto in Sagittarius continues to motivate you to initiate positive personal change and grants you the willpower and determination to overcome obstacles. This year you're on the verge of completion, ready to make almost the final move into the future, having gradually transformed your life outlook during the past eleven years. Next year Pluto will enter Capricorn, your career sign, so now is the time to gain the knowledge you need to launch yourself into this new phase. If you're a student, give it your all with a goal of completing your studies by year's end. If education separates you from a step up, take action and use your high energy to make it happen. This may be one of the most positive steps of your life. Keep the faith!

This year's solar and lunar eclipses occur in Virgo and Pisces, your solar Sixth and Twelfth Houses. The emphasis is on work, service, health, and the unseen. You can develop a deeper appreciation for the other side of life—a slower pace than your norm. With that comes an interest in self-renewal, a healthier lifestyle, and treating yourself and others with the ultimate in kindness.

If you were born between March 19 and March 31, you're the first of your sign to experience the "reality check" that arrives as Saturn enters Virgo, your solar Sixth House, this fall. Take heart! By the time other Aries experience the effects of Saturn the taskmaster, you'll be an old pro. Try to focus on the excitement that accompanied your recent career gain and hang onto it as Saturn in Virgo pushes you to live up to expectations. Although it will be an adjustment, you can do whatever it takes to prove yourself. But be aware that you're probably in for a somewhat thankless job and little recognition even though you deserve far more. Persist! A few years from now you'll be glad you did when, almost as if by magic, you begin to earn rewards for past efforts. With so much on your plate, it's even more important to treat yourself well. Sleep, exercise, and time to rest and relax should be equal priorities—they can be if you budget your time accordingly. Key dates: October 13, November 30, and December 6 and 19.

If you were born between March 31 and April 10, Uranus in Pisces nudges your deepest inner self to life from your solar Twelfth House. Don't be surprised if you feel the urge to make significant personal changes, as well as more global ones. The shift will center more on your attitudes and insights than on events, and you're likely to find yourself questioning some of your long-held beliefs and searching for new truths. Your sixth sense will push you in this direction and trigger hunches that help you in practical ways every day. The more you listen, the stronger your intuition will become.

Reading a few books or taking a class just for the fun of it can also strengthen your sixth sense. Key dates: January 22, February 7, March 4 and 31, April 27, June 8, September 4, October 8, and November 25.

If you were born between April 6 and April 21, Saturn in Leo puts you in touch with the past as it encourages you to look beyond today. Your life experience is especially valuable now and although you might feel your self-expression is mildly restricted, it will be only if you allow it to be. Now more than ever, you're in charge of yourself and your life direction. So accept that awesome responsibility, set your path, and go after what you want—a family, a new business, a healthy body, a job or promotion, or financial security. Once you do, you're likely to find yourself in a positive growth stage, whatever your age. Where before you were limited, you now will find yourself moving forward, slowly but surely, to claim the rewards you've earned through weathering the tough times. With this growth could come a rise in status that you've long desired but been unable to grasp. Now you can. Yet it is only the start of greater things to come, and what you do now will determine your future. Be bold! Be yourself! Be an Aries pioneer! Key dates: January 20, February 10, March 22, April 19, May 9, July 1 and 30, August 13 and 20.

If you were born between April 7 and April 13, you get the benefit of Neptune in Aquarius in favorable alignment with your Sun. The synergy of this alignment could motivate you to get involved in or increase your commitment to a charitable organization. You'll have the satisfaction of knowing you've made a difference, even in a small way, as compassionate Neptune touches your heart. But there's also the possibility you could become disillusioned with a group, especially if your perceptions are based more on an ideal than reality. If that happens, your best choice might be to part ways and consider it a lesson learned. Neptune also can inspire you to find a new outlet for your creative energy. If there's a hobby you've always wanted to try, now is the time. Although this new activity might be more challenging than expected, you'll also feel great about what you accomplish and benefit from the relaxation.

Hobbies are great way to get your mind off the stresses and strains of everyday life. Key dates: January 20 and 26, February 9, April 5, May 6 and 13, June 26, August 12, September 23, November 23, and December 20.

If you were born between April 15 and April 20, Pluto in Sagittarius boosts your personal power and gives you easy access to this planet's transformative energy. Whatever you wish to do, to change, to learn, is more than possible this year. Although there are no guarantees from the universe, with Pluto and determination on your side, you can achieve what you set out to do. You'll also attract powerful people—movers and shakers who can become influential supporters. Cultivate these contacts. They can have a major impact on your career life after Pluto enters Capricorn next year. Key dates: February 19, March 18, April 8, May 12, September 19, November 5, and December 10.

Aries/January

Planetary Hotspots

January arrives with the Sun in Capricorn, your career sign, so get set to dive in and make your mark. You'll gain momentum as the month unfolds and be ready to peak the week of New Moon in Capricorn, January 18, which occurs two days after your ruler, energetic Mars, enters the same sign.

Wellness and Keeping Fit

Get started January 3 with the Full Moon in Cancer if you're ready to shed holiday pounds. Increase motivation and the potential for success by joining forces with a family member or friend. Slow the pace a little the last five days of the month when Venus in Pisces, your solar Twelfth House of self-renewal, encourages a brief step out of the social whirl. Take time for yourself.

Love and Life Connections

Friendship and relationships are also strong themes this month, with the Sun joining Mercury, Venus, and Neptune in Aquarius on January 20. Welcome new people into your life and see longtime friends, but be prepared for ups and downs as some delight and others disappoint you. A close relationship will prompt more questions than answers; this is not the month for commitment.

Finance and Success

January's career focus may be the best of the year, so set high goals and give it your all. If your aim is a promotion or new job, get things started the first week of the year when the Sun aligns favorably with Mercury and Uranus. Networking is key, but be selective about whom you tell, as even a friend could be a competitor. Money matters require moderate caution, especially around mid-January. What sounds like a winning proposition may or may not be, and it'll be month's end before all the facts are revealed. Go slowly.

Rewarding Days

5, 6, 8, 10, 12, 14, 15, 16, 17, 18, 19, 21, 24

Challenging Days

1, 3, 11, 13, 20, 22, 23, 26, 28, 29

Aries/February

Planetary Hotspots

February is another fast-paced career month, as well as one that features socializing and the desire for time to yourself. Strive for balance, but also make the right and responsible choices and keep your future in mind. With Mercury turning retrograde February 13 and karmic Saturn active at the same time, decisions made now will come full circle at the end of March.

Wellness and Keeping Fit

Your thoughts turn inward as Mercury arrives in Pisces, your sign of self-renewal, February 2, followed by the Sun on February 18. The combined influence encourages you to quiet your mind and listen to your inner voice during this insightful period. Although the process will continue into April, take note of your initial impressions, especially regarding your work life.

Love and Life Connections

Carefree moments with friends continue to delight you, and your social calendar gets a boost from Mars, which begins its six-week trip through Aquarius, your friendship sign, February 25. However, a close relationship or group involvement may not be on such positive footing. A long talk and compromise could be a good short-term solution, but time apart to sort out your feelings might be a better alternative. Ultimately, you should do what's best for you.

Finance and Success

Heightened intuition is a positive factor in your work life this month. Watch, wait, and listen. You're likely to hear confidential information, only some of which is true or, at best, subject to change. Keep it to yourself and await further developments. Do the same if a financial opportunity pops up. Protect your resources.

Rewarding Days

1, 6, 7, 12, 13, 15, 16, 17, 20, 27

Challenging Days

4, 5, 10, 18, 19, 21, 23, 25

Aries/March

Planetary Hotspots

Spring arrives as the Sun enters your sign on March 20, bringing with it renewed enthusiasm for personal plans and goals. Use the time before then to consider what you want to achieve in the next twelve months of your life. Although other opinions can be helpful in this process and it's wise to listen with an open mind, your own insights are ultimately the best guide. You'll also want to be cautious the third week of March, when a planetary lineup involving impulsive Mars advises against risk-taking and legal matters.

Wellness and Keeping Fit

Tune into your body and soul as this month's eclipses emphasize your health sectors, Virgo and Pisces. Get a checkup and initiate a change in diet and lifestyle if that's the best choice for you. Even moderate exercise several times a week can have immediate and long-term benefits. Laugh!

Love and Life Connections

With Mars in Aquarius all month, friends and social events continue to fill your nights and weekends with happy memories, but a rocky relationship could become even more so. It might be time to let go and move on. For couples in love, the second week in March is ideal for a weekend getaway, while some singles launch a long-distance romance.

Finance and Success

Money matters are on the upswing March 17, as Venus enters Taurus, your sign of personal resources. Overall, a conservative attitude is the wisest one, especially with investments; unexpected expenses could pop up. You'll also want to use a tactful approach with supervisors and co-workers, and document information as necessary.

Rewarding Days

1, 2, 5, 6, 10, 11, 12, 13, 15, 16, 20, 27

Challenging Days

9, 14, 18, 22, 25, 29, 31

Aries/April

Planetary Hotspots

You sparkle and shine in the spotlight of this month's New Moon in Aries, April 17. It's accompanied by Mercury, also in your sign from April 10–26, so step out with confidence and pursue your dreams. Bright ideas and new directions are featured, but back up sudden impulses and insights with facts, and balance optimism with reality. If in doubt, seek the advice of a trusted friend or professional at the end of the month.

Wellness and Keeping Fit

Set aside time every day to unwind. It's one way to counteract the stress and frustration that can build with Mars, your ruler, in sensitive, watery Pisces. Equally important to your health is making the effort to turn off your mind and to limit caffeine before bedtime so you can recharge your body with a solid night's sleep.

Love and Life Connections

A close relationship could reach a turning point at the Full Moon in Libra on April 2, when Venus in Taurus clashes with Saturn and Neptune. But a chance encounter at month's end could spark a whirlwind romance or an instantaneous friendship with a soul mate as Venus and Mercury connect you with intriguing people.

Finance and Success

Friends, romance, relatives, and money are a poor mix the first two weeks of the month. Be cautious with investments and spending, and resist the pressure if you're asked for a loan or donation. All that changes by month's end, when you could earn a raise, bonus, or promotion, or receive a long-awaited payment or settlement.

Rewarding Days

3, 7, 9, 10, 11, 12, 16, 17, 25, 29, 30

Challenging Days

1, 5, 13, 18, 20, 21, 27, 28

Aries/May

Planetary Hotspots

Your usual fast-paced lifestyle moves into ultra-high gear May 15, when Mars arrives in your sign. Stamina and determination are your secrets to success, but this influence also triggers impatience and impulsiveness. Keep that in mind as you lay the groundwork for potential personal and career gains this summer and fall. The more supporters you can line up now, the smoother things will go and the more people you can call on for favors.

Wellness and Keeping Fit

Common sense is your ally after Mars enters your sign. This risk-taking influence could prompt you to push the envelope in everything from exercise to daily activities, as you rush through life. Be especially careful with tools in the kitchen and on the road.

Love and Life Connections

Family relationships benefit from the Sun, Venus, and Mercury as this trio travels in Gemini, your communication sign, and Cancer, which guides your domestic life. Couples delight in time together at home, being lazy and working on home improvements. Home is also the best place to socialize, so consider hosting a holiday get-together for friends and neighbors at month's end.

Finance and Success

This month's May 2 Full Moon in Scorpio and the New Moon in Taurus on May 16 emphasize personal and family finances. Although extra expenses could stretch your budget, your bank balance should end up in positive territory by month's end. But if you're contemplating a major domestic purchase (including a new home), try to avoid the lure of easy credit. Even better, postpone the decision until July.

Rewarding Days

3, 4, 6, 8, 11, 14, 15, 17, 19, 21, 22, 29

Challenging Days

5, 9, 10, 12, 18, 20, 25, 30

Aries/June

Planetary Hotspots

New horizons beckon as the June 1 Full Moon in Sagittarius highlights travel and learning. Take a summer class for the fun of it, or start looking at vacation options. If other commitments prevent a week or two away, or even if they don't, your best option might be a weekend getaway around the June 15 New Moon in Gemini, your sign of communication and quick trips. But double-check reservations and have your car serviced early in the month because Mercury turns retrograde June 15. Whether at home or away, family mix-ups and misunderstandings are possible, so choose your words with care and be extra sensitive to the moods and feelings of others.

Wellness and Keeping Fit

Summer is the perfect time to get involved in a sports league, learn tennis or golf, or go for a daily walk, swim, skate, or bike ride. It's more fun and motivational with a partner, so ask your mate, a neighbor, or friend to join you.

Love and Life Connections

You're at your social best thanks to Venus, which enters Leo, your solar Fifth House of pleasure, June 5. This alignment is also a major plus for your love life, whether you're single or committed. If you're searching for romance, socialize with friends where you can meet other singles and ask a pal to introduce you to someone who might be a good match.

Finance and Success

Mars charges into Taurus on June 24 with all the energy you need to boost your bank account between now and early August. But this influence also can trigger impulse buys, so focus on addition rather than subtraction. Mars, along with the June 30 Full Moon in Capricorn, your career sign, could trigger a pay raise, possibly in early July.

Rewarding Days

1, 5, 10, 13, 14, 17, 18, 23, 27, 29

Challenging Days

2, 3, 6, 8, 12, 19, 21, 26

Aries/July

Planetary Hotspots

Life is relatively calm in comparison to recent months. July's major planetary event involves Venus, which turns retrograde in Virgo, your sign of daily work, July 27. Depending upon your perspective that's a plus or a minus. If you're free to play your way through summer, you'll be glad to see the work pace slow. But if you're involved in a major project or anticipating career developments, prepare to be frustrated.

Wellness and Keeping Fit

You can put Venus' retrograde period to good use to "remodel" yourself if you're ready to shed pounds, strengthen your muscles, and improve your overall health. Join forces with a partner—your mate or best friend—and challenge each other to step out with a new look by the time Venus turns direct in September. Make it fun. Join a gym or take a yoga class.

Love and Life Connections

With Venus in Leo, your sign of romance, through July 14, and the Sun entering the same sign July 22, you're more or less guaranteed an active social life this month. Both are positive influences for your love life, especially if you're committed. If you're single and searching for love, the first week of July offers the best opportunities. Get out and about and meet new people.

Finance and Success

Look forward to job success and progress before Venus turns retrograde, July 27, and after Mercury resumes direct motion July 9. If you travel in early July, try to take a few extra days for yourself. Finances are primarily positive with Mars in Taurus, your sign of personal resources. But extra expenses are possible at month's end.

Rewarding Days

1, 7, 8, 15, 17, 20, 21, 22, 25, 26, 30

Challenging Days

3, 6, 10, 12, 18, 19, 23, 31

Aries/August

Planetary Hotspots

August action centers in your solar Fifth House of romance, leisure, creativity, and children. Expect happy times and challenging ones as the Sun, Mercury, and Venus in Leo contact each and most of the outer planets. With Venus retrograde all month, first in Virgo and then in Leo on August 11, close relationships are up and down, and each day will be a new adventure, especially mid-August. This is not the month for major relationship decisions. If you're a parent, get more involved in your children's lives, meet their friends, and help them discover their creativity as you explore yours.

Wellness and Keeping Fit

The Full Moon in Pisces on August 28 encourages you to look within, to think, and get in touch with your inner voice. Make self-understanding your goal during this spiritual period, when new truths can emerge along with flashes of insight. What was previously a mystery now becomes clear.

Love and Life Connections

Be somewhat cautious about what you say to whom this month. That's especially important on the job and with friends. Someone you trust may not have your best interests at heart. Friends will both disappoint and delight you, and you'll feel deeply connected to someone who shows you a different side of life.

Finance and Success

Your work life will be hectic at month's end, when a sudden opportunity sends you into high gear. But be careful not to take on too much and make it a point to include others. If you travel on business, have a back-up plan for a delay or cancellation, and drive with care, especially the last week of August.

Rewarding Days

3, 7, 11, 12, 16, 17, 18, 22, 23, 25, 26, 30, 31

Challenging Days

2, 6, 8, 15, 20, 21, 27, 28, 29

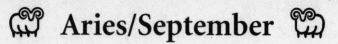

Aries/September

Planetary Hotspots

Saturn, your career planet, enters Virgo, your sign of daily work, September 2. This two-year influence also has a long-term effect; it can launch your rise to the top ten years from now. Keep that in mind as September gets off to a rocky start. Difficult planetary alignments push your limits in the days leading up to the New Moon in Virgo, September 11. Strained relationships can trigger conflict and you could find yourself caught in a power struggle. Sidestep the skirmish as best you can and try to align yourself with supporters.

Wellness and Keeping Fit

Virgo is also one of your health signs, so tune in to Saturn as it enters that sign and take a close look at your lifestyle. If it's less than optimum, take action to reverse the trend. Start with a checkup, modify your diet, and ease into an exercise program. If you want to lose a few pounds, get started at the September 26 Full Moon in your sign.

Love and Life Connections

Romance and socializing regain momentum as Venus turns direct in Leo on September 8. That's as much of a plus for the close relationships in your life as is Mercury moving into Libra, your partnership sign, September 5, followed by the Sun on September 22. Communication flows, so take advantage of the opportunity to talk out recent concerns and issues.

Finance and Success

Money matters also benefit from Venus turning direct, but it'll be next month before you see much of its positive effect. Until then, be conservative with spending and begin thinking about how to better manage family funds when Mercury enters Scorpio, your sign of joint resources, September 27.

Rewarding Days

4, 6, 7, 8, 12, 13, 14, 18, 20, 22, 27

Challenging Days

2, 3, 11, 16, 17, 19, 21, 26

Aries/October

Planetary Hotspots
Challenges and changing conditions describe your October work life. You'll also have some high points and get a better idea of what to expect from Saturn in Virgo the next two years. You might be asked—or you could offer—to take on added responsibilities that could require some quick learning to get up to speed. It's well worth the time and effort even though you'll feel stretched thin at times. Consider it an investment in yourself.

Wellness and Keeping Fit
Take a little time this month to get up to date on the latest health trends and steps you can take to help ensure long-term wellness. Then open your mind and willingly make any necessary changes. If you need added incentive, form a liaison with your partner or a close friend.

Love and Life Connections
Family and personal relationships continue to bring happiness this month as the Sun travels in Libra through October 22. Welcome new people into your life, see friends, and regularly touch base with relatives. Be aware, though, that Mercury turns retrograde in Scorpio on October 11, and slips back into Libra on October 23. That increases the chance for misunderstandings, so choose your words with care.

Finance and Success
Money matters are in mostly positive territory this month with Mercury in Scorpio, your sign of joint resources, through October 22, the day before the Sun enters the same sign. Expect gains and a possible raise or bonus for you or your mate. But with Mercury traveling retrograde part of the month, you should avoid loans and contracts and postpone major decisions.

Rewarding Days
4, 6, 10, 11, 14, 16, 17, 18, 20, 21, 27, 30

Challenging Days
2, 8, 9, 15, 19, 22, 23, 24, 28, 29

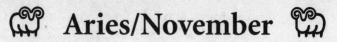

Aries/November

Planetary Hotspots

November will be a relatively quiet month with routine challenges in your daily life. There is one exception, however. Mars, your ruler, turns retrograde November 15 in Cancer, your solar Fourth House of home and family. Although you'll experience occasional domestic tension, this influence is more likely to be internal rather than external. You'll feel as though nothing is moving forward in your personal life. Instead of seeing that as an obstacle, consider it a gift from the universe to kick back and enjoy life and the holidays with your favorite people.

Wellness and Keeping Fit

Although the Thanksgiving holiday isn't the best for travel, you could benefit from a few days off this month. Try for the first weekend even if you stay home instead of heading out of town. It'll be a welcome break and the timing is perfect to strengthen ties with loved ones as Mercury turns direct in Libra on November 1.

Love and Life Connections

You're a people magnet this month, thanks to Mercury in Libra through November 10 and Venus in the same sign from December 18 on. That's a definite plus for love and romance and socializing with friends. If you're single, a new love interest could enter your life at month's end. Ask a friend to set you up.

Finance and Success

Money flows your way with the Sun and Mercury in Scorpio part of November, but it can disappear just as quickly. Be kind to your budget and don't feel obligated to help a friend or relative or donate to someone's favorite cause. It's also possible you could lose a treasured item, so take precautions.

Rewarding Days

2, 7, 10, 12, 13, 15, 16, 17, 20, 25, 26, 28

Challenging Days

5, 6, 11, 18, 21, 23, 24, 27

Aries/December

Planetary Hotspots

Communication with career contacts, in-laws, and other relatives will test your patience off and on throughout December as the Sun and Mercury clash with Mars and several other planets. You'll also want to avoid travel if at all possible, especially the first half of the month when delays and cancellations are likely.

Wellness and Keeping Fit

Try to put your fast-paced lifestyle on hold now as the year comes to a close so you can cherish special moments with those you love. With Mars still retrograde in Cancer, your domestic sign, you'll continue to benefit from laid-back hours this month just as much as you did in November.

Love and Life Connections

Create beautiful memories of togetherness with your partner the first few days of December before Venus departs Libra, your partnership sign, to enter Scorpio on December 5. It might be your last chance this month for the ultimate in quality togetherness time because planetary alignments promise lots of holiday socializing with friends and co-workers. If you need to consult a professional, such as an attorney or CPA, do so while Venus is in Libra.

Finance and Success

Circle December 18 on your calendar. It's a banner day! Lucky Jupiter enters Capricorn, your solar Tenth House of career. This year-long influence can elevate your status and bring a fabulous promotion or job offer in 2008. Give some thought to where you'd like to be twelve months from now and set plans in motion to achieve your goals. Finances get a boost from Venus in Scorpio from December 5–29, and you could receive a sizable bonus or cash gift from a family member.

Rewarding Days

4, 5, 9, 10, 11, 12, 14, 16, 18, 19, 21, 25, 26

Challenging Days

1, 2, 3, 6, 8, 13, 17, 22, 27, 30

Aries Action Table

These dates reflect the best—but not the only—times for success and ease in these activities, according to your Sun sign.

	JAN	FEB	MAR	APR	MAY	JUN	JUL	AUG	SEPT	OCT	NOV	DEC
Move							10-21			8-10		
Start a class					19-27			7-22	23-27			
Join a club	15-31		9-16	11, 12		5, 6						14
Ask for a raise			19-21	27-30			17-19					
Look for work	3-13	5-9						24-31	3, 4	8-10	6-8	21-28
Get pro advice	11	6, 7	7	2, 3, 29, 30	27, 28		20, 21		12-14	2-5	6, 7	3, 4
Get a loan	14	10	9		3, 30		24		16	3, 4	9, 10, 12-15	6, 7
See a doctor	9	7	19, 20	26	7	7	17, 18		10	8	19	28
Start a diet		4, 5	3, 4							7, 8	4, 5	1, 2, 28, 29
End relationship	10, 11	6, 7	5, 6	2, 3					26, 27		7	4
Buy clothes	6	1, 28	1, 28, 29	24, 25	21	9, 13	11, 12		12, 18, ,27	5, 6	29	26
Get a makeover	23, 24	20, 21	1, 2, 20	15, 16		9, 10			8, 9	6		
New romance		28	1	17		17, 18	7		13, 26	6, 11		
Vacation	15, 16	11, 12	10, 11	7, 8	4, 5, 31	1, 28, 29	25, 26	11, 12, 22	17-19		11, 23-30	3-19

TAURUS

The Bull
April 20 to May 22

♉

Element:	Earth
Quality:	Fixed
Polarity:	Yin/Feminine
Planetary Ruler:	Venus
Meditation:	I trust myself and others
Gemstone:	Emerald
Power Stones:	Diamond, blue lace agate, rose quartz
Key Phrase:	I have
Glyph:	Bull's head
Anatomy:	Throat, neck
Color:	Green
Animal:	Cattle
Myths/Legends:	Isis and Osiris, Cerridwen, Bull of Minos
House:	Second
Opposite Sign:	Scorpio
Flower:	Violet
Key Word:	Conservation

Your Ego's Strengths and Weaknesses

Without a doubt, determination ranks among your greatest strengths. This unwavering willpower sees you through as you build toward success in your every endeavor. Little, if anything, can steer you off course once your path is set.

Security is of utmost importance to you, and those in your inner circle rely on your steady, practical nature for reassurance. Like a harbor, you're a safe haven in the ups and downs of life and a caring, concerned friend and partner.

The flip side of determination is stubbornness—and only a select few don't experience this aspect of your personality at one time or another. For you, it's a matter of learning when it's advantageous to dig in your heels and when you should go with the flow—not an easy task when your mind is set!

The same is true of change, which you prefer to avoid. You enjoy routine and life's little comforts because they provide the security that is so essential to your nature. But change can be good! Besides motivating you to move forward with your life, it can provide a refreshing opportunity to embrace all that is new and different.

Possessions are important to you—sometimes too much so. Emotional insecurity can prompt you to cling not only to things, but to people. Learn to let go and place a higher value on yourself and your considerable talents. That, in turn, will invite more love and lasting relationships into your life.

Your Venus-ruled sign has a great appreciation for lasting, enduring beauty, and your artistic ability is strong. You could get great satisfaction from painting, gardening, decorating, or refinishing furniture to improve your surroundings.

Slowly but steadily you can build a financial fortune if you want. Always thrifty, you nevertheless spend willingly on creature comforts and what pleases your senses. You won't, however, let go of even a dollar if you feel something is overpriced. Value is the key.

Shining Your Love Light

You're content to let others play the field while you concentrate on one romance at a time. Even managing that can be a stretch because you're ultraselective, somewhat reserved, and happy with the status quo. Dating, after all, is a risk that requires a change in routine.

But once someone captures your heart, your innate tenderness and sensuality emerge. You expect commitment and loyalty from a partner and willingly give the same. That's terrific as long as you curb a tendency toward possessiveness and jealousy, which is usually unfounded. Try to remember that no relationship is static and will grow, evolve, and deepen if you adapt and welcome change.

An Aries will liven up your life, but you might find this sign too fast-paced for your steady, measured approach. Life with another Taurus can be pure delight or just the opposite if stubborn egos clash, and you both may be too set in your ways. You will appreciate Gemini's lightness and wit although this changeable sign can have you constantly at loose ends.

Cancer shares your need for security and your love of home and family, and can benefit from your practicality as you gain a freer expression of emotion. In Leo you will find a generous, loyal, and loving mate, but where you seek lasting value in possessions, Leo goes for glitter and glitz. Virgo's earthy sensuality mirrors your own, and you're both practical and realistic. You and Libra have a common love of beauty, but this sign is more social than yours and also prone to indecision, whereas you have firm opinions.

Magnetic Scorpio stirs your passions and shares your sensuality and need for commitment, but is also prone to jealousy. While Sagittarius thrives on adventure and encourages you to broaden your horizons, you'd rather be comfy at home. You can learn from Capricorn, who is as practical and security-minded as you are; but while you are thrifty, this sign can pinch pennies. While free-spirited and spontaneous, Aquarius might be too detached and aloof for your tastes. In Pisces you find a sensitive, creative soul whose dreamy qualities balance your sensible ones.

Making Your Place in the World

You're most comfortable in a career that's safe and secure, so you could easily stay with the same company your entire working life. Although not entirely outside the realm of possibility, it's improbable in today's world. This can actually be to your benefit. Let the pursuit of stability and steadily increasing income and benefits encourage you to take a few calculated risks to advance your status.

Personally pleasing surroundings and congenial co-workers are factors important to your day-to-day job happiness and productivity. You also do best in an environment that promotes idea sharing, compromise, and teamwork.

Among the many career fields that might interest you are construction, carpentry, landscaping, farming, massage therapy, real estate, and the music industry. Your innate financial skills could lead you to a career as an accountant, bookkeeper, loan officer, teller, or investment adviser.

If you have creative talent, you could excel as an artist, hair stylist, flower designer, cabinetmaker, or interior decorator. You also might enjoy working as a museum curator or in an art gallery. Food-service careers are another option—you could be an excellent pastry chef or candy maker.

Putting Your Best Foot Forward

You put your best forward in so many ways, day in and day out. Steady and reliable, you're the rock others depend on to bring calm to their topsy-turvy lives. Ever patient, people appreciate your listening skills, sensitivity, care, and concern. You're a natural psychologist who can help others identify and resolve their core concerns.

In order to make the most of these fine personality traits throughout your life and daily activities, you need to welcome change and accept that it's inevitable. If you wait too long, that golden opportunity may pass you by, so be proactive—take a chance and go after what you want. By learning to go with flow and be more flexible, you also can more easily adapt to the ups and downs of your personal and professional lives. And give yourself permission to be frivolous once in a while.

You do nothing halfway, as you believe anything worth doing is worth doing well. Determination and unwavering pursuit of your goals also gives you a head start in nearly every endeavor. But when it becomes stubborn determination, you lose the benefit of other viewpoints and information, which can simplify problem-solving and trigger your imagination and creativity. So make an effort to keep an open mind and to see things from another perspective.

Almost anything is possible if you start slowly. Take a different route to work, shop at a different store, or sample another culture's cuisine. And with your willpower, it's a given you can achieve whatever you set out to do. Go for it!

Tools for Change

One of this year's themes is relationships. Friends, children, colleagues, relatives, and neighbors have a stronger presence. In their own way, each can bring something into your life, and you can do the same for them.

Friends can help you redefine yourself and your career goals. Their insights will amaze you and provide the impetus to embrace change. This is especially valuable to you now because you may feel somewhat directionless from time to time. An equally important component is visualization. What you think, imagine, and wish for only needs to be transformed into concrete reality. Dream big and use your talent for planning and organization to set things in motion.

Friends and colleagues can enhance your career growth through networking. Consider joining a professional organization or club to widen your circle and build a network of contacts, any one of whom could be your link to a sudden step up.

Relatives can test even your patience as these relationships go through an evolutionary process. Each brings a learning experience, the chance to gain flexibility, and undeniable proof that you can choose your friends but not your relatives!

Your immediate family offers you similar, albeit more positive, growth opportunities. You may discover they are an even larger part of the solid foundation that contributes greatly to your security needs and that they are your most valuable assets. The stronger these relationships become, the more willing you will be to expand your comfort zones.

You can stretch yourself in other ways as well. Travel to see the world or explore nearby locations. Take a class for fun to learn another language. Or, acquire the how-to skills for home improvements that will reward you with a sense of accomplishment.

Affirmation for the Year

People beautify my life,
and we bring joy to each other.

The Year Ahead for Taurus

Think green, gold, and glitter as Jupiter travels in Sagittarius, your solar Eighth House of money. This fortunate period, which happens only once every twelve years, ups the financial odds in your favor. With luck, you can greet December 18, the date Jupiter moves on to Capricorn, with a fatter bank account than you had at the start of 2007. Your paycheck could become significantly larger, and you might benefit from a windfall such as an inheritance, lottery or contest win, settlement, or gift from a relative. But curb the urge to splurge with credit unless you find a zero-interest deal that you can pay off by the deadline. Otherwise, save up and pay cash for big-ticket items. Shop around to get the best mortgage rate if you plan to purchase or build a new home (or improve your current one) and seal the deal before September 2, when Saturn enters Virgo.

Saturn is in the final stretch of its two-year trip through Leo, your solar Fourth House of home and family. You may have already relocated, purchased property, or remodeled your home. If finances have held you back before, Jupiter could change that. But buy less rather than more so you can afford to travel next year, which you'll want to do, and help pay or save for your children's college expenses. Do-it-yourself decorating and home improvements can save dollars if you have the skills. If not, positive planetary alignments can help you gain the know-how. This year you may take on extra responsibilities involving an elderly relative, including the possibility of someone moving in with you. Although sharing your home might seem workable, it probably won't be a long-term solution, so look for an alternative if you have a choice.

You'll have many opportunities to widen your circle of friends, just as you have had the past four years when Uranus began traveling through Pisces, your solar Eleventh House of group activities. Fill your weekends with socializing and consider joining a club or professional organization to meet people and network. You could meet a soul mate unexpectedly this year who becomes a friend or romantic interest. Although the relationship will have its challenges, realize that you were brought together for a reason. Learn from each other about life, people, change, new directions, and what you hope to achieve. Even if you're together only a short time, you'll feel as though you've made a major difference in each other's lives.

What you know is as important as who you know this year as Neptune continues its fourteen-year tour of Aquarius, your solar Tenth House of career. You can expect the typical career ups and downs, successes and challenges, disillusionment and inspiration, but the positives can far outweigh the negatives if you use visionary, intuitive Neptune to your advantage. Some people will support your efforts, others won't, so don't put all your faith in a single supporter. Line up as many backers as you can and be sure each is aware of your skills and talents. Then use your marvelous common sense, create a plan, and make your big dreams reality.

Pluto is nearing the end of its long Sagittarius transit and will enter Capricorn next year. You've undoubtedly had a wide range of financial experiences in the past twelve years as the planet of transformation focused its energy on your solar Eighth House of other people's money. What you have learned will be especially important this year. The universe, in a sense, will test your knowledge and challenge you to make wise use of Jupiter's largesse. That should be a snap for you and your sensible approach to money matters, though the temptation to spend will be stronger than usual. But go ahead and splurge on yourself once in a while. It's OK.

This year's solar and lunar eclipses in Virgo and Pisces spotlight your Fifth and Eleventh Houses. Social events, children, romance, hobbies, and other leisure-time activities will delight you. Do what you enjoy and enjoy yourself doing it!

If you were born between April 20 and 30, you'll enjoy the steady influence of Saturn from September 2 on, when it enters Virgo, another earth sign. A dating relationship could become more serious, or you might have a change of heart and decide it's in your best interests to move on. If you're a parent, one of your children could embark on a new life phase as a college student, but if you have teens at home, reassure yourself by getting acquainted with their friends. If you're ready to start a family, your wishes could be fulfilled this year or next. Do something for yourself, too. Take up a new hobby or sport, something you've always wanted to try but never had the time to do. Or, return to school for the fun of it. You might stumble into a new career or gain skills to advance in your current one. Key dates: October 13, November 30, and December 6 and 19.

If you were born between May 1 and 10, Uranus nudges you to seek new opportunities, revisit your life and career goals, and develop beneficial contacts. Now is the time to be proactive and initiate change before it's thrust upon you. Although you're usually more comfortable with the status quo, action taken this year will give you the edge in 2008, when you'll have fewer choices and some events will seem fated. In essence, what you do now can trigger positive gains next year. Networking, groups, and shared resources are your lucky charms, and the more contacts you make, the better prepared you'll be to reap well-deserved rewards. Stretch yourself, especially later this year, and get involved in a professional organization, club, your children's activities, a volunteer effort, or other events where you can meet people. One or more of them could be your unexpected link to success. Key dates: January 22, February 7, March 4 and 31, April 27, June 8, September 4, October 8, and November 25.

If you were born between May 7 and 22, Saturn in Leo will contact your Sun from your solar Fourth House. This marks the start of the second phase of Saturn's lengthy zodiacal cycle of twenty-eight years, which began seven years ago when it joined your Sun in Taurus. You'll probably need more sleep than usual to maintain your usual stamina and might even feel as though you're treading water and making little progress toward your worldly goals. Take heart! Although this might feel like a low point in your life, it's actually the beginning of an upward trend that will culminate fourteen years from now. You will feel the full effects of Saturn if you were born near May 7, including the potential for domestic and career issues. Your home may need renovations, or you may decide to undertake a major remodeling project, or simply relocate. If a home purchase is in your plans, make it contingent upon a professional inspection. Key dates: January 20, February 10, March 22, April 19, May 9, July 1 and 30, August 13 and 20.

If you were born between May 8 and 13, Neptune in Aquarius is challenging your Sun from your Tenth House of career and status. You may feel a bit adrift, unable to clearly define your worldly aspirations, yet have an increasing desire to find a new avenue for your skills and talents. But this year isn't the best for a major career shift. What looks good one day loses its luster the next as your interests shift, so this is a better time to explore your options rather than commit to a new direction. If you're tempted to accept a new position, ask yourself if the offer is too good to be true. On another level, you should take precautions to avoid the murky waters of misunderstanding. Your notable common sense and caution are the top assets here, and qualities that can help protect your position. Avoid assumptions, document everything of importance, and leave no room for misinterpretation. Take note that someone you consider a friend could be the opposite, so keep confidential matters to yourself. Neptune, however, can enhance your natural creativity. Tap into this inspiration and find new outlets to use your innate inventiveness freely in personal and professional activities. Key dates: January 20 and 26, February 9, April 5, May 6 and 13, June 26, August 12, September 23, November 23, and December 20.

If you were born between May 16 and 22, Pluto in Sagittarius stimulates a desire to break free from old patterns and habits. Identifying what to change and when is the challenge, which could prompt you to go for all or nothing to fulfill your need for personal growth. Not a good idea! Tackle one thing at a time, but even so, only after giving much consideration to your feelings. Even with this positive approach, adjusting to the idea of change might take a while, so move slowly and give yourself a chance. The more comfortable you are with change, the easier it will be. If, for example, your greatest desire is a slimmer, trimmer, in-shape you, start slowly and gradually move into a healthy regimen of diet and exercise. You will feel all the better for it if this slow, but steady, transformation takes all year to as you achieve a new look from head to toe. The healthy lifestyle is also more likely to become a permanent life pattern and one that will have you feeling terrific, inside and out, for years to come. Key dates: February 19, March 18, April 8, May 12, September 19, November 5, and December 10.

Taurus/January

Planetary Hotspots

Finances can become an issue this month as Mars and Pluto align in your solar Eighth House of joint resources. Seek an expert's advice if you and your partner need help with debt management or even basic money matters. It's also possible you'll need to assist an elderly relative. If you're anticipating an insurance settlement or inheritance, be prepared for a few hurdles before everything is finalized. Stick with it.

Wellness and Keeping Fit

Fitness can be a challenge in the winter months when cozy nights at home are more appealing than a workout. Try an alternative. Ask a few co-workers to join you for a quick lunchtime walk several days a week. Besides being good for you, it's a great opportunity to get better acquainted and to develop supportive relationships.

Love and Life Connections

This month's January 3 Full Moon in Cancer and the New Moon in Capricorn on January 18 emphasize communication and have you in contact with many people, near and far. Romance could develop with a friend or someone you meet through your career. If you're committed, you'll greatly appreciate your partner's support, especially because some other family relationships may be difficult.

Finance and Success

Career gains can be yours this month as three planets join Neptune in Aquarius: Venus on January 3, Mercury on January14, and the Sun on January 20. At the least you'll be an attention-getter; at best you may earn a promotion or be offered a position that requires relocation. Ask questions to clarify your role and responsibilities before you accept.

Rewarding Days

2, 3, 8, 12, 14, 15, 17, 18, 21, 25, 30, 31

Challenging Days

1, 6, 11, 13, 20, 24, 26, 28, 29

Taurus/February

Planetary Hotspots

Career stress can trigger strained relationships at home and on the job in the two weeks following the February 2 Full Moon in Leo, when career and domestic responsibilities demand equal attention. Although it will be nearly impossible to prevent all causes of turmoil, you can minimize the effect through open communication that promotes support and understanding.

Wellness and Keeping Fit

Venus, your ruler, enters Aries, your solar Twelfth House of well-being, February 20. Diet and exercise are important, and this transit also encourages you to share your skills and talents for the good of others. A volunteer activity can provide needed stress relief and leave you feeling great about yourself and your contributions. With the Sun in Pisces, your friendship sign, after February 17, further involvement in a charitable organization is also a great way to meet new people.

Love and Life Connections

Pick up the phone and get things started! An active social life is yours all month, thanks to Venus in Pisces, your friendship sign, through February 19, and the Sun's arrival there the day before. Mercury is in Pisces from February 2–25, but the communication planet turns retrograde February 13, so you'll want to confirm dates, times, and places.

Finance and Success

A financial matter that pops up within the first few days of the month will require more attention as February draws to a close. But it will be mid-March before it is resolved. This could involve earned income, an expense, or loan. With Mercury retrograde, be sure to pay bills early and carefully examine statements for errors.

Rewarding Days

3, 6, 7, 8, 9, 12, 13, 14, 20, 22, 27

Challenging Days

5, 10, 11, 15, 19, 23, 28

Taurus/March

Planetary Hotspots

Career competition is stiff with Mars in Aquarius all month. The fiery planet also fuels your determination, but give yourself a periodic reality check because tunnel vision can distort the true picture. You'll also want to be cautious about whom you trust. Someone who appears to be a friend and supporter may not be. Much will be revealed after March 7, the date Mercury turns direct in Aquarius.

Wellness and Keeping Fit

The Sun enters Aries, your sign of self-renewal, March 20. Use the following four weeks to re-energize yourself through daily meditation or time alone to review the past 12 months. That's the first step toward new goals and your new Solar Year, which begins next month when the Sun enters your sign.

Love and Life Connections

Your social life begins to pick up mid-month with the arrival of Mercury in Pisces, your friendship sign, March 18. Even better is Venus, which begins its annual Taurus tour March 17. This stellar influence lights up your powers of attraction and whatever you wish for—love, money, happiness, and more—can be yours in the weeks ahead if you have faith and believe in yourself. Turn on the charm and make the connection.

Finance and Success

Although you'll experience tension in your work life this month, planetary alignments favor financial gain, possibly through a raise or bonus. At least as likely, and maybe more so, is a lucky find or win. You could discover hidden treasure, such as a collectible or family heirloom that's worth far more today. Try the lottery or enter a contest the first full week of March.

Rewarding Days

4, 7, 12, 13, 17, 19, 21, 25, 26, 30, 31

Challenging Days

1, 2, 8, 9, 11, 16, 22, 24, 29

Taurus/April

Planetary Hotspots

A possible financial setback in early April frustrates you as it challenges your need for security. Work through these money matters one step at a time, knowing that it won't last forever. You also should be extra cautious with financial information (even with friends and organizations you trust) and check your credit report for errors.

Wellness and Keeping Fit

With Mercury in Aries from April 10–26, your have a perfect opportunity to reprogram your mind to embrace a healthier lifestyle. As the ruler of Virgo, your sign of recreation, Mercury also encourages you to ease your way into an exercise routine. Try yoga or join a gym. If you want to shed a few pounds, get started April 2 with the Full Moon in Libra and you'll begin to see results by the time the Sun enters your sign April 20.

Love and Life Connections

You'll enjoy an active social life this month thanks to Mercury in Pisces, your friendship sign, through April 9, and Mars in Pisces after April 5. Networking can result in a beneficial career contact early in the month, when you also could be surprised by a friend who expresses interest in a romantic liaison. Be firm but gentle if it's not the right relationship for you. Do the same if a pal asks for a loan.

Finance and Success

The recent hectic pace at work begins to ease after April 5 when Mars exits Aquarius, but not without one final push, so be prepared to move into high gear the first few days of the month. Although finances are in flux as April arrives, you can look forward to more stability after Venus enters Gemini, your sign of personal resources, April 11. Unexpected good news is possible at month's end, when Venus aligns with Jupiter, Saturn, Uranus, and Neptune.

Rewarding Days

3, 8, 9, 10, 11, 16, 17, 19, 22, 24, 26, 30

Challenging Days

5, 7, 12, 13, 18, 20, 23, 27, 28

Taurus/May

Planetary Hotspots

You know you're a determined soul, as well as a stubborn one at times. The choice is yours to be one or the other, or both, when planetary alignments the first two weeks of May put you to the test as frustration, delay, and confusion alternate with solid thinking, flashes of insight, creativity, and momentum. Stay the course and you'll be set for a fresh start at the May 16 New Moon in Taurus.

Wellness and Keeping Fit

If you began a new health regimen last month, or even if you didn't, Mars encourages you to re-commit to the effort when it enters Aries, your solar Twelfth House of wellness, May 15. But you'll want to exercise earlier in the day because working out at night could make it tough to get to sleep at a reasonable hour. The same is true of your mind. Try to turn it off an hour before bedtime to help ensure a restful night.

Love and Life Connections

You're on the go seeing friends and socializing the first two weeks of May as Mars travels in Pisces, your friendship sign. After that, the pace slows and you'll enjoy quiet, quality time with your closest pals and partner. If you're searching for love, someone fascinating could appear as if by magic after Venus enters Cancer on May 8. Introduce yourself to neighbors and be alert as you run errands and go about your daily activities.

Finance and Success

Your work life perks along this month, especially once you jump a few hurdles in early May. Money matters are active with a good chance for gain as Venus advances in Gemini through May 7, and Mercury is in the same sign May 11–27. With the Sun in Gemini after May 21, funds flow your way.

Rewarding Days

1, 6, 7, 8, 11, 15, 20, 24, 29

Challenging Days

5, 9, 10, 12, 18, 22, 25, 30

Taurus/June

Planetary Hotspots

Two slow-moving outer planets, Saturn and Neptune, form an exact alignment the end of June in your solar Fourth and Tenth Houses of home and career. Be sure your home is covered by adequate insurance, and maintain a low profile on the job into early July. If you're tempted to start a home-based business, hold off until later this year. Conditions are less than ideal, especially for an endeavor that requires an up-front investment.

Wellness and Keeping Fit

Last month's emphasis continues through June 24, when Mars exits Aries and enters Taurus. Sleep and time to relax and unwind becomes, if anything, more important now, with this high-energy planet in your sign. Although you're usually safety-conscious, this influence could prompt even you to take physical risks. Try not to push yourself too hard. It's easy to overdo it now.

Love and Life Connections

Your love life benefits from favorable planetary lineups that stir passion and romance. But deciphering the feelings of family members may be tough, especially at month's end, when Venus in Leo aligns with Saturn and Neptune. Communication can be a challenge after Mercury turns retrograde June 15, so clarify your thoughts and words and avoid assumptions. If you meet someone intriguing, keep the thought. It might be mid-August before you get together.

Finance and Success

The June 1 Full Moon in Sagittarius and the June 15 New Moon in Gemini spotlight joint and personal resources—your money, family funds, spending, debt, savings, retirement, and investment accounts. Although usually in sync with money matters, even you can benefit from a periodic financial assessment. Do that this month.

Rewarding Days

5, 7, 13, 15, 16, 17, 18, 23, 25

Challenging Days

3, 4, 6, 12, 19, 20, 24, 26

Taurus/July

Planetary Hotspots

With summer in full swing, the last thing you want is a slowdown in your social life. Unfortunately, that's just what may happen when Venus turns retrograde in Virgo on July 27. It's likely to have the same effect on your love life, so it'll be tough to launch a new romance. Because Venus is also your personal ruler, this is not the time for new personal directions. Think, plan, and explore options so you're ready to move forward when Venus resumes direct motion in September.

Wellness and Keeping Fit

Home life delights you and you'll enjoy entertaining friends with Venus in Leo, your domestic sign, through July 13, followed by the Sun on July 22. Stay cool and comfortable at home and gear up for a major decluttering session the weekend of July 7, when you can easily let go of unneeded items. The end result will free your mind even more than your space. Take the best to a consignment shop or have a yard sale.

Love and Life Connections

Take the initiative to get better acquainted with neighbors after Mercury, your personal romance planet, turns direct in Cancer on July 9. You could meet someone fascinating. With Mars in your sign all month, though, patience and flexibility will get you much farther with family members and on the job.

Finance and Success

Expect some job-related frustration at month's end when a project is put on hold and people are disagreeable. Quit while you're ahead rather than try to change minds. Finances are in positive territory much of July, but postpone major purchases and decisions until after Venus turns direct in September.

Rewarding Days

1, 4, 8, 9, 13, 14, 17, 22, 27, 28

Challenging Days

2, 3, 6, 10, 12, 16, 19, 23, 31

Taurus/August

Planetary Hotspots

The domestic scene and, to a lesser extent, your career life receive a major share of your time, attention, and effort this month as four planets travel in Leo, the sign of the August 12 New Moon. On a practical level, you should check your home for potential repairs and keep the structure and its contents well insured against loss. You'll also have increased interaction with family, some positive and some less so, and you may need to become involved in the daily affairs of an elderly relative. All this could of course affect your work life so be sure to keep your employer informed.

Wellness and Keeping Fit

Life will be beyond hectic at times this month, especially around mid-August, so make stress management a priority. Even thirty minutes a day to yourself can help you re-center your body and soul. Try for meditation or quiet thought before bedtime. If that's unrealistic, try for lunchtime.

Love and Life Connections

Venus, your ruler and the universal love planet, is retrograde all month, first in Virgo, your sign of romance, and then in Leo from August 11 on. A new romance will get off to a slow start at best, and you'll probably be more content at home than out and about. Invite a few close friends to join you for dinner at your place during the week of the August 28 Full Moon in Pisces, your friendship sign.

Finance and Success

Mars enters Gemini, your solar Second House of personal resources, August 7. That can put more money in your pocket, but also encourages impulse buys. Be kind to your budget.

Rewarding Days

1, 5, 9, 10, 11, 16, 17, 18, 19, 23, 24, 30

Challenging Days

2, 6, 8, 12, 13, 15, 20, 27, 28, 29

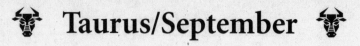

Taurus/September

Planetary Hotspots

The emphasis shifts to Virgo, your solar Fifth House of romance, children, and creativity. Besides the Sun, Mercury, and September 11 New Moon in that sign, Saturn arrives there September 2 to begin its two-year transit. Learning and travel will interest you, and you might profit from a hobby or teaching a community class. Plans will begin to come together next month when Venus, which turns direct September 8, advances into Virgo.

Wellness and Keeping Fit

If you haven't yet scheduled an annual checkup, let the September 26 Full Moon in Aries, your Twelfth House of health, motivate you to pick up the phone. The lunar energy is also an asset if you want to lose a few pounds before the holidays.

Love and Life Connections

Romantic relationships will be more serious, but also more secure and stable for the next two years with Saturn in Virgo. But it will be easy to get into a comfortable rut rather than move forward with someone who could be a lifelong soul mate. Don't rush, but don't delay. You also could welcome a new family member or become an empty-nester.

Finance and Success

You could net a fatter paycheck later this month when Mercury in Libra, your sign of daily work, aligns with Jupiter and Pluto in your solar Eighth House of joint resources. That's an equally positive influence for job recognition and success. Before then, however, you can expect extra expenses related to children or leisure-time activities. If vacation travel is in your plans, firm up costs before you go.

Rewarding Days

1, 5, 6, 10, 15, 20, 22, 24, 27

Challenging Days

2, 3, 11, 16, 19, 23, 26, 28

Taurus/October

Planetary Hotspots

You might choose to end a dating relationship, friendship, or group involvement this month as Venus in Virgo, your sign of romance, aligns with Saturn and Uranus. Values are the basic issue, and money may also have a role. Ultimately, you should do what's right for you even if it means cutting long-standing ties. If in doubt, postpone the decision until November.

Wellness and Keeping Fit

If you wanted to but didn't begin a diet in September, the universe offers you another chance this month. Put all your determination behind the effort around the October 26 Full Moon in your sign. While not exactly easy, you'll at least find it easier to keep your goal in sight.

Love and Life Connections

This is one of the best months of the year for love and commitment. If you're part of a couple, romance your partner at every opportunity. The only catch is Mercury turns retrograde in Scorpio, your partnership sign, October 11, and slips back into Libra on October 23, the date the Sun enters Scorpio. While that keeps the energy flowing all month, misunderstandings can destroy the mood. Think before you speak and try not to jump to conclusions.

Finance and Success

Get set for a terrific month at work that signals maximum success and could include a raise or promotion. If you're searching for a new position, you could land a lucrative one. Keep in mind, though, that Mercury will be retrograde in Libra, your solar Sixth House of daily work, through the end of October. Discuss details and be sure all is locked in before you move on.

Rewarding Days

3, 4, 7, 12, 16, 17, 18, 20, 21, 26, 27, 30

Challenging Days

6, 9, 15, 19, 22, 25, 28, 29, 31

Taurus/November

Planetary Hotspots

You're not far off if you feel as though life and the information flow are grinding to a halt mid-month. Mars, the ultimate action planet, turns retrograde in Cancer, your communication sign, November 15. Expect plans, projects, and decisions to be put on hold, so gear up and do all you can before then.

Wellness and Keeping Fit

You'll probably find yourself lost in thought while Mars is retrograde. As the ruler of your solar Twelfth House of self-renewal, this is an excellent time to slow your mind, tune out extraneous information, and tune in to your inner voice. It also will help you manage the periodic stress and frustration when Mars delays progress.

Love and Life Connections

The November 9 New Moon in Scorpio, your partnership sign, lights up the close relationships in your life. You'll especially enjoy the company of loved ones from November 11 on, when Mercury returns to Scorpio. Take it one step further and get acquainted with new people. Socialize with friends and neighbors and consider hosting a holiday get-together this month or next.

Finance and Success

Job communication improves somewhat as Mercury turns direct November 1 and Venus enters Libra, your solar Sixth House, November 8. But you'll want to be a little cautious about what you say to whom. The very planets that promote success also clash with Neptune in Aquarius, your career sign, and that can prompt some people to stretch the truth or even try to put the blame on you. Cover yourself with documentation.

Rewarding Days

3, 4, 7, 8, 9, 15, 22, 26, 28

Challenging Days

5, 6, 11, 18, 21, 23, 24, 30

Taurus/December

Planetary Hotspots

Jupiter takes off for new horizons December 18, when it departs Sagittarius and arrives in Capricorn, your solar Ninth House of travel and learning. Do as much of both in 2008 as you can. See the world or a piece of it, return to school to complete or pursue a degree or advanced certification, or renew your library card and take a class for the fun of it. What you learn in the next year will benefit your career in 2009.

Wellness and Keeping Fit

Continue to kick back some evenings and weekends this month to enjoy quality time with your favorite people. Listen more than you talk and welcome the chance to learn more about yourself in the process. You might also ask for feedback about your thoughts about life, spirituality, and what you'd like to achieve in the new year.

Love and Life Connections

Workplace relationships are upbeat and the enthusiasm contagious, and you'll have many opportunities to socialize with co-workers and friends as the holiday season moves into full swing with Venus in Scorpio, your partnership sign, December 5–30. You could reconnect with a former love this month, someone you had a serious relationship with in the past. Take it slowly if you're interested.

Finance and Success

Tempting as it is to toss out your usual conservative financial attitude this month—don't go there. You'll undoubtedly regret it when the bills begin to arrive in January. Establish a firm gift budget and stick to it. If you buy electronics, consider an extended warranty to protect your investment.

Rewarding Days

4, 5, 7, 12, 14, 15, 16, 19, 25, 28, 29

Challenging Days

2, 3, 6, 9, 13, 17, 22, 23, 30, 31

Taurus Action Table

These dates reflect the best—but not the only—times for success and ease in these activities, according to your Sun sign.

	JAN	FEB	MAR	APR	MAY	JUN	JUL	AUG	SEPT	OCT	NOV	DEC
Move	5, 6	1, 2		24, 25	21-27		23- 25		10-26			
Start a class	3,4, 29,30		25, 26		22-24	1-4	12-19					
Join a club	28-30	2-12,19,20	2-9, 27-30	10-12								
Ask for a raise				20	22-24	14, 15						
Look for work	19-26		10-16	11, 12					12-14, 22-26			
Get pro advice	12	9			2,3, 28-30						8, 9	6, 7
Get a loan	15,16					27-29			17, 18		11, 12	3,4, 8,10
See a doctor	10, 24	7		16, 17, 30					12, 13	10	7	3, 4
Start a diet	10, 11	6, 7	5, 6						27	10	6, 7	3, 4
End relationship	12, 13	8, 9	8, 9	4, 5	1, 2					26, 27		
Buy clothes	7, 8	5	31	26			17, 18		10, 11	8	4, 5	1, 2
Get a makeover	26, 27	22, 23	18-31	1-10, 27-30	15, 16		9			26-27		
New romance	7, 8		21, 30, 31		16				10, 11		3, 4	
Vacation	1-13		13	9	6-8	30	1				14, 15	22-31

GEMINI

The Twins
May 22 to June 21

♊

Element:	Air
Quality:	Mutable
Polarity:	Yang/Masculine
Planetary Ruler:	Mercury
Meditation:	I explore my inner worlds
Gemstone:	Tourmaline
Power Stones:	Ametrine, citrine, emerald, spectrolite, agate
Key Phrase:	I think
Glyph:	Pillars of duality, the Twins
Anatomy:	Hands, arms, shoulders, lungs, nervous system
Color:	Bright colors, orange, yellow, magenta
Animal:	Monkeys, talking birds, flying insects
Myths/Legends:	Peter Pan, Castor and Pollux
House:	Third
Opposite Sign:	Sagittarius
Flower:	Lily of the valley
Key Word:	Versatility

Your Ego's Strengths and Weaknesses

As a Gemini, you're the multitasker of the zodiac. That's a definite plus for juggling the many demands of a hectic twenty-first century lifestyle—something you do exceptionally well. Even you are amazed by how much you can accomplish in a day. Your secret to success is, of course, organization. Without this key ingredient, your energy is scattered and your strength diminished. So treat your calendar and those to-do lists as your best friends.

You're also an information-seeker, a master at tracking down what isn't already stored in your active, Mercury-ruled mind. Trivia fascinates you as much as fact-finding, and many Geminis are avid readers who also enjoy puzzles, computer games, writing, and taking hobby classes. But decision-making sometimes can be a challenge because it's easy to get bogged down in the pros and cons of conflicting data. Zero in on the most pertinent facts and set deadlines.

No matter how busy you are, boredom is never far away. There's always something more interesting to do or say or see to satisfy your curiosity. When something grabs your attention, however, your concentration kicks in and you stick with the matter at hand until your inquiring mind is ready for the next adventure. Unfortunately, life is full of tasks and responsibilities you—and everyone else—would rather avoid. In these situations, your mercurial nature is an advantage: Unique approaches help maintain interest, as does periodically switching activities. More variety, better results!

Witty and charming, you're a natural in social and business situations, with a knack for networking and bringing people and plans together. Others respond to your lighthearted, youthful aura—whatever your age—and enthusiasm for new experiences. Remember, though, well-thought-out change is usually more productive than acting on a whim. That approach, along with listening to other viewpoints and your intuition, also generates support for the brightest of your bright ideas.

Shining Your Love Light

You're fun and flirtatious, lively and sociable. Friendship and playing the field delight you, but you're happiest when paired with a date. Initially attracted by good looks, charm, and sophistication, intellectual rapport is a must in any lasting relationship, as is someone who shares your love of spontaneity and adventure. Yet try to be aware that mutual interests and casual talk are no substitute for dealing with and expressing your deep feelings.

Your desire for freedom is strong and you need plenty of space to just be yourself and explore your interests. Thus, a relationship with a supportive mate built on trust that allows you to be you is very important to your personal happiness. You also do best with someone who's not only in tune with your spur-of-the-moment ideas, but who can offer alternatives to expand your thinking. Listen! Welcome different viewpoints and advice!

You have a natural bond with the other air signs, Libra and Aquarius, who value communication as much as you do. Libra's finesse and refinement attracts you, but too much togetherness can leave you feeling trapped. Innovative Aquarius shares your need for independence and encourages you to view life and love from a new perspective. Romance with another Gemini can bring out the best in each of you, provided you both listen as much as you talk.

Aries' freshness energizes and motivates you to stretch yourself and to pursue concrete goals. Sensual Taurus adds stability, but could be too slow-paced for your active lifestyle. Although Cancer can be nurturing, this sign's emotional, protective nature can be overwhelming. Dramatic and generous Leo inspires creativity and romance, and you'll delight in being treated like royalty. Virgo's practicality can stifle your spontaneity, but your strong mental connection with this Mercury-ruled earth sign promotes understanding and awareness of individual needs.

You're attracted and intrigued, although puzzled, by Scorpio's intensity and mysterious silence. The magnetic lure of Sagittarius can be irresistible, but be prepared to experience a double-dose of your own wanderlust. Although you can learn valuable life lessons from Capricorn, control issues can emerge with this match. Romantic moments are memorable with Pisces, but this sign's dreamy idealism mystifies you.

Making Your Place in the World

A career that offers variety and mental stimulation is essential, and the more you strengthen your communication skills, the farther you'll go. Planning and goal-setting are equally important, so make it a semiannual habit to look ahead and strategize your next step.

Writing, public relations, advertising, and media careers such as TV or newspaper reporting, are good options for you. Public speaking and the performing arts, including comedy and films, are a natural outlet for your sense of humor and knack for creating audience-pleasing illusions. The travel, customer service, and computer industries are other possibilities, and you might excel as an interior decorator, artist, massage therapist or herbalist, or in sales.

Hands-on careers appeal to some Geminis. If you're among them, consider dentistry, hair styling, construction, or auto mechanics. You also could do well as a school counselor or therapist because you're drawn to psychology and the inner workings of the mind.

If you're torn between two career options, pursue one as a day job and another as a sideline until your true passion emerges.

Putting Your Best Foot Forward

Communication can be your greatest strength, as well as your greatest challenge. Take heart in knowing that this is normal. It is far easier to use the skills and talents that come easily than to overcome obstacles. Where you excel is also where risk-taking feels less chancy.

As the premier communicator of the zodiac, you have a natural affinity for speaking, writing, and other forms of expression. The difficulty arises when these talents overpower—and even suppress—your many other gifts. If you're a typical Gemini, you love to talk and share your thoughts, ideas, and opinions.

But do you also enjoy listening?

Listening is as much a part of communication as talking. When you give others and their words your full attention, you experience a true conversation with all the give-and-take that builds relationships. The bonuses for you are more information for your already sizable knowledge bank and more friends and business contacts.

Even though communication is your forte, your intellectual focus can make it tough to express your deepest emotions. Make no mistake; emotions are just as important and real to you as they are to everyone else. But you think of your feelings more often than not, analyzing them to gain a fuller understanding of your emotions in any given situation. This is very natural to you, and also your comfort zone. And there's no reason to change your very essence.

But you could benefit from a freer expression of your emotions. After all, it's one thing to verbalize your love and quite another to let your heart rule your head. Try it when you're on safe ground with someone who cares as deeply about you as you do about him or her. The object of your affections will adore you for it.

Tools for Change

Powerful tools for change await you this year. Each is significant in itself, and together they offer you an incredible opportunity to expand your knowledge in many areas of life. Focus on your career, your relationships, and your spiritual connections, all of which are intertwined. They mesh beautifully to bring new insights into your place in the world and how people can help you get there.

Expanding relationships can change your life through personal and career contacts, some of whom could be one and the same. You have something to gain from each person who appears or reappears—even from those who are no longer a part of your daily life. Take the time to reflect on what you hear and observe, and be ready to snap up the lucky breaks that come your way.

Your knowledge base will grow in other ways as well. Whether you pursue a degree, take a few classes, or delve into a subject on your own, what you learn will boost your career potential—in obvious and surprising ways—and how you relate to other people. Friends in high places are part of your secret to success, so make connections and be prepared to impress them with your know-how.

On a personal level, look within and without, and create a practical vision for your future. That might seem doubtful upon first reflection. It's not! With your curious mind and interest in human nature, you can look beyond the obvious to shape your ideal path. Faith and an unwavering belief in yourself, your skills, and your talents is the first step. Follow it with a look at the big picture and then the details, which are useful in creative visualization.

Affirmation for the Year

Knowledge is my steppingstone to success.

The Year Ahead for Gemini

Although simple solutions might elude you this year as questions outnumber answers, you're nevertheless well-placed to make significant strides. Success can come through others, and career and relationships can be profitable. It's important, however, to first identify your needs and motivations. Think, dream, talk with—and listen to—people you respect. Clarity then emerges, along with fresh insights and a deeper understanding of yourself and your place in the world.

Bountiful Jupiter traveling through your solar Seventh House can bring lucky personal and professional connections, as well as some life-changing ones. Romantic opportunities link some Geminis with a future mate, and others decide to take a relationship to the next level as marriage and commitment become priorities. Success can come through a business partnership, but thorough research, expert advice, and a conservative financial approach are paramount considerations. December brings a turning point in a close professional or personal relationship. Try to restrain yourself even though you feel compelled to take action. Words spoken and decisions made at this time are final. Jupiter enters Capricorn on December 18, signaling the start of a year-long focus on money matters involving others. Chances are you'll gain financially from this fortunate transit, but you also could end up owing more. Save, and pay down debt.

You can benefit from two lessons as Saturn transits Leo: planning and organization. This emphasis on your solar Third House of communication is also an opportunity to further your education. The tough part is deciding what you want to learn and how it can best benefit your ambitions. You'll also find yourself thinking more about the past as a first step toward resolving what holds you back. Counseling could help identify the key issues as well as creative solutions, especially from February through July. You could meet a soul mate in August or, at the least, someone whose wisdom empowers you to welcome new horizons with strength and confidence. Saturn's focus switches to domestic matters and new beginnings from September 2 on, when it enters Virgo, your solar Fourth House. Begin here to lay the foundation for what you want to achieve in fourteen years, when Saturn can bring well-deserved rewards. If your thoughts drift toward remodeling your home or purchasing a new one, wait until next year to put your plans in motion. Funding will be easier to acquire.

You've probably already experienced the effects of unpredictable Uranus, which continues its seven-year transit of Pisces, your solar Tenth House of career. Now at its midway point, you can expect unexpected opportunities to pop up. A calculated risk—one backed by solid facts and figures—could work to your advantage if you're ready to assume the accompanying responsibilities. Look for initial developments in January, when a chance encounter could set the ball rolling, and await further developments in May and again in October.

Neptune's ongoing multiyear tour of Aquarius inspires you to delve into the mysteries of life and, on a practical level, gain knowledge that can boost your career potential. Travel, also associated with your solar Ninth House, can widen your perspective. Because Aquarius is the universal sign of friendship and groups, your inquiring mind might enjoy a travel-learning tour. The most favorable months are October and November, when timing also is good for a romantic Neptune getaway. Be prepared this year, however, to come face-to-face with truths you'd rather avoid. The smart choice is to be pragmatic rather than dwell on ideals, even when disillusioned. Consider yourself wiser for having learned from the experiences that occur in March and June.

Pluto is nearing the end of its long trek through your solar Seventh House, which it completes next year. This transformative planet prompts you to re-examine all you've learned about relationships in the past twelve years. Mend hurt feelings, even if they're only your own, and nurture fresh starts with the most important people in your life. Endings are also possible as you look to the future and your best interests, but might best be postponed until next year.

This year's four eclipses—two solar and two lunar—highlight your Fourth and Tenth Houses. Each encourages you to find a balance between career demands and your home life, triggering activity and change in those areas. Some Geminis relocate for a job, and others pursue new career opportunities, in part, to establish roots.

If you were born between May 22 and June 1, Saturn in Virgo from September 2 on focuses your attention on home and family. You may decide to purchase a home, remodel your current one, or relocate for a job opportunity. Even though your income should increase next year, it's still a good idea to buy wisely and borrow less than you qualify for. That way you'll have cash available for improvements and furnishings. Be cautious, though, if a roommate seems like a good idea. Whether friend or lover, you may regret the decision by December and subsequently find it difficult to end the living arrangement. It's also possible that an elderly relative will require your help during this time. Key dates: October 13, November 30, and December 6 and 19.

If you were born between June 1 and 11, Uranus in Pisces is pushing you to redefine your career life. That doesn't necessarily mean a job or career change, but that's certainly possible—by choice or circumstance. Be proactive and keep your options open, but resist the urge to make a change for the sake of change. A true star-studded career winner will be easy to spot, in part, because that offer will come with opportunities for personal and financial growth. But be cautious if your thinking turns toward a home-based business, especially one that requires a major up-front investment or a partner. If the draw is irresistible, start slowly and don't give up your regular paycheck—yet! Tap your creativity instead of your financial resources. Key dates: January 22, February 7, March 4 and 31, April 27, June 8, September 4, October 8, and November 25.

If you were born between June 7 and 21, Saturn in Leo brings opportunities for learning and self-understanding. The two are intertwined: the more you learn about life, the better you'll understand your strongest motivations and what you really want to achieve this year. Time alone aids your thought process, and you'll find it much easier than usual to concentrate while reading, working, or studying. You also can be a highly effective and motivational team leader, even in informal settings where brainstorming and cooperative efforts help generate and crystallize your visionary, yet realistic, ideas. Be careful not to align yourself too closely with any one person or group because the least likely supporter might turn out to be your link to bigger and better. On a practical level, you might have to deal with a car, appliance, or other mechanical repair in February, June, or both, and the problem will be difficult to diagnose—even by a reputable, certified pro. Try to hold off until this fall if a replacement or expensive repair is necessary. If that's impossible, carefully check credentials and consider getting a second opinion before you spend. Key dates: January 20, February 10, March 22, April 19, May 9, July 1 and 30, August 13 and 20.

If you were born between June 8 and 14, Neptune invites you to touch the untouchable. If you've never explored your creative urges—or even if you have—this is the year to unleash them. Start by taking a class just for the fun of it. Shoot for something practical that yields concrete results, such as painting, needlework, decorating, woodworking, or writing. This year is also a good time to get in touch with your spiritual side and to delve into metaphysical realms. The more you recognize and value your intuitive thoughts, feelings, and urges, the more you're rewarded with unseen guidance and knowledge that can open new vistas of understanding. Travel is another wonderful outlet for Neptune's positive contact with your Sun and the excursions are even better if combined with learning in a relaxed atmosphere. You might enjoy a visit to Mayan ruins, an alternative-healing seminar at a resort, or weekend trips to nearby historical sites. Wherever you go and whatever you do, welcome the unusual and fresh insights into your life. And don't be surprised as the year evolves if subtle, internal changes begin to occur in how you view your place in the world, as well as your goals and aspirations. Take pleasure in the journey as you redefine your life philosophy, core beliefs, and personal happiness. Key dates: January 20 and 26, February 9, April 5, May 6 and 13, June 26, August 12, September 23, November 23, and December 20.

If you were born between June 16 and June 21, Pluto in Sagittarius intensifies your close relationships. Try to view them with an objective eye because you'll discover much about yourself—both positive and negative—reflected in others. That's especially important in a business or romantic partnership, where you could become overly involved—even obsessed—with the other person. Step back and develop your own interests, your own talents, and your own life rather than link too much of your identity to someone else. Passion could sweep you off your feet if you're single and searching for love, but don't make the leap to commitment until you really know your heartthrob. Sometimes it's easy to get caught up in an infatuation that can be mistaken for the real thing. If you decide that it's time to cut ties and move on, be 100 percent sure of your decision; once made, it's unlikely to be reversed. Key dates: February 19, March 18, April 8, May 12, September 19, November 5, and December 10.

Gemini/January

Planetary Hotspots

Communication is a challenge, primarily mid-month and as January comes to a close. Mix-ups and misunderstandings are likely, but on a deeper level you'll question how to mesh your values with someone's else. Compromise is the solution, but that can be tough to achieve. You'll also want to be careful about what and whom you believe. Some people stretch the truth and others might try to intentionally steer you off course. Ask questions and be especially wary in legal and financial matters.

Wellness and Keeping Fit

With the Sun, Mercury, and Venus joining Neptune in Aquarius this month, there's little you'd like better than to take off for a fun-filled winter vacation. Not the best idea. Delays, hassles, and cancellations can erase the potentially positive stress relief you hope for. Find an alternative, such as a crafts or decorating project or a hobby class to stimulate your creativity.

Love and Life Connections

Mars transiting your solar seventh house through January 15 signals emerging relationship issues centered on individual needs and goals. Talk is the first step toward resolution; knowledge and acceptance are the second. Some singles make a match the week of January 9, when your social life gets a boost.

Finance and Success

Money matters require attention around the January 3 Full Moon in Cancer and the New Moon in Capricorn, January 18. Be proactive rather than reactive, and make a fresh start in budgeting after defining goals. Mars, which enters Capricorn on January 16, adds incentive to increase earnings and pay down debt. A career opportunity could pop up the third week of the month.

Rewarding Days

5, 6, 10, 15, 19, 24, 27

Challenging Days

1, 3, 7, 16, 20, 22, 26

Gemini/February

Planetary Hotspots

What you know sets you apart from the crowd this month. Avoid assumptions and give extra attention to details. You also might benefit from taking a short-term skills class or studying on your own. Anything that increases your knowledge is to your advantage later this month and next.

Wellness and Keeping Fit

Try to squeeze in at least a few vacation days this month. The February 2 Full Moon in Leo prompts a quick getaway for some Geminis, and others travel later in the month. If a business trip takes you out of town at the New Moon in Aquarius on February 17, or after February 24, when Mars is in Aquarius, take some extra days to see the sights.

Love and Life Connections

Plan ahead and seek your partner's support. Mix-ups, career demands, and misunderstandings can trigger family tension after February 12, when Mercury is retrograde. Organization helps you manage it all, as do carefully chosen words. Network as you socialize with colleagues and friends as Venus advances in Pisces through February 19. Traveling singles could make a lucky love match early in the month.

Finance and Success

You're well-situated to catch the attention of decision-makers all month, so do whatever it takes to set yourself up for career gains. Extra effort could net added income at mid-month, when Mars aligns with Venus. That's also a positive time frame to apply for scholarships and loans, but stay on top of deadlines and double-check your paperwork.

Rewarding Days

1, 6, 7, 8, 12, 14, 15, 17, 20, 26, 27

Challenging Days

3, 4, 5, 9, 10, 11, 16, 19, 25

Gemini/March

Planetary Hotspots

Life, communication, and the information flow appear to be back on track when Mercury, your ruler, turns direct March 7. Unfortunately, it's only a lull, with more to come the third week of March, when Mars aligns with Jupiter, Saturn, and Neptune. Cover your bases in between. Line up supporters, confirm facts, and double-check previous work. Take your car in for routine maintenance in the same time frame and try to postpone travel. Drive with care.

Wellness and Keeping Fit

It's easy to lapse into a lazy mood and develop a taste for sweets and comfort food when Venus is in Taurus, the sign it enters March 17. Stop before you get started and stock the kitchen with healthy meals and snacks. Moderate exercise, such as a daily noontime walk, gets you moving and energized.

Love and Life Connections

With Venus in Aries, your friendship sign, most of the month, and the Sun's arrival there March 20, you're set for an active social schedule this month. Host a get-together the week of the March 3 Full Moon in Virgo, your domestic sign, and arrange outings, day trips, and more to fill your weekends with fun and adventure. Or visit friends, attend a reunion, or travel with a group the second weekend in March, when a pal could be your link to love.

Finance and Success

You and your career are in the spotlight, thanks to the Sun in Pisces through March 19, the day after Mercury arrives in the same sign. The dual influence singles you out as an attention-getter and you'll want to snap up every opportunity to impress those who count. The energy peaks at the March 19 New Moon, but with Pluto also involved, take care not to step on toes.

Rewarding Days

5, 6, 10, 12, 15, 16, 19, 20, 21, 24, 27, 30

Challenging Days

2, 8, 9, 11, 18, 22, 28, 29

Gemini/April

Planetary Hotspots

Think twice before you speak and act as April arrives and departs. Stressful planetary contacts between your solar Seventh House of relationships and your solar Tenth House of career signal rising tension and increased conflict potential. Keep your cool and try not to let difficult people and situations get to you. Then you can come out on top and possibly even benefit from your smooth handling of a complicated situation.

Wellness and Keeping Fit

The Sun enters Taurus, your solar Twelfth House, April 20, followed by Mercury, April 27. Use this time and the first three weeks of May to refresh and renew your spirit and energy in preparation for the Sun's arrival in your sign next month. Quiet your mind and look inward as you resolve any regrets or issues from the past year. Then look to the future with optimism.

Love and Life Connections

You could meet a sensational someone through a friend within a few days of the April 12 Full Moon in Libra, your sign of romance. But if a dating relationship isn't working out as you hoped, it might be time to move on. Welcome new people into your life in the two weeks following the New Moon in Aries on April 17, and consider getting involved in a club or organization to widen your circle.

Finance and Success

Mars steps up the pace at work after it enters Pisces on April 6, when it will be easy to overload yourself. Plan ahead, carefully budget your time, and take on only what you're sure you can accomplish on schedule. This placement also brings you to the attention of many, so proceed accordingly and rack up credits. What you do now can pay off in May.

Rewarding Days

3, 8, 9, 11, 16, 17, 19, 22, 24, 26, 29, 30

Challenging Days

1, 5, 6, 13, 18, 21, 27, 28

Gemini/May

Planetary Hotspots

Career and professional relationships continue to be a hotspot the first two weeks of May. Much of the activity—and potential conflict—centers behind the scenes, however. So do what's necessary to protect your position. You also could be involved in confidential talks or learn privileged information. Keep it to yourself. Even hints to a friendly co-worker could have negative repercussions.

Wellness and Keeping Fit

Worries and daily stress can catch up with you as the Sun and Mercury travel in Taurus, your solar Twelfth House of health. Talking out your concerns, walking, or another form of moderate exercise can help ease tension. Light reading or a challenging puzzle can also take your mind off the day's events. The May 2 Full Moon in Scorpio is one of the best times of the year to begin a wellness program if you want to lose a few pounds.

Love and Life Connections

Mars, your friendship planet, zips into Aries, your friendship sign, May 15. That's a terrific influence for your social life, as warmer temperatures encourage outdoor activities with friends. Fill your calendar with dates, events, and outings the next six weeks.

Finance and Success

A positive financial trend begins this month with the May 8 arrival of Venus in Cancer, your solar Second House of personal resources. It's followed by Mercury, which enters Cancer on May 28. Give some thought to how you can increase income with the help of this beneficial influence, which continues into June. If your annual review is coming up, start recording your accomplishments now. Or apply for a promotion or new position.

Rewarding Days

3, 4, 8, 11, 13, 14, 17, 21, 22

Challenging Days

5, 9, 10, 12, 18, 25, 28

Gemini/June

Planetary Hotspots

The June 15 New Moon in Gemini brings out your best, filling you with a fresh perspective and the incentive to pursue new personal directions and goals. With so much going for you this month, it's even more important to take precautions. Communication requires careful handling with Mercury turning retrograde June 15. Equally important, if not more so, is the difficult alignment of Saturn and Neptune, June 25. This can trigger conflict, misunderstandings, and false information. If possible, avoid travel and legal matters.

Wellness and Keeping Fit

Calm evenings and weekends help you unwind, as do even calmer thoughts. Yoga and meditation also can be helpful to counteract the effects of energetic Mars, which begins its six-week tour of Taurus, your solar Twelfth House of health, June 24. Otherwise, this transit could interfere with the solid sleep you need night after night.

Love and Life Connections

June continues to accent your active social life. It gets even better June 5, when Venus enters Leo, the universal sign of romance and your solar Third House of communication. That's the ideal combination to charm your partner or a love interest with all the right words. Express your heartfelt feelings. Long walks and talks are magical.

Finance and Success

You could be in line for a major step up with money to match. Much depends upon your initiative and willingness to compromise. The odds also increase if you know the right people, so identify key players and network with friends and colleagues. Keep spending under control, though, and pay bills early because of Mercury's retrograde status.

Rewarding Days

1, 5, 6, 7, 10, 13, 14, 16, 17, 18, 23, 27, 29

Challenging Days

3, 4, 8, 9, 11, 12, 19, 21, 26, 30

Gemini/July

Planetary Hotspots

July's notable planet is Venus, which turns retrograde July 27 in Virgo, your domestic sign. On a practical level, you might want to postpone any home improvements and decorating projects until September, when Venus turns direct. Otherwise, you could find yourself redoing the work. The same applies to home furnishings. Because Venus is also the universal love planet, you should reconsider and postpone any thoughts of establishing a home with a romantic interest. You might regret the decision.

Wellness and Keeping Fit

Redouble the stress-management techniques you began last month. With Mars still in Taurus, it's in your best interests, especially the last ten days of July when the red planet aligns with Saturn, Uranus, and Neptune. If you need a few days off then, home is a better choice because travel is unfavorable.

Love and Life Connections

New love liaisons get off to a fast start in early July, while couples delight in passion and rediscover how much they have in common. Your social life is equally active during the same period and, with Venus entering Virgo on July 4, consider hosting a holiday get-together. As Venus begins to slow before turning retrograde, so does your social life.

Finance and Success

Finances begin to get back on track as Mercury turns direct July 9, and even more so with the fresh start represented by the July 4 New Moon in Cancer, your sign of personal resources. Look at spending and saving habits, revamp your budget, and set financial goals. You could earn a raise before month's end.

Rewarding Days

7, 8, 9, 13, 14, 15, 20, 21, 25, 26, 30

Challenging Days

3, 6, 10, 12, 16, 19, 24, 31

Gemini/August

Planetary Hotspots

A concentration of planets in Leo, your solar Third House, sends your daily routine into overload when life's little frustrations seem to multiply, especially mid-month. Communication in general is affected and at times it'll be tough to get a straight answer out of anyone. Confirm facts, ask questions, and believe only half, at most, of what you hear. If travel is a must, expect delays and cancellations, and drive with care. Mechanical problems also are possible, so take your car in for routine maintenance and check home appliances.

Wellness and Keeping Fit

You benefit from the high energy and incentive of Mars as it travels in your sign the next six weeks. You'll be amazed at all you can accomplish in a short time, but this influence also increases the odds for accidents. Use common sense, slow down on foot and on the road, and think safety in the kitchen and if you work with tools.

Love and Life Connections

Family relationships are strained at month's end, but you can ease much of the tension if you assume the role of mediator and promote calm, open communication. Find the middle ground, the compromise that everyone can live with. If you're involved in a serious dating relationship, this is not the month for commitment and, if you're wavering, time apart could help you sort out your feelings.

Finance and Success

With Venus retrograde, you could have some extra expenses this month so you'll want to be conservative in spending. Career-wise you can stand out above the rest at month's end when the Full Moon in Pisces spotlights your solar Tenth House of status. Success, however, will be directly linked to changing conditions and your willingness to adapt.

Rewarding Days

1, 3, 7, 10, 11, 16, 12, 17, 26, 30, 31

Challenging Days

2, 6, 8, 13, 15, 20, 21, 27, 28, 29

Gemini/September

Planetary Hotspots

Your attention is focused on home and family as Saturn enters Virgo, your domestic sign, September 2. This influence could prompt you to purchase property or relocate in the next two years. This month, however, is not the best for either, or for other household changes because the Virgo Sun clashes with Mars and several outer planets. If you can hold off, next year is a better choice. The same is true if you're considering a home-based business.

Wellness and Keeping Fit

Take the initiative to increase your wellness knowledge after Mercury enters Scorpio, your Sixth House of health, September 27. Bone up on the latest trends and information and how you can modify your daily activities and diet to promote a healthier lifestyle.

Love and Life Connections

Your social life gains momentum as Venus turns direct September 8. Communication also benefits, and you'll be motivated to get out and about and connect with people. Mercury in Libra, September 5–26, enhances the effect, as does the Sun in the same sign from September 22 on. The energy continues to flow into October, thanks to the September 26 Full Moon in Aries, your friendship sign. That's a terrific week for couples in love and singles searching for romance. Ask a friend to arrange a date.

Finance and Success

Money matters are fairly stable this month with the possible exception of domestic expenses. If you make a major purchase, consider an extended warranty. Look forward to a possible financial boost next month, when you'll reap the most benefit from Mars, which enters Cancer, your sign of personal resources, September 28.

Rewarding Days

4, 6, 7, 8, 12, 13, 14, 18, 22, 27

Challenging Days

2, 3, 9, 11, 16, 17, 19, 26, 30

Gemini/October

Planetary Hotspots

Just when you thought life would return to normal after a hectic few months, Mercury in Scorpio turns retrograde October 11. Since Mercury is your ruler, you're well aware of the mix-ups and misunderstandings that the communication planet can trigger, which at this time center on your work life. Be sure to confirm appointments and information, double-check details, and plan ahead the best you can for indecision and delays.

Wellness and Keeping Fit

The October 26 Full Moon in Taurus, your Twelfth House of self-renewal, encourages you to look within for answers to life questions. Quiet time enhances the search and your intuition, and it's also good for you to periodically still your mind. Try walking meditation or yoga.

Love and Life Connections

Your love life and your social life are stellar, thanks to the October 1 New Moon in Libra and beneficial solar contacts. Keep your calendar up to date, especially after Mercury turns retrograde and slips back into Libra on October 23, so you don't miss out on any events. This month could fulfill your wish if you're searching for love, and some singles get engaged. Couples are in sync and in the mood for romance. If you can manage it, try for a weekend getaway designed for two.

Finance and Success

Despite retrograde Mercury, planetary alignments accent success. A job search could yield spectacular results, and you might be in line for a promotion or raise as decision-makers suddenly realize and recognize your contributions and know-how.

Rewarding Days

4, 6, 7, 10, 11, 14, 16, 20, 21, 27, 30

Challenging Days

2, 9, 15, 17, 19, 22, 23, 24, 28, 29

Gemini/November

Planetary Hotspots

Work and relationships bring you a few challenges this month, but nothing that a few precautions won't prevent or resolve. Try to stay on the sidelines if you see signs of a power struggle developing, and be cautious of anyone who comes on too strong or tries to play to your ego. Chances are, there's a hidden motive involved—one you want no part of. Be up-front if you run into complications with a project; it will add to your credibility.

Wellness and Keeping Fit

You'll have the willpower if you want to lose a few pounds or at least limit holiday treats, thanks to the November 24 Full Moon in your sign. With Mercury, your ruler, resuming forward motion in Libra, your social and recreation sign, a gym membership might be a good investment, for both health and the opportunity to meet new people.

Love and Life Connections

Social events, dates, outings, and more continue to fill your calendar this month, with Mercury and Venus in Libra. Close relationships—family, partner, and best friends—are in focus from November 22 on, when the Sun enters Sagittarius, your partnership sign. Although you can expect a minor rough spot at month's end when communication falters, you can do much to smooth things over.

Finance and Success

You might want to scale back on holiday spending because Mars turns retrograde in Cancer, your personal money sign, November 15. Your budget will thank you for it next year when few bills arrive. Unfortunately, there's also a chance this influence could rule out, delay, or limit a holiday bonus or raise.

Rewarding Days

2, 4, 7, 9, 10, 12, 15, 17, 20, 25, 28

Challenging Days

3, 5, 11, 18, 21, 23, 24, 30

Gemini/December

Planetary Hotspots

You'll experience all the ups and downs associated with relationships this month as five planets travel in Sagittarius, the sign of the December 9 New Moon. Although you'll feel the effects in your personal life, stressful contacts are primarily related to your work. In both, however, you'll also enjoy many satisfying and productive days when everyone is on the same wavelength.

Wellness and Keeping Fit

Retrograde Mars returns to Gemini on December 31, just in time to commit to a New Year's resolution to emphasize health and wellness, as well as personal goals, in 2008. Give yourself a month to clearly define what you want to achieve and get set to go when Mars turns direct January 30.

Love and Life Connections

Take time this month to strengthen ties with your partner and other loved ones. Talk out concerns and issues, celebrate love and life, and reconnect on a spiritual level. Mercury in Sagittarius from December 1–20 enhances communication, as does the Sun in the same sign through December 21.

Finance and Success

Think green and gold! Jupiter arrives in Capricorn, your solar Eighth House of joint resources, December 18. This beneficial influence can boost your assets in the coming year. Use it wisely. Build security. Save as much as you can, invest for the long term, and pay off debt rather than give in to the temptation to incur more. As wonderful as it would be to have this influence forever, it only lasts a year! Make the most of it and make the money work for you.

Rewarding Days

4, 5, 14, 15, 16, 18, 21, 25, 26, 29

Challenging Days

1, 2, 6, 8, 11, 17, 22, 23, 30

Gemini Action Table

These dates reflect the best—but not the only—times for success and ease in these activities, according to your Sun sign.

	JAN	FEB	MAR	APR	MAY	JUN	JUL	AUG	SEPT	OCT	NOV	DEC
Move							17, 18	24-31	1-3		3-4	
Start a class			28, 29	24, 25				7, 8, 11, 17				
Join a club	23, 24			11-18								17, 18
Ask for a raise	29				29, 30		13			2		
Look for work	28-31	2-9	17-19		11, 29, 30		22-24				8, 9, 11, 21	
Get pro advice	15, 16		12	6	4	1	25, 26		19		12	
Get a loan	2-12, 17, 18			10	6, 7				20, 21		14, 15	
See a doctor		9	19, 20		2, 3, 15, 30			6			9	5-7
Start a diet	12, 13	8, 9			2, 3						8	6, 7, 21
End relationship	14-16	11, 12	10, 11	7, 8	4, 5, 31	1						8
Buy clothes		7		29, 30	26				12, 13		6, 7	3, 4
Get a makeover	28		23, 24	19, 20	17		12		4, 30	1	25	3, 4
New romance		6, 7		28-30	26, 27				12-14	11		
Vacation	15-31		10-16	11, 12		5, 6			22, 23			1, 14

CANCER

The Crab
June 20 to July 21

♋

Element:	Water
Quality:	Cardinal
Polarity:	Yin/Feminine
Planetary Ruler:	The Moon
Meditation:	I have faith in the promptings of my heart
Gemstone:	Pearl
Power Stones:	Moonstone, chrysocolla
Key Phrase:	I feel
Glyph:	Crab's claws
Anatomy:	Stomach, breasts
Color:	Silver, pearl white
Animal:	Crustaceans, cows, chickens
Myths/Legends:	Hercules and the Crab, Asherah, Hecate
House:	Fourth
Opposite Sign:	Capricorn
Flower:	Larkspur
Key Word:	Receptivity

Your Ego's Strengths and Weaknesses

You'd care for the entire world if you could. Since that's impossible, your family and close friends—those you consider family—reap the full benefit of your nurturing personality. This soft, sensitive side of you, although very real, is also an illusion that belies your powerful inner strength. Woe be to those who underestimate your ability to take a stand. Once riled, you rarely retreat.

Like the changeable Moon, which rules your sign, you can be happy one moment and feel low the next. Yet only those closest to you experience the entire spectrum of your emotions because you have the ability to fit your "mask" to the occasion. You use the same protective shell to safeguard your deeply sensitive inner self, outwardly detaching yourself from your surroundings.

Cancer, a water sign, is highly receptive to the environment. You sense what others miss—the undercurrents and vibrations in a room, situation, or between people. This is often an advantage, but be sure to protect yourself. Whatever you feel you can also absorb, so learn to draw in the positive energy and block the negative.

The quest for security is a driving force in your life. Strong family ties, a loving partner, and a warm, welcoming home are integral to your self-confidence and contentment. A sizable bank account, investments, and retirement funds complete the picture. The challenge is to know when enough is enough. Because your emotional and material security needs are higher than most, you can become stuck in a cycle of needless worry. Give yourself a periodic reality check with the help of someone close whose opinion you value.

Loyal and sentimental, you have a long memory for those who are considerate and kind, and will repay their thoughtfulness, though sometimes years later. The reverse also is true. You rarely give anyone a second chance.

You effortlessly put people at ease, and here, too, your intuitive side emerges to sense what others need. This gives you a talent for entertaining as well as dealing with the public. People trust you and feel comfortable in your presence.

Shining Your Love Light

Your ideal is a devoted partner who shares your love of family. Closeness, both emotional and physical, is vital to your well-being, and you cherish every moment of togetherness. Warm and affectionate, you freely express your emotions once someone captures your heart.

At times you sacrifice your needs for your mate's. Although this is part of the compromise for any long-lasting bond, being too accommodating can result in a lopsided relationship that's unhealthy for both parties. Strive for a fifty-fifty partnership, and be sure your individual hopes, wishes, and desires are fulfilled. Doing so will also strengthen your mutual love and commitment.

You're a passionate romantic who delights in the sensual side of life and long, leisurely hours with the one you love. When you're ready to settle down, you may resonate best with someone who is mature, in attitude if not in age, and who can provide the emotional and material security so important to you.

Strongly attracted to the fast pace of life with Aries, you may struggle with this sign's fondness for taking risks. With Taurus, you feel safe and secure, although household clutter could get the best of you. Gemini is pure fun, but prefers an intellectual focus to your emotional one.

You're naturally compatible with Cancer and the other water signs, Scorpio and Pisces. Although your needs are in sync with another Cancer, your changing emotions may not be. Scorpio's intensity draws you like a magnet, and Pisces can spark your creativity and intuition in a spiritual union.

Romantic, loyal Leo loves all your attention, but you may not receive an equal share in return. Life with Virgo might be too narrow for your tastes even though your values are compatible. With Libra you'll have an active social life, but lack the emotional connection you need.

Adventuresome Sagittarius encourages you to broaden your horizons, to move beyond home and family into the world. Your opposite sign, Capricorn, may be the best match, and together you can build a secure future. With Aquarius, you experience friendship at its finest, but this sign may be too independent and aloof for you.

Making Your Place in the World

The career world is a perfect match for your competitive instincts, which come alive as you race for the top. Backed up by high energy and enthusiasm, little stands between you and success.

You prefer a fast-paced career environment that has plenty of opportunities for advancement. If that comes too slowly, or the chance for promotion is slim, you're quick to move on. That can be to your advantage as long as job-hopping doesn't become a habit.

The freedom to be a pioneer in thought and action is an important job component, as is the independence to structure your daily work within a loose framework. A hovering boss is not for you!

You could excel in real estate or politics, or as a surgeon, obstetrician, or florist. Hotel management, domestic services, human resources, home furnishings, antiques, and social work also might be good choices. Your financial savvy could be an asset in mortgage banking or investments, and your family focus might lead you into childcare, teaching, or work as a nanny. If the food-service industry appeals to you, a job as a chef, baker, server, or caterer could fulfill your career goals.

Putting Your Best Foot Forward

You're in touch with people, attuned to their needs, and aware of their cares and concerns. Family members, close friends, and even co-workers benefit from your warmth and sensitivity, and come to depend upon you to soothe hurt feelings and help them weather life's ups and downs. When someone needs a hug or a kind word, you're usually the first to offer it.

This is part of your life mission, and you feel very worthwhile when fulfilling it. But how often do you put yourself first? Probably not often enough!

Even though it might not seem so, you will be better able to care for your extended family if you're content with yourself and your own life. When you feel centered and your needs have been met, your emotions may fluctuate less and your powerful inner voice will become stronger.

There's another important reason to give yourself equal time. At their best, Cancers are the nurturers of the zodiac, people who encourage and empower others to become their best. All that changes, however, when love exceeds "normal" bounds and becomes "smother love." Then what should be nourishing can stifle growth. By allowing those you love to stumble and learn through experience, you do them and yourself a favor. This is, of course, far easier to do when you have your own life, career, hobbies, and other interests, and your self-esteem is more closely tied to your own achievements rather than your family. And, after all, you'll be there to help them get back on their feet!

Tools for Change

What you value comes into question this year as you're encouraged to take a close look at two major life themes: emotional and financial security.

Financial security is important to almost everyone, but more so to you. How you define it, however, can cover a broad spectrum of feeling from caution to thrift to penny-pinching.

Your challenge is to find and maintain a middle ground that's both healthy and financially sound. Start by banishing "austerity thinking," and replacing it with thoughts of abundance, which is really a matter of perspective. When you feel and think you're wealthy, you are; when you don't, you aren't. Then you can move on to identify your financial goals, including income, savings, investments, and retirement funds. Be realistic and specific.

Self-knowledge is an equally valuable tool for self-understanding. Self-help books, support groups, and even talking with your partner or close friends can help you gain the knowledge to better understand yourself and why you react the way you do, both emotionally and financially. The more know about yourself, the better prepared you will be to deal with the ups and downs of daily life.

So look within to discover what you value—what's really important to you—in relationships, personal goals, happiness, and financial security. You likely already know many of the answers, but the ones yet to be found on your journey of discovery will amaze you.

Affirmation for the Year

I value myself and feel secure in my life.

The Year Ahead for Cancer

Jupiter in Sagittarius through December 17 accents your solar Sixth House of work and health. This happy, upbeat planet associated with good fortune and opportunity can help you beat the odds in the game of life. But there are no guarantees! Sometimes Jupiter promises more than it delivers or compounds what would otherwise be a manageable situation. Keep that in mind as the year unfolds and you're tempted to snap up every lucky job break that comes your way. Examine the opportunities, though, because it's possible, for example, that excessive work—the desire to do it all—could negatively affect your health. But Jupiter can be just the motivation you need to adopt a healthier lifestyle, including moderate, stress-reducing exercise and a more nutritious, balanced diet. And as your energy rises, so will your life outlook, which, in turn, will attract more of Jupiter's beneficial energy.

Saturn completes its trek through Leo, your solar Second House of income, this year. By now you've experienced some of the ups and downs that accompany this transit, which has challenged you to address your financial attitudes. Given your strong need for financial security, Saturn's influence can trigger austerity thinking when what you really need is tighter budgeting and knowledge to more effectively manage your resources. That includes the principle of letting your money circulate. With good intentions and a positive attitude, what you spend or donate—within reason—is more than likely to be returned to you several times over. But start slowly and test the waters rather than jump in feet first, if for no other reason than to convince yourself. Give someone you love (maybe you?) a small gift for no reason other than to express affection. Or amaze and delight your children by indulging their latest whim—even if it's overpriced by your standards. Gradually, you'll detect a subtle shift as you begin to think and embrace abundance. After Saturn enters Virgo on September 2, your focus begins to shift from money to knowledge and communication. Learn all you can in the next two years, whether through a class, reading on your own, or talking with and observing people. At times your thoughts will focus on the past, but stop short of regrets. Find the message in the memories instead, learn from them, and put the experience to good use in daily life, relationships, and your career.

Uranus, now in its fifth year in Pisces, continues to touch your spiritual heart as it encourages you to broaden your physical and mental horizons. Travel, delve into metaphysics, or study a subject that's always tickled your fancy. If business sends you out of town, take a few extra days to explore the area, and aim for a luxury trip later this year or next. Consider a learning vacation, such as a week at a gourmet cooking school, a walking tour of ancient ruins or one of the world's major capitals, or a hands-on seminar to develop your creative talents. Uranus also can lead you in unexpected directions as it boosts your sixth sense and invites fresh insights into life, love, and what you value most. Your outlook will evolve as the year advances and you begin to discover new truths and, with them, the desire to share your newfound knowledge with others. This could manifest as an interest in teaching in a traditional or nontraditional setting, or as the passion to pursue your true calling in life, starting with the education that will help you realize your dreams.

Where Saturn in Leo emphasizes your money, Neptune in Aquarius spotlights joint resources, including inheritance, insurance, investments, benefits, retirement accounts, and partnership funds. Neptune is as much the planet of illusion and confusion as it is of enlightenment. But it can be tough to look through the haze to identify which is which. Although realistic Saturn aids that process this year, it's still wise to consult well-qualified, certified professionals before making major financial decisions that can have long-term consequences. You, your partner, or both may have already experienced some of Neptune's effects because it's been in Aquarius since 1995. If so, benefit from that knowledge, especially what you learned seven years ago when Saturn contacted your Sun from practical Taurus, a sign that's as security- and value-conscious as you are. On another level, spiritual Neptune encourages you to have faith and to trust in the universe. Not blindly, but as an extension of yourself that's based on wisdom, facts, and the belief that you deserve the best from life.

This year is the last of Pluto's long transit through Sagittarius. During the past twelve years your work life has undergone many changes as this transformative planet sometimes pushed you to take bold steps and at other times to retreat and regroup. You've undoubtedly learned the ins and outs of workplace politics and how best to manage everything from your time and talents to the boss and co-workers. Now it's time to cash in! This year is the one you've been working and waiting for, when all your hard work can pay off. With luck and opportunity on your side, you're set for a step up—one that will have you on your way to ever-increasing gains over the next five years. There are, however, two caveats to this rosy picture. Take on only what you're sure you have the knowledge and experience to handle. Otherwise you could lose, rather than gain supporters who can benefit you this year and next. As you make your mark, also try to remember that no one, including you, is invincible. Commitment can become obsession, and overconfidence can trigger power struggles. Maintain your perspective and empower others as you share the load and the credit.

This year's eclipses—two solar and two lunar—are in Virgo and Pisces, your solar Third and Ninth Houses. They reinforce the emphasis on learning and education, as well as travel. If a long vacation is out of the question, consider periodic weekends away without your cell phone or computer.

If you were born between June 20 and July 2, you will be among the first of your sign to experience the positive benefits of Saturn in Virgo, your solar Third House, from September 2 on. This influence brings out your natural analytical ability, but also your tendency to worry. Try to keep things in perspective and be realistic, and quickly replace negative thoughts with serene ones, such as your favorite vacation spot or an uplifting moment. You might consider a return to school for a degree or advanced certification that can lead to career gains in a few years. If that's your desire, your family will be supportive and your partner willing to take on extra domestic responsibilities. Key dates: October 13, November 30, and December 6 and 19.

If you were born between July 2 and 12, Uranus in Pisces, your solar Ninth House, encourages you to initiate positive personal change. Although you prefer the safety of the status quo, with Uranus in a fellow Water sign, you'll be more open to the idea. Not that you'll have to be. It's likely to happen with or without your action, as you grow into your true self, no matter your age, and really get to know yourself. A year from now you'll see the difference and how far you've come without being fully aware of the process. You can enhance this evolution by exposing yourself to new information and people, different cultures, and other lifestyles. All can spark new insights about yourself, your life and your place in the world. Key dates: January 22, February 7, March 4 and 31, April 27, June 8, September 4, October 8, and November 25.

If you were born between July 9 and 15, Neptune is in Aquarius, your solar Eighth House of joint resources, so the focus is on money matters involving other people. That includes your partner (business or personal), debtors, insurance companies, and inheritance. Because Neptune often signals confusion, you should be extremely careful when signing contracts, and if you file an insurance claim, it could take considerable persistence for it to be resolved in your favor. Confirm that all premiums and taxes have been paid and that professionals you consult have the proper certification. It's also possible a partner's income or benefits could be reduced. Key dates: January 20 and 26, February 9, April 5, May 6 and 13, June 26, August 12, September 23, November 23, and December 20.

If you were born between July 9 and 21, Saturn in Leo will contact your Sun before it enters Virgo on September 2. Although possessions and other assets are of utmost importance, you may begin to question what you most value in life. Security might be the first intangible that comes to mind, but have you ever considered your skills and talents as assets? They may be your most valuable resources, along with your unique personality traits. Your challenge this year is to identify what at first might seem indefinable: your personal strengths. Start by making your own list and then ask others you trust and respect for their feedback. You might be surprised to discover that the list is long and includes more than a few characteristics you never considered. It's possible you're more aware of your weaknesses. That's OK and natural. But emphasize the positive and determine which traits you can change and which ones you can minimize. Key dates: January 20, February 10, March 22, April 19, May 9, July 1 and 30, August 13 and 20.

If you were born between July 17 and 21, you may have to deal with a difficult person in the workplace—most likely a boss or co-worker—as Pluto in Sagittarius contacts your Sun. The situation will not be easy to resolve and you really have only two choices: live with it or look elsewhere. But before you move on, remember that Jupiter is also in Sagittarius. Although this dual influence can compound the situation, it could trigger a fabulous promotion as well as a new job at another company. Health concerns also are possible, so treat your body well and get a checkup. Key dates: February 19, March 18, April 8, May 12, September 19, November 5, and December 10.

Cancer/January

Planetary Hotspots

January's hotspot is finances. Save rather than spend early in the month so you'll have extra cash if unexpected expenses pop up the last two weeks. Although you'll see more money go out, whatever you need will likely be there when you need it. This is not the month to apply for a loan or run up debt. But with a little luck, which you'll have, you might even earn a raise or bonus. Think prosperity!

Wellness and Keeping Fit

With Mars, Jupiter, and Pluto in Sagittarius, your solar Sixth House of health, you can succeed with an exercise program launched at the January 3 Full Moon in your sign. Start slowly, though, because you'll have a tendency to push yourself too hard. Besides being good for your body, physical activity can help you better manage stress during this fast-paced work period.

Love and Life Connections

You're drawn to people and they to you as several planets travel in Capricorn, your sign of close relationships and this month's New Moon on January 28. Devote extra hours to loved ones, your partner, and close friends. If you're ready to take a dating relationship to the next level, the New Moon could trigger talk of a commitment. Mars in Capricorn from January 16 on stirs passions, but conflict is also possible. Know when to back off.

Finance and Success

Your work life is hectic and your work load heavy the first two weeks of the year, with Mars, your career planet, in expansive Sagittarius. The pace eases after that and you can settle into a normal routine or daily tasks.

Rewarding Days

2, 5, 8, 10, 12, 17, 18, 21, 22, 25, 31

Challenging Days

1, 11, 13, 16, 20, 23, 26

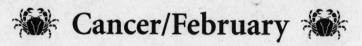

Cancer/February

Planetary Hotspots

Although finances continue to challenge you, this month's hotspot is communication. Frustration can get the best of you mid-month, when Mercury turns retrograde in Pisces and then slips back into Aquarius, your sign of joint resources, February 28. Money matters you consider resolved will resurface, and getting information will be tough. Travel also can be disrupted, so try to avoid trips, especially the second week of February.

Wellness and Keeping Fit

The Sun, Mercury, and Venus travel in Pisces, your solar Ninth House of knowledge at various times this month. Use this trio for self-understanding. The more you know about yourself and what makes you tick, the more effective you can be in the world, your personal life, and relationships.

Love and Life Connections

What seems perfectly clear to you may not be to others when Mercury is retrograde. Clarify thoughts, be patient, and encourage questions to help prevent misunderstandings. This is especially important with loved ones, business associates, and professional consultants. Socialize with colleagues after Venus enters Aries on February 20. Among them could be a new romantic interest.

Finance and Success

Your star is on the rise February 20, when Venus enters Aries, your career sign. Make it a point to talk with decision-makers and others who can promote your strengths and talents. However, impulsive Mars is in Capricorn through February 24, so use a subtle, tactful approach as you strive to gain supporters.

Rewarding Days

6, 7, 8, 9, 11, 13, 14, 20, 21, 22, 27

Challenging Days

5, 10, 15, 16, 19, 23, 25, 28

Cancer/March

Planetary Hotspots

Financial challenges begin to ease as Mercury turns direct March 7, but expect one more hurdle at month's end. The same applies to communication, which is highlighted by the March 3 Full Moon in Virgo, and the March 19 New Moon in Pisces. Take the initiative to clear up recent misunderstandings, although it will take all your people skills to accomplish that with a difficult co-worker.

Wellness and Keeping Fit

Let Mercury motivate you to expand your knowledge about diet and nutrition after it enters Pisces on March 18. Take a class for the fun of it to learn new and easy techniques to create healthy meals and snacks. If you're already an expert, consider teaching a community class this summer.

Love and Life Connections

You'll be ready to socialize when Venus enters Taurus, your friendship sign, March 17. Chances are, you'll click with someone exciting and have an instant rapport. Whether this person is a new pal or a romantic interest, you can form a strong and lasting bond. Couples in love might want to plan a summer trip or dash off for a romantic weekend before the Sun completes its Pisces transit, March 19.

Finance and Success

You continue to catch the attention of important people as Venus advances in Aries and the Sun enters the same sign March 20. So gear up for what promises to be a terrific career month, with the chance for a raise, bonus, or step up. If your goal is a new job, send out résumés now and you could land the ideal spot in April.

Rewarding Days

4, 6, 10, 12, 13, 17, 19, 21, 25, 26, 27, 30

Challenging Days

1, 9, 16, 18, 22, 23, 24, 29

Cancer/April

Planetary Hotspots

Communication, primarily with friends and co-workers, is a challenge early in the month. You might feel as though it's next to impossible to please anyone and frustration rises as a result. Maintain a low profile, go with the flow, and quit while you're ahead. Stubborn people do not want their minds changed. Travel is subject to delays and cancellations during the same time frame, so plan accordingly. Postpone legal matters as well.

Wellness and Keeping Fit

Time at home is especially satisfying this month. It's a comforting haven, the place to unwind, be yourself, and retreat from the world, which you'll want to do at the April 12 Full Moon in Libra, your domestic sign. The influence continues as Venus enters your solar Twelfth House of self-renewal on April 11. Enjoy your own company and relaxing hours with those you love.

Love and Life Connections

With the Sun, Venus, and Mercury in Taurus, you may receive more social invitations than you have the time—or desire—to accept. Choose the best of the best, as well as leisurely get-togethers with your closest friends, which you'll enjoy far more than large gatherings later in April. If you want to host a get-together, plan it for next month.

Finance and Success

You and your career continue in the spotlight with favorable odds for financial gain. That's a plus if your sights are set on a step up or you're interviewing. Everything comes together the last two weeks of the month, thanks to the April 17 New Moon in Aries, your career sign, and Mercury's beneficial planetary contacts from the same sign.

Rewarding Days

3, 4, 9, 11, 16, 17, 19, 22, 23, 26, 29

Challenging Days

5, 8, 12, 15, 20, 21, 27, 28

Cancer/May

Planetary Hotspots

Friends, groups, money, and values clash early this month. You'll see a previously unseen side of someone that will disappoint you as you discover your goals differ greatly. Learn from the experience and move on. Put yourself and yours first if a friend leans on you for a loan or a group expects a donation. Don't feel obligated to stretch your budget. You're unlikely to see a return any time soon, if ever.

Wellness and Keeping Fit

Your inner voice speaks strongly May 11–28, as Mercury in Gemini encourages you to look inward. Your thoughts and intuition are extremely powerful now. Listen closely and fill your mind with positive, uplifting thoughts to attract what you wish for. You also should make an effort to protect yourself from negative environments and people because you'll be unusually sensitive to your surroundings.

Love and Life Connections

May brings you many opportunities for love, romance, and carefree days with friends. TLC and intimate moments link hearts, minds and passions for couples the week of the May 3 Full Moon in Scorpio as Venus completes its Gemini transit. The same time frame brings a new romantic interest to some singles. If you're debating the merits of a dating relationship, finances may be the deciding factor.

Finance and Success

Mars advances into Aries, your career sign, May 15, after which you can expect a fast pace and the need for quick action. Take advantage of the opportunity to showcase your leadership skills, and volunteer for projects that stretch your skills. You'll be pleasantly surprised at just how much you can do. Even if you don't see an immediate financial gain, you'll earn the trust of someone who can help further your aims.

Rewarding Days

1, 3, 6, 7, 8, 11, 15, 19, 24, 29

Challenging Days

5, 10, 12, 16, 18, 22, 25, 26

Cancer/June

Planetary Hotspots

Life is fairly smooth with one exception. Financial challenges resurface as Saturn and Neptune form an exact alignment. Your usual savvy and caution should see you around any obstacles. Even so, this is not the month for major money moves and decisions. Advice may be false or misleading, so check credentials if you consult a professional. On the upside, you could receive a long-awaited check.

Wellness and Keeping Fit

This month's June 1 Full Moon in Sagittarius and the June 15 New Moon in Gemini highlight your solar health sectors. If a slimmer, trimmer, in-shape you is your goal, get started at the Full Moon. If interest begins to wane, reinforce your resolve at the New Moon. Ask a friend to join you in daily exercise and motivate each other.

Love and Life Connections

Your summer social life gets off to a fast start June 24, when Mars enters Taurus, your friendship sign. Be alert for networking opportunities as you meet new people, but choose your words with care. Mercury in Cancer turns retrograde June 15, increasing the odds for a misunderstanding. June has two Full Moons. The Blue Moon on June 30 in Capricorn, your solar Seventh House of close relationships, triggers talk of commitment for some singles. If you're among them, listen to your inner voice and do what's right for you. If you're unsure, postpone the decision.

Finance and Success

Career kudos accompany Mars, which completes its Aries transit June 23. Positive alignments with Jupiter early in June and several planets mid-month signal success as well as possible talk of a promotion, additional responsibilities, or a job offer. Listen carefully and closely. Be sure you understand all facets before you accept.

Rewarding Days

1, 5, 7, 10, 13, 15, 16, 18, 23, 25, 27

Challenging Days

2, 3, 6, 9, 12, 19, 20, 24, 26

Cancer/July

Planetary Hotspots

Expect minor mix-ups and misunderstandings as Mercury, your communication planet, travels retrograde through July 8. Enjoy it while it lasts because you'll get a similar effect after July 27, the date Venus reverses direction in Virgo, your communication sign. So you'll want to continue to confirm dates, times, and places, and to choose your words with care, especially with friends and family and in other close relationships.

Wellness and Keeping Fit

Celebrate your new Solar Year on July 4, the date of July's New Moon in your sign. Give some thought to what you want to accomplish in the next twelve months, for yourself, your well-being, your career, your family, and your home. Then set your plans in motion after Mercury turns direct.

Love and Life Connections

You'll question the future of a friendship at month's end when Mars in Taurus, your friendship sign, clashes with Saturn and Neptune. The issues will be money and values and will involve a third person. As tough as it will be to walk away, you'll have the strength to do that if it's the right choice. The planetary alignment also could affect a business relationship, so you should be cautious about sharing your ambitions with just anyone.

Finance and Success

Venus in Leo, your sign of personal resources, through July 13, and the Sun in the same sign after July 21, increase earning potential. But with universal money-planet Venus turning retrograde after it enters Virgo this month and then slipping back into Leo in August, you'll want to be cautious about spending.

Rewarding Days

1, 4, 5, 9, 13, 14, 17, 21, 22, 25, 27, 28

Challenging Days

2, 3, 6, 7, 10, 16, 19, 23, 24

Cancer/August

Planetary Hotspots

Finances occupy your time and attention, especially in mid-August when the Sun, Venus, and Mercury in Leo contact most of the outer planets, including Saturn in Leo. Be careful and cautious with money matters and let your natural financial savvy be your guide. Although risks and major decisions are unwise, this influence can be positive or negative or a little of both. However, it also could bring you a lucky windfall, so take a chance on the lottery.

Wellness and Keeping Fit

Mars arrives in Gemini, your solar Twelfth House of well-being, August 7. Put it to work for you with an exercise or stress-management program to release the bottled-up tension that accompanies this transit. You'll also want to take the time to relax and unwind before bedtime to ensure easy and restful sleep.

Love and Life Connections

You can expect a quiet month on the social scene with Venus retrograde, but at the same time you'll delight in more evenings and weekends in the company of loved ones. Communication requires extra care and understanding at month's end, however, when Mercury is active in Virgo and the August 28 Full Moon in Pisces has people at odds, primarily at work. Avoid travel at that time if possible, and drive with care.

Finance and Success

All your hard work could pay off this month with a major promotion or fabulous job offer as Saturn forms a beneficial contact with Pluto in Sagittarius. You also could receive an award in recognition of career achievements or your efforts for a good cause.

Rewarding Days

1, 3, 5, 9, 10, 16, 17, 18, 19, 23, 24, 30, 31

Challenging Days

2, 6, 8, 12, 13, 15, 20, 21, 28, 29

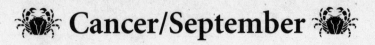

Cancer/September

Planetary Hotspots

Saturn enters Virgo, your solar Third House, September 2. This two-year influence accents learning and communication, and could bring you in contact with a soul mate who has important knowledge to share. You could do the same for someone else, possibly without realizing it at the time. Take a class if you're motivated to master a subject or your career would benefit from it.

Wellness and Keeping Fit

Pluto, your recreation planet, turns direct in Sagittarius, your solar Sixth House of health, September 7. That's all the reason you need to dive into an exercise program to firm and tone muscles and improve your overall health. Join a gym, take tennis lessons, or try water aerobics to get your blood moving.

Love and Life Connections

Family relationships are upbeat and uplifting, thanks to Mercury in Libra, your domestic sign, September 5–27, and the Sun's arrival in the same sign September 22. You'll especially enjoy the relaxing, supportive atmosphere at home because workplace communication will be a challenge. There you can expect power struggles and difficult people whose main mission is to block progress. Stay out of the power plays as much as possible. Also continue to drive with extra care.

Finance and Success

Finances are on the upswing as Venus turns direct September 8, but you'll want to be a little cautious the third week of the month when Venus contacts illusive Neptune. Snap up an opportunity to rise above the rest the week of the September 26 Full Moon in Aries, your career sign. You'll be ultramotivated then because Mars, your career planet, arrives in Cancer two days later. Go for it!

Rewarding Days

1, 5, 6, 7, 12, 13, 14, 15, 18, 20, 27

Challenging Days

2, 3, 16, 17, 19, 21, 23, 24, 26

Cancer/October

Planetary Hotspots

On October 11, the New Moon in Libra, your domestic sign, could spark the urge to redecorate or remodel. Your motivation is the desire for change, but this month is better for planning than initiating projects because Mercury turns retrograde October 11 in Scorpio and returns to Libra on October 23. Chances are, you'll change your mind next month, so use this time for planning, clearing out storage spaces, and general de-cluttering.

Wellness and Keeping Fit

Take the initiative to resolve regrets or outstanding issues with friends or family members as Venus travels in Virgo from October 8 on. Whatever the reaction, which might surprise you, what's most important is for you to put the matter behind you so you're free to move on.

Love and Life Connections

Your social life picks up, thanks to Mercury in Scorpio, your solar Fifth House of romance and play, through October 22, the day before the Sun advances into the same sign. Even better is the October 26 Full Moon in Taurus, your friendship sign. Call friends, line up dates, and plan to host an event next month to kick off the holidays. Be patient if you meet someone fascinating. It might be November before you get together.

Finance and Success

An exact alignment of Jupiter, Uranus, and Neptune spotlights your finances and work life. This potentially lucky influence could trigger a step up the career ladder, a fatter bank account, or both, this month or next. Listen, observe, and use your intuition to pick up on undercurrents.

Rewarding Days

3, 4, 6, 7, 8, 10, 11, 14, 18, 26, 27, 30

Challenging Days

2, 9, 12, 15, 17, 19, 22, 23, 24, 28, 29

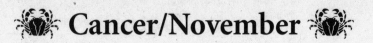

Cancer/November

Planetary Hotspots

Life and events may not progress as quickly as you'd like after Mars turns retrograde in your sign, November 15. Emphasize patience and curb frustration, rather than attempt to get things moving. For whatever reason, now is not the time, so kick back, enjoy the holidays, and let matters develop at their—and the universe's—pace.

Wellness and Keeping Fit

Remind yourself to schedule routine checkups the week after the November 24 Full Moon in Gemini, your solar Twelfth House of health. Besides peace of mind, you'll gain the incentive to adopt a healthier lifestyle at next month's New Moon.

Love and Life Connections

Holiday socializing moves into high gear thanks to the November 9 New Moon in Scorpio, which sparks a new romance for some singles. That's a great weekend to host a party because both Venus and Mercury will be in Libra, your domestic sign. You'll also want to celebrate family life this month. Plan some special evenings in honor of yourself, your partner, and your children, as well as a get-together for extended family.

Finance and Success

With Mars, your career planet, retrograde later this month, you can expect a slowdown at work, but not totally. The Sun in Sagittarius, your sign of daily work, from November 22 on, will help you complete unfinished projects. But leave room for revisions. They're likely, even into February. If you're waiting to hear about a job offer or promotion, it also may be put on hold until next year.

Rewarding Days

3, 4, 7, 8, 9, 10, 12, 15, 18, 19, 22, 26

Challenging Days

5, 6, 11, 14, 21, 24, 30

Cancer/December

Planetary Hotspots

A gift from the universe arrives December 18 when lucky, expansive Jupiter enters Capricorn, your solar Seventh House of close relationships. This year-long influence is terrific for love and romance, as well as professional consultations and partnerships. If you're single, your status may change in 2008. If you're committed, Jupiter renews your celebration of love.

Wellness and Keeping Fit

Dust off the stress-management techniques you acquired in August when Mars was in Gemini. The red planet, still retrograde, does a rerun and slips back into Gemini on December 31. Carry the energy into the new year and make it a way of life in 2008 for your health and well-being.

Love and Life Connections

If you want to host a holiday party, try for the first weekend in December when Venus in Libra aligns with Jupiter and Pluto. Venus moves into Scorpio on December 5 to keep your social life active through year's end. It's also a marvelous influence for your love life, whether you're in search of someone new or in a committed relationship. Set aside a few special evenings just for the two of you after Jupiter arrives in Capricorn.

Finance and Success

Progress alternates with setbacks and delays at work, where decision-makers seem to do anything, but information is tough to come by. You could receive a holiday bonus, although maybe not as much as you hope for. Keep that in mind if you're tempted to splurge on gifts for family and partner. Use your imagination, rather than money, to create gifts for co-workers and neighbors.

Rewarding Days

4, 5, 7, 10, 11, 12, 14, 16, 19, 25, 28, 29

Challenging Days

1, 2, 3, 6, 8, 9, 15, 17, 22, 23

Cancer Action Table

These dates reflect the best—but not the only—times for success and ease in these activities, according to your Sun sign.

	JAN	FEB	MAR	APR	MAY	JUN	JUL	AUG	SEPT	OCT	NOV	DEC
Move		6, 7		29, 30					13, 23-26	9-11	6, 7	3, 4
Start a class	7, 8			26, 27			17, 18	24-31	1-3			28, 29
Join a club		21-23	21, 22	27-30	1-9. 15, 16							
Ask for a raise		28		24, 25		18			7	5	28, 29	
Look for work	15, 23, 24	20, 21		16, 17		9, 10	25, 26	21, 22	18	15, 16		8-10
Get pro advice	2, 17-19	13, 14	13, 14	9, 10	7		27	23, 24	20, 21	17, 18	13-15	11, 26-30
Get a loan	15-26		10-16	11, 12		5, 6						14
See a doctor	15, 16, 29		12	20	16, 17	1, 14, 27, 28	11, 12	7, 8, 22				
Start a diet	15, 16				4, 5	1					24, 25	
End relationship	3, 17		13, 14	9, 10	6, 7	2-4						
Buy clothes	13	10	8, 9	4	2, 28-30		22		15		8-10	5-7
Get a makeover	30, 31		26		19			12-14		2, 30	27	24
New romance	13	8, 9		5	29, 30	25	22				9	5, 6
Vacation	28-31	17-19	17-19			7	4, 5	2			18, 19	15, 16

The Lion
July 22 to August 23

♌

Element:	Fire
Quality:	Fixed
Polarity:	Yang/Masculine
Planetary Ruler:	The Sun
Meditation:	I trust in the strength of my soul
Gemstone:	Ruby
Power Stones:	Topaz, sardonyx
Key Phrase:	I will
Glyph:	Lion's tail
Anatomy:	Heart, upper back
Color:	Gold, scarlet
Animal:	Lions, large cats
Myths/Legends:	Apollo, Isis, Helios
House:	Fifth
Opposite Sign:	Aquarius
Flower:	Marigold, sunflower
Key Word:	Magnetic

Your Ego's Strengths and Weaknesses

Outgoing, generous, honest, and loyal, you light up a room the way the Sun, your ruling planet, brightens the world. People delight in your cheerful optimism. You're ambitious and seek outlets for your natural leadership ability, which plays well on center stage and keeps you in the middle of the action. So it's no surprise that your unique style and flair dazzle people wherever you go.

With so much attention focused your way, it's easy to forget that others also enjoy being in the limelight. Everyone delights in an ego boost, and praise coming from you carries a lot of weight. You also shine when you're a motivational team player who shares the glory and the credit.

You're both a starter and a finisher because Leo is a fixed fire sign. That gives you the spark of initiative to get things moving, plus the follow-through to deliver as promised. So even though you prefer the status quo, you also understand the need for change—as long as you're in charge of the change!

Although generally broad-minded, you do have your moments. Determination and stubbornness get equal billing, depending upon the situation. You're unwilling to compromise your strong beliefs and have the courage to defend them. The same is true once you've formed an opinion. But you never know. Someone else just might have a better idea.

You cherish your play time, and it's such a part of your life that you usually have a joke or a witty story to share. Evenings and weekends are the best times for you, and your popularity makes you a party headliner. Hobbies, sports, and other recreational activities are terrific outlets for your creative talent.

You're drawn to glitter and glitz, and want only the real thing. That's great incentive to wisely manage your money and investments rather than risk a loss. Overall, you can do well financially if you look at the big picture while handling the details. Plan ahead, budget, and keep your goals in sight.

Shining Your Love Light

Romance is your specialty. Charming words, warmth, affection, and a flair for the dramatic is the right combination to wow and woo anyone who catches your eye. Playing the field is just your style and you can take generosity to the point of extravagance to win the attention and adoration of a potential mate until that special someone walks into your life.

You have the soul of a romantic, and the one lucky enough to win your heart revels in the royal treatment. Spontaneity, playfulness, and passion keep your love alive, and you think nothing of dashing off at a moment's notice to rekindle the sizzle that brought you together.

Lasting love could be yours with Aquarius, your opposite sign, but you'll have to accept Aquarius' need for autonomy within the relationship. Manage that and your bonus is a wide variety of friends to enrich your life.

You click with the high energy of the other fire signs—Aries and Sagittarius—or another Leo. Aries is always on the go, so it might be tough to find quieter moments to explore your love. With Sagittarius, your spirit of adventure can reach new heights, but you prefer to travel in luxury. Sparks fly with another Leo, although sharing the spotlight could be a challenge down the line.

Taurus' earthy sensuality captivates you, but resistance to change could have you at odds. Lively, flirtatious Gemini enhances your fun factor and is mentally stimulating if you can adjust to the sometimes scattered energy. Virgo might be too reserved for you, although that gives you more chances to shine. Loyalty is a strong draw.

Libra shares your social needs, and you're attracted to the glamour, style, and class of this sign. Smoldering passion can be yours with Scorpio, but possessiveness and emotional intensity can outweigh the inner strength you appreciate. Capricorn may be too career-oriented and structured to be your ideal playmate even though this sign's stability appeals to you. Spirituality and romance can reach ultimate heights with sensitive Pisces, although you'll probably never truly understand each other's needs.

Making Your Place in the World

You play hard and work hard and rarely do anything halfway. Never one to shy away from responsibility, you see each challenge as bringing you closer to the top spot to satisfy your lofty ambitions. Your take-charge attitude accelerates the rise, but you should periodically remind yourself that moving from entry-level position to big cheese is not an overnight process. A well-planned, steady climb is far more to your benefit.

If you choose to use it, you have the persistence to stick with a company, career, or job as long as you see opportunities for the future and receive recognition along the way. You also expect to be well paid for your skills, talents, expertise, and experience, and should always negotiate for a higher salary or additional benefits.

You and your leadership skills are an ideal match for a supervisory position. That means you can excel in almost any career that appeals to you and the odds favor increasing levels of authority.

The business world, politics, and the gaming industry are good choices, as is the entertainment industry, where you could be an actor, theater or club manager, director, producer, costume designer, or make-up artist. If you have the talent, you could become a professional athlete or coach in a team or individual sport.

You might find your niche as a fundraising executive, motivational speaker or facilitator, or as a TV or radio personality, jewelry designer or manufacturer. Event planning and promoting is another area where you could shine, or you might enjoy the fast-paced lifestyle of a stockbroker.

Putting Your Best Foot Forward

In the language of royalty, which Leo rules, there are two options: be a benevolent monarch or a controlling, overbearing one. The choice is obvious. The first will get you much farther in life and you'll build a strong network of supporters along the way.

Personal success is linked to your self-esteem and your willingness to promote the talents and accomplishments of others as you would your own. The more aware you are of other people's needs, the more aware you will be of the ways you can help fulfill their hopes, wishes, and goals. Even better, it also will please your warm, generous heart. And that makes you feel terrific!

When you share your life stage—and kingdom—with others, you set in motion what can be a perpetual cycle. Your motivational skills are among the best and it takes only a kind word in private or a rally for public praise to encourage others as they too strive for success. And as you bask in the reflected glory, you also get an ego boost. This recognition-reward cycle, once begun, will keep your life filled with uplifting relationships, marvelous career contacts, and a wide circle of friends. It's also personally motivating and opens up new paths to follow as you pursue lifetime achievements.

Try it! You'll like it! And you'll also like the applause!

Tools for Change

You have so much going for you now, and your life is liable to be more hectic than ever this year. So it's essential to give your health and well-being some extra attention. You are your most valuable resource—far more important than the people, places, things, and events in your life.

Make it a priority to take time for yourself, even if only thirty minutes a day. Exercise your body or your creativity, read, walk, or re-center through meditation. What you do isn't as significant as putting family and career demands on hold to focus on your needs. It will do wonders for you, your relationships, and your job success.

Your body will reward you with increased energy if you also focus on an overall healthier lifestyle. Track your diet. If it's heavy on fast food or less than nutritionally balanced, take the plunge and make the switch to tasty, nourishing meals. Add plenty of sleep, and find the stress-management techniques that work for you.

On another level, knowledge gained about yourself will mirror what you learn about others, especially those closest to you. United, you can explore new vistas of learning and togetherness. What at first seems mysterious and out of reach will become clear if you free your emotions and get in touch with your true feelings. This inner journey can be a spiritual experience for both of you, and one that restores or enhances your faith in love and personal responsibility. Above all, you will learn what it means to be true to yourself.

Willingness to consider the idea of change is, of course, integral to success even though that's hardly your favorite life experience. Give yourself a chance to get used to the idea by taking small steps rather than giant leaps. The more you do, the easier it will become, and you might even grow to like the idea—or at least accept it.

Affirmation for the Year

I am healthy and happy, and welcome positive change.

The Year Ahead for Leo

Jupiter lights up your love life in 2007, as it travels in Sagittarius, your solar Fifth House of romance, and favorably contacts your Sun. This beneficial influence, which occurs only every twelve years, boosts dating potential for singles and renews the sizzle for even long-committed couples. Socializing is equally in focus and will fill many days, nights, and weekends with hours of pleasure and new adventures. Jupiter here also enhances your creativity, bringing the urge to produce a tangible product—the outward manifestation of your inner drive. If you're like many people, you define creativity only as artistic talent. In reality it's so much more. Explore this side of yourself this year. Try your hand at crafts, jewelry-making, scrapbooking, decorating, or writing; join a community theater group or develop an innovative procedure at work. Because the Fifth House also is associated with children, you might enjoy coaching youth sports, leading a scout group, or helping with your children's after-school activities. If you're a parent, this year offers the ideal opportunity to form a strong bond with your children as they amuse and delight you. If you hope to become a parent, your wish could be fulfilled. Fill your life with fun and laughter this year so you're ready to focus on your work life from December 18 on, when Jupiter enters Capricorn, your solar Sixth House.

Saturn completes its two-year transit of your sign this year. Although this influence may not be one you'd care to repeat anytime soon (it will be another twenty-eight years), there is an upside. This practical planet can bring the ultimate sense of accomplishment, mostly because you feel you've earned whatever you achieve during this time, having strived long and hard to achieve it. So it's only natural that with Saturn in your Sun sign, you'll want to assess your life progress and ambitions. Realign your goals with a focus on work and relationships. Saturn urges—even demands—that you accept responsibilities, even those you wish you could ignore. But because your Sun-ruled sign enjoys being in charge, you could run yourself ragged trying to do it all. Give yourself permission to ask for help when you need it. Share the load more often than not. That's especially important because your physical energy may be low until September 2, when Saturn enters Virgo, your solar Second House of personal resources. Although your income could decrease in the next three years, that's not a given. Saturn's message—and lesson—is about learning to manage and maximize your personal and financial resources. Don't be surprised if you begin to place a higher value on your skills and talents, as well as building a savings cushion.

As Saturn in Virgo will highlight personal resources later this year, Uranus continues to influence joint resources. Now midway through its long transit of Pisces, your solar Eighth House, Uranus represents change, surprise, and opportunity. A windfall is as possible as a loss when this quirky planet influences finances, so you should be more conservative than bold with investments and family funds. A similar scenario applies to your partner's income, which could soar or plummet, although gains are more likely. It's equally possible either or both of you will benefit from an inheritance or lucky win. Overall, though, it's a wise idea to keep close tabs on credit, loans, and insurance matters and to build up savings for unexpected expenses. If debt has become an issue, you might want to look into credit counseling or debt consolidation to speed up the payoff process. Think carefully, though, before you put your home at risk or take on a sizable mortgage.

Neptune entered Aquarius, your solar Seventh House of partnership, in 1998. As it begins its tenth year in this sign, close relationships will benefit more than ever from an emphasis on communication. Idealism continues to dominate, but this year you will begin to see another side of your business or romantic partner (or potential partner). That may be positive or negative, but there's no doubt it will lead to a better understanding of what you both need and expect from a relationship. February and June will be key months in this process. It's possible you will suddenly view your partner in a more realistic light. This may be tough to accept because on some level it will burst the bubble of perceived perfection. Consider it a learning experience. You'll also want to carefully check credentials before consulting a professional, such as an attorney, accountant, financial adviser, or medical personnel. If in doubt, get a second opinion.

Where Jupiter in Sagittarius invites you to expand romantic and creative opportunities, Pluto in its last year in Sagittarius encourages self-empowerment. This positive growth process began in

1995, the last time Jupiter and Pluto were in Sagittarius, and concludes this year with both planets again in your solar Fifth House. The journey will come full circle this year as you fully realize how much you've evolved during that time with ever-increasing confidence and self-understanding. As your inner strength peaks, you might contemplate a major life change. If you decide to make the move, be 100 percent sure. Once you make the move there will be no turning back.

This year's solar and lunar eclipses in Virgo and Pisces reinforce the 2007 focus on personal and shared resources. They occur in August, September, and March, months that will bring money matters to your attention.

If you were born between July 22 and August 3, Saturn in Virgo will contact your Sun from September 2 on. Be proactive right from the start and take charge of your personal finances, including debt, earnings, and saving and spending habits. If you've never had a budget, or taken it seriously, change that. Track spending for a month to see where your dollars go. You might be surprised to discover how many expenses you can cut. It'll be easier than you think. Use the savings to build a nest egg and pay down debt. Your thoughts also will turn to increased income—not so much because you want more money, but because you feel you're worth it. If you're happy with your current position, be prepared with a list of accomplishments prior to your annual review; if not, send out résumés. Key dates: October 13, November 30, and December 6 and 19.

If you were born between August 2 and 12, you should be particularly cautious when money matters involve other people. This includes not just outsiders, such as insurance agents and investment advisers, but also family members. Anyone can make a poor decision, and erratic Uranus in your solar Eighth House of joint resources can trigger significant changes, up or down. You'll also want to take extra precautions to safeguard credit cards and accounts. Check your credit report for errors, and limit debt. On the upside, Uranus accents a wonderful opportunity for you and your partner to define—or redefine—how best to work together for mutual gain. Talk, take your time, seek professional help (if necessary), compromise, and develop a new model that works for both of you. Key dates: January 22, February 7, March 4 and 31, April 27, June 8, September 4, October 8, and November 25.

If you were born between August 9 and 16, Neptune in Aquarius touches your softer, more emotional inner self as it encourages a spiritual connection with your partner. If you and your mate are in love, this year could be one of the most romantic. But if you're questioning a union, disillusionment could prompt you to think about breaking ties. In the process, you might consider it your responsibility to try to "repair" the relationship. It's not. That belongs to both of you, so accept only your share. Neptune also can affect other close relationships in your life; some people will disappoint you and others will be an inspiration. Key dates: January 20 and 26, February 9, April 5, May 6 and 13, June 26, August 12, September 23, November 23, and December 20.

If you were born between August 9 and 23, Saturn in Leo through September 1 offers you the opportunity to set your sights on new achievements that can maximize your strengths, skills, and talents. That's ambitious in itself, but not from Saturn's perspective. You're more than capable of the task if you take it one step at a time. Let your thoughts drift first to the past. Look without regret at where you've been, what you've learned and experienced, the people who've influenced you, and your greatest rewards. From there you can define a new path. Because Saturn will directly contact your Sun, it's vital that sleep, rest, and relaxation are priorities. It will take longer to recoup your energy, which will wane more quickly than usual. This is even more important if your birthday is within a few days of August 10. Try to arrange the perfect Leo luxury vacation in March or April, or at least a long weekend away with friends or a romantic one with your partner. Key dates: January 20, February 10, March 22, April 19, May 9, July 1 and 30, August 13 and 20.

If you were born between August 18 and 23, you will experience Pluto at its best. As this powerful planet of transformation contacts your Sun, it will urge you to go for bigger and better, to be the best you can be. With Jupiter in Sagittarius amplifying the effect, especially at year's end, you could gain through a significant lifetime opportunity. Think carefully about what you most want to achieve this year. Then make it happen. Key dates: February 19, March 18, April 8, May 12, September 19, November 5, and December 10.

Leo/January

Planetary Hotspots

Close relationships test your people skills with loved ones and close friends and on the job. Misunderstandings are likely, and it's easy to jump to conclusions. You may question the future of a romantic relationship, but if fear of commitment holds you back, talk can help you identify the reason why. A business partnership can prompt similar thoughts; if in doubt and if money is involved, listen to your common sense. Carefully check credentials before you consult a professional.

Wellness and Keeping Fit

If all those holiday treats were irresistible (or even if you're one of the few who said "no" to temptation), the January 3 Full Moon in Cancer and the January 18 New Moon in Capricorn, focus your attention on wellness. Resolve to get in shape, emphasize nutrition, and manage stress in 2007. With only a little effort and determination you can adopt new habits and a healthier lifestyle.

Love and Life Connections

Singles searching for romance could encounter a soul mate as Mars in Sagittarius energizes your love life through January 15. The fiery planet stirs passions for couples, who will delight in intimate moments at home. But with stresses and strains affecting even the best relationships this month, open communication is vital. Share your concerns and find a compromise to satisfy both your needs.

Finance and Success

You're in sync with some co-workers this month, but not others. The challenge will be to know who's who. Use your intuition, knowledge, and experience. Then ask questions and be wary of anyone who tries to play to your ego while sidestepping the issues. If a new job is your goal, send out résumés the last week of January.

Rewarding Days

1, 4, 5, 6, 8, 10, 15, 16, 19, 24

Challenging Days

11, 13, 18, 20, 22, 23, 26

Leo/February

Planetary Hotspots

Although relationships are more easygoing, expect a few rough spots the second week of the month. If you're still wavering about a personal or business alliance, a Sun-Saturn-Neptune lineup will likely prompt a decision. You'll also experience some minor financial challenges when unexpected expenses pop up. But the same planetary energy could trigger a lucky win around February 7 or 19.

Wellness and Keeping Fit

Exercise is a great way to de-stress before or after this month's many long days with a heavy workload. Even a quick lunchtime walk can be beneficial. Ask a co-worker to join you and amuse each other with stories and jokes guaranteed to make you laugh.

Love and Life Connections

Breathe fresh energy into your closest relationships the week of the February 17 New Moon in Aquarius. Reach out to others and take the initiative to resolve any recent upsets. Then look to the future and invite new people into your life as Mars sparks incentive after it enters Aquarius on February 25. Take care, though, not to come on too strong at work or at play. Enthusiasm and impatience could encourage you to push too hard, especially when deadlines turn up the heat.

Finance and Success

Although you prefer solo work while Mars is in Capricorn through February 24, that's not the best option. Try to include others because teamwork will get you much farther. Venus in Pisces, your sign of joint resources, through February 20, and the Sun in the same sign from February 18 on, are positive financial influences. But Mercury in Pisces turns retrograde February 13, so mix-ups and delays are likely. Put major money moves on hold until the end of March.

Rewarding Days

1, 6, 7, 12, 14, 15, 17, 20, 22

Challenging Days

4, 5, 10, 16, 23, 25, 28

Leo/March

Planetary Hotspots

During this mostly easygoing month, you'll experience a few communication and financial challenges. A home or appliance repair could temporarily stretch your budget, and delays interfere with work and personal progress. Determination sees you through, as does the ability to shift focus and adapt to changing conditions.

Wellness and Keeping Fit

Internal tension rises as values-based questions and decisions test your faith in yourself and the universe. Do what's right for you rather than let others persuade you to lower your standards, despite your strong sense of loyalty. There is no perfect solution other than the one that leaves you feeling good about yourself and stress-free.

Love and Life Connections

Mix-ups and miscommunication are almost a given with Mercury retrograde in Aquarius through March 6. Minimize the effect by listening closely to what others say and fully explaining your own thoughts and ideas. With Mars also in Aquarius, patience is equally important. Strive for compromise with a caring and understanding attitude the third week of March to help avoid conflict.

Finance and Success

Knowledge and information are your keys to career and financial success this month. Seek both and share your talents with others so you're fully informed when Venus arrives in Taurus, your career sign, March 17. Know-how may be the path to a lucky connection that can boost your bank account. You'll also want to take a close look at personal and family finances as the Full and New Moons in Virgo and Pisces, your money signs, are also eclipses. Review spending, credit, and monthly expenses and develop a realistic budget that includes debt reduction, if necessary.

Rewarding Days

1, 5, 6, 7, 10, 11, 12, 16, 19, 20, 21, 27

Challenging Days

2, 8, 9, 14, 18, 22, 28, 29

Leo/April

Planetary Hotspots

Finances cover the spectrum this month, from extra expenses to potential windfalls. Gains can come through a friend or lucky win; the lottery is worth a try and a group purchase can increase the odds. But you'll want to limit spending and shopping as much as possible so you can cover the unexpected. Staying away from the mall also minimizes the urge to splurge, which will be strong all month.

Wellness and Keeping Fit

Take a hint from April's New and Full Moons: plan a vacation or at least a weekend away whether or not you think you need it. Chances are you do, and even a few days can ease the stresses and strains of daily life. Go for a change of scenery, try somewhere new. Just be sure to get a recommendation from someone you trust and a firm price quote in writing before you go.

Love and Life Connections

Friendship and socializing fill more of your leisure hours after Venus enters Gemini on April 11. Reconnect with pals you haven't seen in months or even years and widen your circle with new faces. Among them could be someone who becomes a lifelong soul mate. Your heart could zing with love at first sight as you instantly click with a friend of a friend, or you might suddenly view a pal as a potential mate. Romance is superb for couples the first week of April, when Mars completes its Aries transit.

Finance and Success

You're an attention-getter, thanks to the Sun, Venus, and Mercury in Taurus. With all three influencing your solar Tenth House of career and status, you'll want to take the lead whenever possible and showcase your know-how for decision-makers. Knowledge and experience set you apart from the crowd, as does teamwork.

Rewarding Days

3, 9, 11, 12, 15, 16, 17, 19, 23, 24, 26, 29

Challenging Days

1, 4, 5, 6, 7, 8, 13, 27, 28

Leo/May

Planetary Hotspots

Expect to be pushed to the max at work the first ten days of May. You'll have your hands full between deadlines and difficult people who compound the situation with indecision and attempts to block progress. Be clever and creative and tap resources to find a way around stumbling blocks.

Wellness and Keeping Fit

Venus enters Cancer, your sign of self-renewal, May 8, followed by Mercury on May 28. Both planetary influences are excellent for quieter moments with your partner, as well as close friends. Step off the treadmill of life some nights and weekends to enjoy quality time in a relaxed atmosphere.

Love and Life Connections

You can choose to socialize with friends any time you wish this month. There will be plenty of opportunities with Mercury, your friendship planet, in Gemini, your friendship sign, May 11–27. Ask a pal to arrange a date around the time the Sun enters Gemini, May 22. The setup could be the start of a whirlwind romance with the soul mate you're searching for. If you're committed, surprise your mate with a weekend or evening adventure and a dazzling gift.

Finance and Success

This month's New Moon in Taurus, May 16, has you in the spotlight for success. This is the time to launch new endeavors, whether that's a project or a new job. Make networking part of your plan, and consider getting involved in a club or organization where you can widen your circle of contacts. You also could net some extra cash this month through a bonus or lucky win. But don't risk funds, especially on investments.

Rewarding Days

3, 4, 7, 8, 13, 14, 15, 17, 21, 22, 27

Challenging Days

2, 5, 9, 10, 18, 20, 25, 28, 30

Leo/June

Planetary Hotspots

June perks along with beautiful days and fun-filled weekends—until the last week of the month. A rocky relationship becomes more so as Saturn forms an exact alignment with Neptune, and even the best partnership is likely to feel the strain. Although it will be a challenge, try to view events, situations, and viewpoints form the opposite perspective. A loving, caring approach may be what's needed, rather than one that's purely practical.

Wellness and Keeping Fit

Welcome the opportunity to look within to resolve past and current issues after Mercury turns retrograde June 15. It's a terrific time to do that as a first step toward redefining your goals, hopes, and wishes. Discover what is truly important to you, your secret desires, your motivators, and what holds you back. Try meditation and self-help books to get started.

Love and Life Connections

An active social life continues to be yours, thanks to the New Moon in Gemini, June 15. The week of the June 1 Full Moon in Sagittarius, which guides your love life, could bring a new romance through or with a friend. Be alert if you travel around that time and, if you're half of a couple, try to dash off for a few days of togetherness.

Finance and Success

Mars energizes your career sector when it zips into Taurus on June 24. Expect a busy and sometimes hectic six weeks. This month's second Full Moon, June 30 in Capricorn, your sign of daily work, sets the pace, so plan ahead to give it your all as June draws to a close. Embrace success!

Rewarding Days

1, 5, 6, 10, 13, 14, 17, 18, 23, 27, 28, 29

Challenging Days

2, 4, 8, 11, 12, 19, 20, 22, 24, 26

Leo/July

Planetary Hotspots

Let common sense be your career guide the last ten days of July. A moneymaking opportunity could turn out to be more hassle than it's worth. You'll also want to tread lightly in the week leading up to the July 30 Full Moon in Capricorn, your sign of daily work, when Mars in Taurus, your career sign, clashes with Saturn and Neptune. Go with the flow even when frustration rises as people try to push your hot buttons.

Wellness and Keeping Fit

Take some time for yourself between the New Moon in Cancer, July 4, and July 9, when Mercury turns direct in the same sign. With both events occurring in your solar Twelfth House of self-renewal, it's a wonderful time to tune out the world and look within. Listen to your inner voice as you re-center, body and soul.

Love and Life Connections

You're at your most irresistible, with Venus in your sign through July 13. Turn on the charm and attract someone special or romance your partner under the stars. Be patient if a new liaison doesn't get off to a fast start. Venus enters Virgo on July 14 and turns retrograde July 27 before slipping back into Leo next month. A soul mate is worth waiting for.

Finance and Success

You'll want to keep a close eye on your budget. With Venus turning retrograde in Virgo, your solar Second House of personal resources, the money flow slows somewhat and, more importantly, it's easy to run up debt without realizing it. Try to postpone major purchases and financial decisions until early October, when Venus will return to Virgo.

Rewarding Days

7, 8, 9, 13, 15, 17, 20, 21, 25, 26, 30

Challenging Days

2, 3, 6, 10, 12, 16, 19, 23, 24, 31

Leo/August

Planetary Hotspots

Welcome to what could be your most fabulous month of 2007. Much depends on your motivation and determination, the people in your life, and luck, which is definitely on your side. The August 12 New Moon in Leo activates four planets in the same sign, which contact nearly all the other planets. Personal change is nearly a given, so it's up to you to decide where and how you want to direct the energy. Ground your dreams in reality and place your trust only in those who have proven themselves and earned it.

Wellness and Keeping Fit

Take a breather once in a while during this hectic month to recenter and renew your objectivity. It will help you identify your personal priorities and examine them from every angle, in addition to providing some healthy stress relief when August events begin to unfold.

Love and Life Connections

If there's one thing you should think twice about this month, it's commitment. The stellar lineup in your sign could trigger, among other events, the desire to elope or move in together. Don't go there! Universal love-planet Venus is retrograde. Move forward if you still feel the same in late September. True love will wait.

Finance and Success

It's not outside the realm of possibility that this month's potentially life-changing Leo alignment could fatten your bank account into a life of leisure. But don't bet on it, at least not with more than a single lottery ticket—it only takes one to win. The downside is someone could play to your generous nature, so make it a firm policy to protect resources now.

Rewarding Days

3, 5, 7, 11, 12, 16, 17, 22, 26, 30, 31

Challenging Days

2, 6, 13, 15, 20, 21, 27, 28, 29

Leo/September

Planetary Hotspots

Money and values are highlighted as Saturn begins its two-year trip through Virgo, your solar Second House, September 2. With the New Moon, Sun, and Mercury in the same sign, now is the time to identify the best use of your personal resources, including your skills and talents. If you feel you're underpaid or underemployed, set a goal to change the situation in the upcoming year, when opportunities will multiply.

Wellness and Keeping Fit

Give yourself the gift of a few days off around the time of the September 28 Full Moon in Aries. Even better, since this is your travel sign, head out of town for a week or long weekend with family, your partner, or close friends. Consider indulging in the royal treatment at a spa.

Love and Life Connections

Turn on the charm! Your social and love life come alive as Venus turns direct in Leo on September 8. Fill the month with outings, events, dates, and more as Mars travels in Gemini, your friendship sign, through September 28. If you're searching for someone special, a pal could be your link to love, or you might find yourself falling for someone you've always considered just a friend.

Finance and Success

Try to plan ahead. You could have some unexpected expenses this month, as well as the periodic urge to splurge. But the biggest risk is investments and entertainment. Don't take chances and don't feel obligated to pick up the check. Treat yourself with generosity and stash cash in savings.

Rewarding Days

1, 4, 7, 8, 9, 12, 13, 18, 22, 27

Challenging Days

2, 3, 11, 16, 17, 19, 24, 26, 30

Leo/October

Planetary Hotspots

Home life is both hectic and delightful with the Sun entering Scorpio, your domestic sign, October 23, the same date retrograde Mercury retreats into Libra. You'll want to spend more time at home in the company of loved ones despite the chaos and probable mix-ups and misunderstandings. However, what you don't want to do during this time frame is begin a home improvement or decorating project. Do that and you're more likely to experience frustration than laughter.

Wellness and Keeping Fit

Find an outlet for stress, which can sneak up on you with Mars in Cancer, your solar Twelfth House of health and well-being. Try yoga, meditation, reading, or a hobby that brings you great pleasure. The goal is to relax and unwind every evening to ensure a restful night's sleep for high-energy days.

Love and Life Connections

You'll enjoy entertaining friends at home far more than being involved in the social scene. Besides, it's a great way to ensure plenty of return invitations during the holiday period, which promises to be an active one this year. Include a few neighbors. Among them could be a new romantic interest.

Finance and Success

Money flows your direction the first half of October, when favorable Venus in Virgo contacts also could deliver a long-awaited check. But some of it is likely to disappear just as fast at month's end, when an unexpected expense is possible. Although you can't control that, you can monitor spending and put credit cards in a safe place other than your wallet. Give the lottery a try the last week of October.

Rewarding Days

4, 5,6, 10, 11, 14, 16, 20, 21, 26, 27

Challenging Days

9, 12, 15, 17, 19, 22, 24, 25, 28, 29

Leo/November

Planetary Hotspots

Because yours is an action-oriented fire sign, it can be tough to adapt to a slower pace. That's your challenge this month after high-energy Mars turns retrograde in Cancer on November 15. You and the rest of the world will experience a slowdown as projects, plans, and decisions are put on hold. Save yourself the frustration. Go with the flow and let it happen.

Wellness and Keeping Fit

Remember to take time to de-stress before bedtime. That's even more important now that Mars is retrograde, so take it a step further. As the ruler of your solar Ninth House of spirituality, Mars encourages you to delve deep within and get in touch with your innermost desires and motivators, as well as what blocks personal success during this powerful period for self-understanding.

Love and Life Connections

You get the best of both this month: socializing at home and out and about. Mercury enters Scorpio, your domestic sign, November 11, two days after the New Moon in the same sign, and the Sun moves on to Sagittarius, your sign of romance and leisure, November 22. Even better, the November 24 Full Moon in Gemini, your solar Eleventh House of friendship, adds more dates to your social calendar.

Finance and Success

Your work life is mostly routine, but you can expect meetings and talks to take more time than usual with Mercury and Venus in Libra, your communication sign, part of November. You'll also want to review, revise, and update previous work and check it for errors after Mercury turns direct November 1.

Rewarding Days

1, 2, 7, 10, 12, 15, 17, 20, 21, 22, 25, 28

Challenging Days

5, 6, 11, 14, 16, 18, 19, 23, 29, 30

Leo/December

Planetary Hotspots

A big event happens December 18. Lucky Jupiter enters Capricorn, your sign of daily work. Think big! This year-long influence can help you land a terrific and lucrative job or promotion in 2008. You'll also enjoy your work life more and look forward to every new project and opportunity. But this enthusiastic planet can prompt you to take on too much because you just want to do it all. Guard against that or you could quickly be overloaded.

Wellness and Keeping Fit

With the holidays in full swing and expansive Jupiter entering Capricorn, which is also your solar Sixth House of health, the pounds can creep on before you know it. Go for moderation rather than attempt to deprive yourself of all those irresistible goodies.

Love and Life Connections

Family ties are heartwarming with Venus in Scorpio, your domestic sign, December 5–29. Make it a point to share your love, time, and attention with your favorite people, near and far. You'll also receive many social invitations, with the Sun and Mercury in Sagittarius, the sign of the December 9 New Moon. But planetary alignments throughout the month advise caution on the road and the importance of a designated driver. Have fun! Be safe!

Finance and Success

Cross your fingers for a nice year-end bonus, thanks to Jupiter, the Sun, and Mercury in Capricorn the third week of December. You also can expect a few last-minute deadlines, which you'll make in the nick of time despite delays along the way. Others will be glad to lend a hand, so ask for help if you need it and then be sure to return the favor.

Rewarding Days

4, 5, 9, 12, 14, 16, 18, 19, 21, 25, 26

Challenging Days

2, 3, 6, 11, 13, 17, 22, 23, 30

Leo Action Table

These dates reflect the best—but not the only—times for success and ease in these activities, according to your Sun sign.

	JAN	FEB	MAR	APR	MAY	JUN	JUL	AUG	SEPT	OCT	NOV	DEC
Move	13				28-30		22-24				3-5, 8-10	5-7
Start a class		6, 7			21-27			16, 17	12, 23-26		6, 7	3, 4
Join a club	27, 28			19, 20	18, 21-27			7, 8			24, 25	
Ask for a raise			30		24		17, 18			8	5	
Look for work	17, 18	13, 14		27-30	7, 16, 17					8	5	
Get pro advice	19, 20, 24		15, 16	11, 12								14
Get a loan	29-31	3-9	8, 9		11, 12			1, 2			18, 19	
See a doctor	12 17, 18		26		7		13, 17, 18				14, 15	
Start a diet	3, 4		13, 14			2, 3	1					
End relationship			15, 16	12		6	3					
Buy clothes	15		11	7		28			17, 18	15	12	8, 9
Get a makeover	5, 6			24, 25	21					5, 6		28, 29
New romance						28, 29			17, 18			8, 9
Vacation	23, 24	21-28		11-18		9, 10			26, 27			

The Virgin
August 22 to September 22

♍

Element:	Earth
Quality:	Mutable
Polarity:	Yin/Feminine
Planetary Ruler:	Mercury
Meditation:	I can allow time for myself
Gemstone:	Sapphire
Power Stones:	Peridot, amazonite, rhodochrosite
Key Phrase:	I analyze
Glyph:	Greek symbol for containment
Anatomy:	Abdomen, intestines, gall bladder
Color:	Taupe, gray, navy blue
Animal:	Domesticated animals
Myths/Legends:	Demeter, Astraea, Hygeia
House:	Sixth
Opposite Sign:	Pisces
Flower:	Pansy
Key Word:	Discriminating

Your Ego's Strengths and Weaknesses

You have the inside track on practical productivity. Concrete results please and motivate you, and your conscientious attention to detail yields phenomenal results.

Your strong work ethic is beyond admirable; in part, because you're inspired by duty and service. A methodical approach, matched with superb analytical skills, helps you zero in on the task at hand. And you usually outdo yourself.

Even though you might define yourself in terms of work, there's so much more to life in general and yours in particular. Your friends and loved ones might not see it this way, but even you appreciate time off—and to yourself—now and then. To them, your leisure-time pursuits probably seem all too much like work. Who cares! If herb gardening, furniture refinishing, patio building, volunteer service, or tinkering in your workshop please you, go for it. What relaxes and satisfies you matters most.

Virgo has a reputation for neatness. Some are; some aren't. This perception is rooted in organization, but not necessarily neatness. Whether you're a messy Virgo or a neat one, what you have a knack for is keeping tabs on everything. And that's no exaggeration, as you well know. Many Virgos forego a calendar and rely on their incredible memory. All born under your sign can produce paperwork in a flash, even if it's buried in a foot-high stack sandwiched between yesterday's newspaper and tomorrow's extensive to-do list.

Your Mercury-ruled sign has an amazing hidden talent: perceptive intuition. It can give you the edge in almost situation, from work to friends to family. In essence, it's as simple as 1+1=2. Your keen powers of observation are the starting point—a piece here, a piece there, a snippet of conversation, body language, casual comments. All this unconnected information is meaningless to others; to you, it's all part of the bigger picture. Your active brain stores the data and then, in a sudden flash of insight, it all comes together, and you're far ahead of the crowd. Listen to your inner voice.

Shining Your Love Light

You have a certain indefinable sensuality that attracts many admirers. Few, however, have the chance to capture your heart. In love, as in life, you're highly selective, with exacting standards.

You're also an idealistic romantic. That's positive if you and your partner lead a charmed, carefree life. But that's rare, so a long courtship is a wise idea. Then you can see your love at his or her best and worst. Otherwise you open yourself up to hurt feelings and disillusionment when fantasy is shoved aside by reality. Perfection is nonexistent.

A strong mental rapport is a must before you will consider a serious relationship. Without that, you feel there is no common ground on which to build long-lasting ties. You also need someone who will respect and support your work ethic, and pick up the slack when you're pressed for time.

You may find yourself in a romantic playground with Pisces, your opposite sign. This match can be heavenly if you handle the daily details of life as your mate contributes spiritual support.

You have a natural bond with the other earth signs—Taurus and Capricorn—as well as other Virgos. Taurus is down-to-earth, conservative, and stable, all of which reflects your mindset; but you're more easygoing and not as set in your ways. Capricorn's sensible, cautious nature appeals to you, although career ambitions could limit time together. With another Virgo, life is pure delight if you can tone down your mutual desire for perfection.

Aries stimulates you to take action, but could be too much of a risk taker. Lively Gemini can lighten up your life, although planning and organization might be a challenge. Life with Cancer can be comfortable and secure even though freely expressed emotions can unsettle you.

Leo's flamboyance might exceed your comfort zone, but you can benefit from this sign's enthusiastic optimism. Thoughts are easy to share with Libra, a socially active sign, although Libra buys for beauty and you opt for what's useful. Scorpio's depth intrigues you and boosts your sense of security, but this sign tests your flexibility.

Adventuresome Sagittarius can encourage you to balance work and play, but you might have a tough time with the spontaneity. Aquarius is free-spirited and independent in contrast to your careful, measured approach, although you'll appreciate all the new friends in your life.

Making Your Place in the World

When a job needs doing, you're usually the first to roll up your sleeves and dig in. Work satisfies you, especially finite tasks with a clear beginning, middle, and end that allow you to use your powerful analytical skills and feel an immediate sense of accomplishment. A tangible result is a reward in itself.

Many Virgos have dual careers—a day job and a sideline—and others switch their career focus several times, depending upon current interests and trends. That's great as long as you remember that overall success is partially linked to longevity and a steady climb.

The freedom to take a job and run with it is a key factor in job happiness because this is your area of independence—you need a great deal of autonomy. Nothing can make you send out resumes faster than a hands-on, micromanaging boss, so try to decipher management styles during the interview process.

Congenial co-workers also are important, although you usually keep your work and personal lives separate.

You might enjoy a career in the health care field as a massage therapist, lab tech, homeopath, physician, nurse, or physician's assistant, or in social services. Veterinary medicine or another career working with animals might appeal to you.

Writing, publishing, editing, and other communications careers might catch your interest, and you could excel as an accountant, bookkeeper, administrative assistant, or nail technician. Scientific research, or statistical or systems analysis might be excellent outlets for your logical mind.

Construction, the building trades, drafting, engineering, and auto mechanics attract some Virgos, as does shipping and receiving, the postal service, and package delivery.

Putting Your Best Foot Forward

Virgo has a corner on the worry market. If you could bottle and sell it, you'd be a megamillionaire and one who's far less stressed on a daily basis. It's worth a try, but chances are that's beyond even your brilliant mind!

There is little that doesn't at one time or another prompt you to worry. Although it's a challenge to change your basic nature, you can learn to better manage your cares and concerns. That's very possible, but it takes time and effort.

Start by identifying the stress factors in your life. Relationships? Security? Family? Job and career? Transportation? Health? Friends? Co-workers? Money? If you find it difficult to zero in on specifics, track and record your thoughts for a day or two. What are the common themes?

Then move on to the specifics. For example, if you find money is a stressor, is it because expenses exceed income, you need more in savings, you feel insecure about retirement funds, or something else? Once you discover your triggers, you're well on your way to counteracting them.

Positive thinking is an incredible tool. When a negative or worrisome thought pops into your mind, replace it with a positive one or a mental image that calms you, such as the ocean, forest, or a favorite vacation destination. Then be proactive and tackle each of your major worries individually. What specifically can you do to eliminate each one? If job skills limit income, for example, you could return to school or search for a position that better fits your experience and the offers growth opportunities you need.

Also important is time for you and your interests. Make it a habit, along with regular time off, so you're at your best and brightest and as worry-free as possible.

Tools for Change

The universe offers you some marvelous tools for change this year. Heading the list is personal growth and the opportunity to learn more about yourself and how you relate to other people in your personal and professional lives.

Inspiration comes from many sources and almost anywhere you look. Family connections are uplifting and motivational, and loved ones bring joy to your life. The more time you spend with them, the happier you'll be.

A personal or business partner could be the catalyst who opens your eyes in surprising ways if you embrace change and enlightenment. You'll also gain fresh insights by observing the people closest to you. In them, you'll see some of your own qualities, as well as traits and life situations you might want to modify.

Intuition is another key to personal growth. Meditation can help you access your subconscious to identify your innermost hopes, wishes, and needs. Listen closely. The answers are within you, and by recognizing them you will encourage a freer flow of information. You can learn much from the past, so let your mind drift there from time to time. Those experiences, events, and people all form the foundation for your future, and by better understanding them—and putting them in perspective—you can move forward with confidence and embrace a whole new chapter of your life.

Believe in yourself, have faith, and welcome the many gifts of the universe!

Affirmation for the Year

I know and understand myself and the people around me.

The Year Ahead for Virgo

In 2007, you'll experience Jupiter's expansive energy in Sagittarius, your solar Fourth House of home and family. This influence could prompt you to relocate to another community, rent or purchase a home, or remodel your current one. You can look forward to many happy moments with loved ones and enjoying the place you call your own. Also plan to entertain friends throughout the year, especially potential networking contacts, because this transit also can benefit your career. Jupiter advances into Capricorn, your solar Fifth House, December 18. This thirteen-month influence promises to liven up your love life and spark plenty of opportunities to socialize. If you're a parent or hoping for an addition to the family, 2008 could bring many reasons to celebrate.

Unlike some signs, Virgo has a certain comfort level with Saturn's Leo transit. Now in the second of its two-year trip through your solar Twelfth House, you probably have valued time alone in meditation or lost in thought, reflecting on life. But this planetary influence can encourage a hermitlike existence that may not be in your best interests. Try for a balance that includes time for yourself, family, friends, and your partner because you'll have many opportunities to meet people this year. Then you'll cherish hours alone even more. In many ways, this is a completion phase as you prepare to begin a new life journey when Saturn enters your sign September 2. Use the months before then to think about what you would like to achieve in the next few years so you're ready to set plans in motion.

Uranus, in its fifth year in Pisces, your solar Seventh House of relationships, keeps things lively as new and interesting people continue to walk into your life. Each has a purpose—even if it's fleeting—and the potential to spark a flash of insight. Relationships are prone to ups and downs, more so than usual, and you might decide to part ways with someone close to you. That might or might not be the wisest move, so consider carefully before you act. It's possible the very traits you dislike in someone else are ones you'd like to change about yourself—so take a closer look and discover the reason behind your feelings. This is true in both your personal life and on the job, where you will have even more opportunities to meet unique people. Some have the potential to change your outlook.

With Neptune in Aquarius, your solar Sixth House of work, service, and health, you may become interested in alternative healing or get involved in a volunteer effort. Either one is likely to put you in contact with many people, and among them could be a soul mate in friendship or love. But with this year's planetary alignments, it's unwise to take anyone new at face value. Be cautious and use your common sense. This year also brings you many opportunities at work to use your unique brand of creativity that's both practical and ideal for concrete results. If your thoughts turn to a home-based business, however, take it slowly and hang onto your day job until earnings match current income. Although Virgo is a health-conscious sign, it's especially important this year to treat your body well. Sleep, moderate exercise, a nutritious diet, and time to rest and relax will help you maintain physical and mental energy.

Along with Jupiter, Pluto in Sagittarius accents your family and domestic life, effectively doubling the chance for a move or major home remodel. If you're a messy, but organized, Virgo, first use this powerful energy to clean out and clean up your place from top to bottom. Clearing your personal environment is an excellent way to prepare yourself mentally in anticipation of new directions. In combination with this year's other planetary influences, you may find it necessary to manage the affairs of an elderly relative or care for one, possibly in your home. Although stressful, this temporary situation will nevertheless have a positive impact upon your evolving view of relationships, your role as a partner or supporter, and what each of you brings to the other.

This year's eclipses are in Virgo and Pisces, your solar First and Seventh Houses, reinforce the relationship emphasis. Besides adding new friends and acquaintances to your widening circle, this influence will connect you with people who can motivate and inspire you to shift your perspective from the purely practical to one that encompasses the more esoteric aspects of life. If you're single and searching for love, your soul mate may appear at the least expected moment.

If you were born between August 22 and September 1, Saturn will meet your Sun after it enters Virgo on September 2. Your knowledge and experience can bring rewards now, based upon what you have earned and deserve. With it will come increased responsibilities, and at times you may feel you're the only one doing anything. If that happens, take a step back and assess the situation and your approach. Despite Saturn's desire to be in charge, you don't have to do it all yourself. Shift your thinking and put yourself higher on your priority list. Self care is very important because this transit is likely to lower your stamina. Sleep, rest, and schedule time for yourself every day to fuel your mind and body for this period of hard work that can launch you on a path to fulfill your expectations with an unmatched sense of satisfaction. Treat yourself with kindness and positive thoughts and remember that, ultimately, you're responsible only for yourself, your decisions, and your future. Key dates: October 13, November 30, and December 6 and 19.

If you were born between September 2 and 12, relationships are topsy-turvy with one surprise after the next. You'll also find your view of partnership changing through new experiences. If a relationship is solid, Uranus encourages you to spice it up with spontaneity and sizzling romance. Use your imagination and let love sparkle and shine as never before, even if you've been together for decades. But if a relationship is shaky and the two of you have grown in different directions, Uranus could trigger a freedom urge. That might amaze others, but not you. The feeling has been building for several years and now you're ready to make a move. Be sure, because it will be nearly impossible to undo. If you're looking for love, a chance encounter could spark a love-at-first-sight whirlwind romance. Enjoy it to the max, but use common sense. This is not the year to commit; save that for 2008, if you still feel the same. You could dash out of love just as quickly. Key dates: January 22, February 7, March 4 and 31, April 27, June 8, September 4, October 8, and November 25.

If you were born between September 9 and 16, Neptune in Aquarius signals an increasing feeling of dissatisfaction with your work life. The challenge, and one that will be difficult at best, is to identify the root cause. It might be a person or people or the realization that you want more. A job change is unlikely to help you break out of the rut, however. Look instead for ways to make daily tasks more satisfying. That, in turn, will exercise your mind and stimulate your imagination. Along the way you might discover an entirely new career field that interests you, such as health care, the nonprofit sector, or working with animals. If something intrigues you, explore the possibility through volunteer service before you commit. Key dates: January 20 and 26, February 9, April 5, May 6 and 13, June 26, August 12, September 23, November 23, and December 20.

If you were born between September 10 and 22, Saturn in Leo contacts your Sun from your solar Twelfth House of self-renewal. You will benefit from looking within, where you can discover your deepest desires and motivators, as well as what holds you back. Now is the time to use your marvelous analytical mind to work through regrets and resolve past issues so you're free to enter a new life phase when Saturn touches your Sun from Virgo. As you get better acquainted with yourself, you might be surprised to discover more of your creative self emerging. Explore this side of yourself with a new hobby or while volunteering for a good cause. Such internal expeditions will contribute to your overall health and well-being, which is important because Leo is one of your health signs (Aquarius is the other). The more you can do to care for your body, the better, including regular exercise. Key Dates: January 20, February 10, March 22, April 19, May 9, July 1 and 30, August 13 and 20.

If you were born between September 18 and 22, Pluto in Sagittarius forms a powerful connection with your Sun. Change is almost a given with this contact, whether initiated by you or the universe. If the desire to transform yourself or a personal situation has been building for the last several years, you will have the determination now to take that bold step. Someone, such as a parent or an adult child, could move into or out of your home. It's equally possible you could relocate or extensively remodel your place. On a practical level, be sure your home and its contents are fully insured (even if you rent) and keep a watchful eye for potential problems, such as termites or water damage, or the need to replace or repair a major appliance. Key dates: February 19, March 18, April 8, May 12, September 19, November 5, and December 10.

Virgo/January

Planetary Hotspots

With the Sun, Mercury, Venus, and Neptune spending time in Aquarius, January's focus is on work. Many days will be rewarding; others only puzzling and frustrating. Fortunately, you'll come out ahead by month's end. But be selective if you're offered extra projects or responsibilities. More is not necessarily better, and being too optimistic could prompt you to take on too much. Co-worker relationships may be strained at times and it's even possible someone could intentionally mislead you. Be aware. Protect your interests.

Wellness and Keeping Fit

This month's heavy workload makes scheduling time for yourself especially important because it will be easy to get run down, which can make you vulnerable to a cold or the flu. Put sleep before socializing and try to reserve evenings and the first few weekends for home life and hobbies.

Love and Life Connections

Even if time is limited, try to squeeze in a get-together with close friends the week of the January 3 Full Moon in Cancer, your friendship sign. Besides being a good balance for all the hours at work, long talks will net you fresh insights into life and love. If you'd like some new couples friends or want to introduce your mate to your pals, now is the time. Your social life picks up at the January 18 New Moon in Capricorn, which is also a plus for your love life.

Finance and Success

You could get lucky the first week of the new year and cash in on a small windfall. Take a chance on the lottery or enter a contest. You also could net a little more in your paycheck or benefit from additional job perks.

Rewarding Days

3, 8, 12, 14, 17, 18, 21, 25, 30, 31

Challenging Days

1, 6, 7, 13, 15, 16, 22, 26

Virgo/February

Planetary Hotspots

You'll experience nearly every facet of relationships this month, especially with family members and others close to you. Consider the ups and downs to be learning experiences and an opportunity to fine-tune your people skills. Besides difficult alignments involving the Sun and Venus, Mercury turns retrograde in Pisces, your partnership sign, February 13. This can trigger what are likely to be simple misunderstandings even though they'll feel like much more. Choose your words with care and try to avoid assumptions.

Wellness and Keeping Fit

This month both the New Moon (February 17) and Full Moon (February 2) in your solar Sixth and Twelfth Houses of health continue to emphasize the importance of treating yourself well. Sleep and a nutritious diet are a good starting point, but you also need to be aware of your limits. Leave work behind and devote evenings and weekends to relaxation.

Love and Life Connections

Your love life benefits from energetic Mars in Capricorn through February 24. The fiery planet also promotes an active social life, which is a good antidote for long hours on the job. A new romance could catch you by surprise early in February, but think twice if romance overcomes common sense. This is not the time to elope.

Finance and Success

You're at your analytical best and a step ahead of most everyone. But all may not be exactly as it seems the first full week of the month, so it's wise to ask questions and double-check details. If a new job is your goal, résumés submitted the first two days of February could net results by month's end.

Rewarding Days

6, 7, 8, 9, 13, 14, 15, 17, 20, 22, 27

Challenging Days

4, 5, 10, 11, 16, 19, 23, 24, 25

Virgo/March

Planetary Hotspots

Although you'll encounter some obstacles at work and home, March is more or less easygoing. Challenging days, however, continue to involve personal and professional relationships, and it will be up to you to compromise even when you feel it should be the other way around. Talk out any lingering differences after Mercury enters Pisces, your relationship sign, March 18.

Wellness and Keeping Fit

New horizons beckon as Venus enters Taurus, your sign of travel and learning, March 17. That's the best reason to close out the month with a relaxing weekend getaway with your partner or best friend. Better yet, treat yourselves to the royal treatment at a luxury hotel and spa.

Love and Life Connections

Even though relationships are this month's hotspot, heartwarming days will far outnumber challenging ones. You'll be drawn to people and they to you at the March 3 Full Moon in Virgo and the March 19 New Moon in Pisces, both of which are eclipses. Either one could trigger an exciting new romance if you're searching for love, or prompt the decision to take a relationship to the next level. This is not the time, however, to introduce someone new to the family. Wait until next month.

Finance and Success

Finances benefit from Venus in Aries through March 16, which makes this a favorable period to apply for a loan or mortgage, purchase big-ticket domestic items, and shop for insurance. You could receive a significant gift or an inheritance from a relative or net a sizable return on a property deal.

Rewarding Days

4, 5, 6, 7, 12, 13, 16, 17, 20, 21, 26, 30

Challenging Days

1, 2, 8, 9, 11, 18, 22, 23, 29

Virgo/April

Planetary Hotspots

Family members try your patience in early April and again at month's end. Try for open communication and understanding, but don't expect miracles, especially with in-laws. What's most important is that you make the effort. You might need a major domestic repair. If so, get several estimates and check credentials. Also postpone legal matters and travel until next month if you have a choice.

Wellness and Keeping Fit

Everyone needs an occasional break from the daily routine, including you. The Sun, Mercury, and Venus all in Taurus, your solar Ninth House of knowledge, presents a great opportunity to fill a few leisure hours with something different. Take a class for the fun of it to learn or perfect hobby skills, study another language, or join a book discussion group.

Love and Life Connections

Although close relationships will again be rocky at times this month, you're in a great position to strengthen ties with co-workers and supervisors. New career contacts are also likely, and a lucky break could connect you with someone who can advance your status. Be alert for a magnetic attraction; it may signal the arrival of a soul mate.

Finance and Success

You're among the favored few, thanks to Venus, which enters Gemini, your career sign, April 11. Be seen and heard and don't hesitate to self-promote, especially if you have your eye on a step up. You could achieve that and more this month, including an award or other recognition. Finances are also on the upswing as the Full Moon in Libra, April 2, and the April 17 New Moon in Aries highlight your solar Second and Eighth Houses.

Rewarding Days

3, 4, 9, 10, 11, 16, 17, 19, 22, 23, 26, 29

Challenging Days

1, 6, 12, 13, 15, 18, 20, 21, 27, 28

Virgo/May

Planetary Hotspots

Dash off in search of new horizons when the Sun and Mercury in Taurus trigger your spirit of adventure. Make it a weekend or plan a week's vacation at a luxury destination. But schedule time away around the New Moon in Taurus on May 16. Travel delays and cancellations are possible before then. The same time frame applies to business trips, presentations, interviews, important talks, legal matters, and communication in general. Be persistent if information is tough to find or if someone intentionally tries to block progress.

Wellness and Keeping Fit

Besides taking at least a few days off to relax and unwind, let the May 2 Full Moon in Scorpio inspire you to get in the habit of a daily walk, skate, or bike ride. Ask a few neighbors to join you in your quest to keep fit. It's a terrific way to keep the motivation high and the energy flowing.

Love and Life Connections

Your social life begins to take off May 8 when Venus enters Cancer, your friendship sign. It's joined by Mercury on May 28, just in time for a holiday weekend get-together. Make a few calls, get things started, and set your sights on meeting new people all month. Venus also increases the odds for a new romance (thanks to a friend) while traveling or involved in a club or organization.

Finance and Success

Reach for the top this month as the Sun and Mercury push you to strive for success. Your efforts peak the week of May 21, so gear up and set plans in motion to achieve your goals. If not this month, you could net a raise in June, thanks to Mars, which enters Aries, your solar Eighth House, May 15.

Rewarding Days

1, 4, 6, 7, 8, 11, 14, 15, 17, 19, 23, 29

Challenging Days

5, 9, 10, 12, 18, 25, 28, 30

Virgo/June

Planetary Hotspots

Life goes your way much of June, but you'll need to be at your adaptable best because Mercury reverses direction June 15. During its retrograde period you'll experience the increasing desire to set new personal and professional goals as you question your current direction. Let the ideas flow, explore options, and look at priorities. Your new direction will all come together by mid-July.

Wellness and Keeping Fit

June arrives with the Full Moon in Sagittarius, your domestic sign. Let it motivate you to get rid of clutter, complete domestic projects, and get your place in shape, inside and out, for summer. Even if you're a neat Virgo, chances are you have storage spaces with boxes that haven't been opened in years. Clean them out. You'll like the results, which will clear your mind as much as your physical space.

Love and Life Connections

With Venus in Cancer through June 4 and the Sun arriving in the same sign June 20, you'll enjoy time with friends this month. But with Mercury retrograde the last two weeks of June, quiet evenings and weekend outings with your closest pals will be more appealing. This month's second Full Moon, on June 30 in Capricorn, could prompt you to move on if a dating relationship isn't working out. Do what's best for you.

Finance and Success

This is your time to shine! The days leading up to the June 15 New Moon in Gemini spotlight your career sector with terrific planetary contacts from the Sun and Mercury. Cross your fingers for a promotion or job offer and a bigger paycheck. Be sure to ask pointed questions if you're offered a step up or a new position. Get the details.

Rewarding Days

1, 3, 5, 6, 7, 10, 13, 14, 15, 16, 18, 23, 25

Challenging Days

2, 4, 8, 9, 12, 19, 20, 21, 24, 26

Virgo/July

Planetary Hotspots

Try to schedule a vacation or business trip before the last ten days of July, when Mars in Taurus, your sign of travel and knowledge, aligns with Saturn, Uranus, and Neptune. That lineup can trigger delays and cancellations, as well as lost luggage and unexpected expenses.

Wellness and Keeping Fit

Learn a new hobby, refinish furniture, join a gym, take a class for the fun of it, or sign up for sports lessons. What you do isn't as important as responding to the energy of the July 30 Full Moon in Capricorn, which encourages you to balance your life with time for recreation and relaxation.

Love and Life Connections

Your earthy sensuality is at its best after July 13, when Venus in Virgo enhances your powers of attraction. There's one slight glitch, however. Venus turns retrograde July 27 and slips back into Leo next month. That actually can work in your favor. You'll have a second chance to reconnect with anyone you meet, especially around the Full Moon. Before then, the New Moon in Cancer on July 4 lights up your solar Eleventh House of friendship, so plan fun-filled and relaxing summer evenings and weekends with pals.

Finance and Success

Projects and plans put on hold begin to regain momentum as Mercury, your career planet, resumes direct motion July 9. But take your time because it will be easy even for you to miss details as others push for completion. Also double-check data. Chances are, your eagle eye will find errors and misinformation.

Rewarding Days

1, 4, 5, 8, 9, 13, 14, 15, 17, 22, 25, 27, 28, 30

Challenging Days

3, 6, 10, 12, 16, 19, 23, 24, 26, 31

Virgo/August

Planetary Hotspots

The action takes place mostly behind the scenes this month, which features a concentration of planets and the July 12 New Moon in Leo, your solar Twelfth House. You'll especially enjoy time alone and with family and close friends. Look within through meditation or quiet time and let your inner voice speak. You're likely to discover a whole other side of yourself, as well as your deepest desires and motivations. Then you'll be ready to embrace the new direction that emerges when the Sun enters your sign next month.

Wellness and Keeping Fit

The New Moon also reminds you to schedule a checkup if you haven't had one recently—it's a good idea to do that periodically. You'll feel better for it, plus you'll have the opportunity to ask questions and get up to speed on the latest wellness information.

Love and Life Connections

You'll be as content with your own company as with others as the Sun, Mercury, and Venus travel in Leo and Virgo, your solar Twelfth and First Houses. Do a little of both, depending upon the day and the invitation. A sensational someone could walk into your life the week of the August 28 Full Moon in Pisces, your partnership sign. But if a relationship isn't all you want it to be, re-evaluate it then. Talk things out.

Finance and Success

Get set for a dynamic six weeks as Mars advances in Gemini, your career sign, from August 7 on. The pace really picks up next month, when you could be well rewarded for your efforts. Give it your all!

Rewarding Days

1, 3, 5, 9, 10, 11, 16, 18, 19, 23, 24, 26, 30, 31

Challenging Days

2, 6, 8, 13, 15, 20, 21, 27, 28, 29

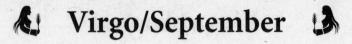

Virgo/September

Planetary Hotspots

Serious Saturn enters your sign September 2, bringing with it the incentive to begin a new chapter in your life. Saturn is noted for taking its time and so should you. You may need most of Saturn's two-year transit through Virgo to fully define a new and ambitious direction. And the final outcome may be far different from what you imagine today. Explore, learn, and stretch yourself to discover new talents, skills, and strengths.

Wellness and Keeping Fit

Saturn in your sign requires some special handling. You may notice an increased need for sleep and should make that a priority when necessary so you don't get run down. Also give yourself the gift of time to relax. If that's something you rarely do, consider it a new skill to be acquired.

Love and Life Connections

People are testy and relationships rocky during the time leading up to the September 11 New Moon in your sign. After that, business and personal contacts bring you luck. Venus in Leo, which turns direct September 8, is perfect for couples in love who want to steal away for a romantic evening or weekend at home or away.

Finance and Success

Mars in Gemini through September 28 has you in full view, an attention-getter who's prime for success. Potential gains are linked to the September 26 Full Moon in Aries, your solar Eighth House of joint resources. Before then, however, you'll have to jump a few hurdles that test your stamina and people skills. Teamwork is key, as is the ability to think on your feet.

Rewarding Days

1, 5, 6, 8, 13, 15, 17, 20, 22

Challenging Days

2, 3, 11, 16, 19, 24, 26, 30

Virgo/October

Planetary Hotspots

Your sharp, analytical mind gets a workout this month after Mercury, your ruler, turns retrograde in Scorpio, your solar Third House of communication, October 11. Listen closely to what people are saying, with your ears and your intuition. They'll inspire and surprise you, and many will challenge your viewpoints as you learn to appreciate the subtle nuances, the shades of gray, that more accurately define an imperfect world. This learning experience is one you'll value throughout the fall and winter months as events continue to evolve.

Wellness and Keeping Fit

Join a group of friends who are committed to regular exercise if you find it difficult to stick to a program on your own. With Mars in Cancer, your friendship sign, all month, you'll get the dual benefit of socializing and the opportunity to meet new people.

Love and Life Connections

Reconnect and rediscover the favorite people in your life—family, partner, and close friends—even those you live with. That's the message of a Jupiter-Uranus-Neptune lineup that links your solar Fourth House of home and family and your solar Seventh House of close relationships. This influence also could prompt you to commit (or recommit) to lifelong love, establish a new home, or launch a whirlwind romance. This is not, however, the time to dash for the altar. Give life and love a chance to develop.

Finance and Success

You'll want to take a few precautions after retrograde Mercury slips back into Libra, your sign of personal finances, October 23. It will be easy to misplace or forget a bill, or lose a cherished possession, but it also could put some extra cash in your wallet.

Rewarding Days

4, 7, 11, 12, 14, 17, 18, 20, 21, 26, 27, 30

Challenging Days

9, 15, 16, 19, 22, 23, 24, 25, 28, 29

Virgo/November

Planetary Hotspots

Your social life begins to slow November 15, as Mars in Cancer, your solar Eleventh House of friendship, turns retrograde. But you'll probably be OK with that and more interested in time with those you love, as well as work and your own interests. What you'll find difficult, however, is a general lack of momentum in many people around you that delays projects, plans, and decisions. Relax and do what you can.

Wellness and Keeping Fit

Journaling is a terrific way to work out stress, resolve personal issues, and explore your hopes, wishes, and desires. With the Sun, Mercury, and the November 9 New Moon in Scorpio, your solar Third House of communication, you'll find it especially satisfying this month. Give it a try.

Love and Life Connections

You'll continue to cherish time with family this month, especially after the Sun enters Sagittarius, your domestic sign, November 22. This month's solar Third House influence also promotes contact with neighbors, among whom you could find a new friend or romantic interest the week of the New Moon. Take a chance on a friend of a matchmaking friend or relative mid-month.

Finance and Success

The work pace picks up a little around the time of the November 24 Full Moon in Gemini, your career sign, although you shouldn't expect too much with Mars retrograde. There's also a chance the lunar influence could trigger a little more in your paycheck, but praise is more likely. Bank it for your next annual review.

Rewarding Days

3, 4, 7, 8, 9, 10, 15, 17, 22, 26, 27

Challenging Days

5, 6, 11, 18, 23, 24, 30

Virgo/December

Planetary Hotspots

Get set to add a lot of fun to your life December 18. That's the date lucky Jupiter arrives in your solar Fifth House of pleasure, children, creativity, and romance. This year-long influence gets off to a fast start within a few days, when Mercury and the Sun join Jupiter in Capricorn. Fill 2008 with social events where you can meet new people (including potential romantic interests), hobby projects, sports activities, and other leisure pursuits. If you're a parent, or hoping to become one, 2008 could bring many reasons to celebrate.

Wellness and Keeping Fit

Embrace Jupiter and wrap up the year with time off, or, if that's impossible, evenings and weekends focused on your partner, your children, friends, and your favorite after-hours activities. Even better, make play time one of your new year's resolutions.

Love and Life Connections

You'll experience every facet of human nature this month as the Sun, Venus, and Mercury contact nearly every other planet in the zodiac. Some will make you smile, others will test your patience, and still others will fill your heart with love. Welcome each one, even those that fall in the category of "good learning experience," because each will benefit you in some way.

Finance and Success

Set a budget and stick to it if you shop the first weekend in December. Bargains will be few and the urge to splurge strong. If you can wait, try the next weekend instead. You could receive a year-end bonus around the same time, but it's likely to be less than you hope for with Mars still traveling retrograde. Look forward to February, when money begins to flow your way.

Rewarding Days

4, 5, 11, 12, 14, 16, 18, 25, 28, 29

Challenging Days

2, 3, 6, 9, 17, 22, 23, 30

Virgo Action Table

These dates reflect the best—but not the only—times for success and ease in these activities, according to your Sun sign.

	JAN	FEB	MAR	APR	MAY	JUN	JUL	AUG	SEPT	OCT	NOV	DEC
Move	15, 16	10			31	1					28, 29	1-4, 8-12
Start a class	12, 13	8-10		4, 5	29, 30				15, 16		11-21	6, 7
Join a club	29-31		25, 26				11-21			2, 30, 31	26, 27	
Ask for a raise	10			30		22			12, 13		7	3, 4
Look for work	15-19		16	11, 12, 19	21-25							13, 14
Get pro advice	30, 31		19, 20	13		7	4, 5	1			19	
Get a loan	23, 24			16								17-19
See a doctor	19		15, 16	11, 12	21, 22							14
Start a diet			15, 16	11, 12			30, 31					
End relationship			17, 18	13, 14	11, 12			28				
Buy clothes	1-3, 17, 18			9, 10					20, 21	17		10
Get a makeover	7, 8		30		24		18		10, 11	7	3	
New romance	1, 2						27		21	17	13, 14	
Vacation		22, 23	18-31	27-30	15, 16				2			

LIBRA

The Balance
September 22 to October 23

♎

Element:	Air
Quality:	Cardinal
Polarity:	Yang/Masculine
Planetary Ruler:	Venus
Meditation:	I balance conflicting desires
Gemstone:	Opal
Power Stones:	Tourmaline, kunzite, blue lace agate
Key Phrase:	I balance
Glyph:	Scales of justice, setting sun
Anatomy:	Kidneys, lower back, appendix
Color:	Blue, pink
Animal:	Brightly plumed birds
Myths/Legends:	Venus, Cinderella, Hera
House:	Seventh
Opposite Sign:	Aries
Flower:	Rose
Key Word:	Harmony

Your Ego's Strengths and Weaknesses

Charming, gracious, and elegant, your pleasant manner is a people-magnet. They're drawn to your winning smile and your knack for putting everyone at ease, even in difficult situations. This talent, along with your incredible social skills, makes you a natural mediator who can effortlessly promote harmony.

Libra is often viewed as indecisive, and this may be true at times, just as it is for everyone else. In reality, you're fair-minded and highly principled and thus can see both the pros and cons—and remain impartial. You're a team player who gently, but very firmly and persuasively, guides others to consensus. But you also should remember that indecision is in reality a decision to take no action.

Closely linked is your strength as an idea person who can objectively plan and strategize everything from a simple project to a complex event for hundreds or thousands. This makes you a natural at public relations and cooperative efforts. Rarely the first to offer ideas and solutions, you sit back, listen and observe others, and then mentally pull them together into a cohesive whole that sparkles with imagination.

Beauty attracts you, and, with Venus as your ruling planet, you have a natural flair for design and entertaining. Attractive surroundings are very important to your well-being, and you adorn your home with all the tasteful furnishings, artwork, and décor you can afford. You do the same for yourself because you're image-conscious and understand the value of first impressions.

Many Libras have artistic talent and fill their time with painting, arts and crafts, and attending plays and concerts. Puzzles, word games, and reading are also mentally stimulating and relaxing.

You function best in an environment of peace and tranquility and will do all in your power to maintain harmony. Sometimes too much. But when pushed too far, anger replaces diplomacy and your verbal guns come out blazing. No one can mistake how you feel! Then you just as quickly return to your usual agreeable state and move on in harmony with the world.

Shining Your Love Light

Libra is the sign of partnership, so you're highly motivated to find your one and only. That's great as long as you do it for the right reasons—not just to make your life complete. Take the plunge only if you're sure you're in love, rather than in love with love. Listen to your heart, your intuition, and your common sense, and opt for a long engagement.

Romance is the key to your heart and it keeps love alive from the first date to the fiftieth—or more!—anniversary. A candlelight dinner is among your favorites, but you're equally content in any setting that focuses on togetherness. If you can manage it, set aside an evening and an afternoon every week just for the two of you.

The attraction can be positively sizzling with Aries, your opposite sign. You'll delight in the pizzazz and the freedom to be yourself within a mutually supportive relationship.

You have much in common with another Libra and the other air signs, Gemini and Aquarius. Gemini is outgoing and shares your social nature, but might be too scattered for your more focused energy. Although Aquarius' independence is a mystery to you, love and friendship are magically intertwined. Romance may be at its finest with another Libra, but budgeting and decision-making could challenge you.

Taurus, the other Venus-ruled sign, also is drawn to beauty and romance, although you might find this one too possessive and slow-paced. Cancer's emotional focus can unsettle you even though you appreciate the family emphasis and closeness. Leo shares your love of luxury and the finer things in life, but this sign's great need for attention can wear thin.

Virgo, although not as social as your sign, can fulfill your need for a strong mental connection. Scorpio's intense passion can mesmerize you, but your need for open communication may go unfulfilled. Sagittarius sparks your spirit of adventure and you both enjoy travel, although this sign may be too blunt for you.

Capricorn can be too cautious for you, even though you're attracted to their practical, ambitious nature. Romantic moments can be spectacular with Pisces, whose spirituality and creativity inspire you; however, this sensitive soul requires special handling.

Making Your Place in the World

With your outstanding people skills you can be successful in a wide variety of careers. A congenial, cooperative atmosphere and pleasant workplace are necessities, and you would be unhappy in any job with limited people contact.

When you're content, you also bring out the best in co-workers because you see and encourage their strengths through motivation and praise. This ability to coach others also contributes to your success as a manager or supervisor.

It can be difficult for you to change jobs even when it's in your best interest. Loyalty—to your employer and co-workers—can hold you back. Keep your goals in mind and stay put only if doing so can advance your ambitions. In today's shifting work world it's more important than ever to put yourself first.

You could be successful in the legal field as an attorney, paralegal, judge, or mediator. Public relations and advertising might appeal to you, or you could enjoy a career in retail, customer service, or as a florist or hair stylist.

If the arts attract you, consider a career as a costume or set designer, actor, fine artist, or makeup artist, or in museum, art gallery, or theater management. The fashion industry is another option, or you might find your niche as an interior decorator, counselor, or agent. Human resources and real estate are other fields in which you could excel.

Putting Your Best Foot Forward

Relationships can be joyous, empowering, and motivational, but can also disappoint and limit you. It all depends upon your mindset, self-confidence, and willingness to take a stand.

You strive to please others, in part because you enjoy—and even need—their approval, praise, and support. Although the immediate gratification boosts your ego, long-term satisfaction comes only from within. When you value yourself as highly as you value others, you no longer feel the need to measure your success through someone else's eyes.

Start by giving yourself a daily pat on the back. Focus on all your marvelous skills and talents and the beautiful world around you. With your quick, sharp, and shrewd mind, you can program your brain faster and more easily than most. The more you believe in yourself, the more others will too.

The same need for acceptance encourages you to put others before yourself more often than not. Relationships that are fifty-fifty are much healthier and inspire a closer bond, as do individuality and personal interests. So let your needs prevail rather than put them aside for another day that may never arrive.

Because harmony and cooperation are vital to your well-being, you sometimes go along with plans, events, and decisions just to make life easier. You feel out of sync with yourself and the world when all is not lightness and love. Intellectually you know that's unrealistic, but it's tough to resist your innate role as a diplomat.

Relationships thrive on the give-and-take necessary to fulfill individual and mutual goals and desires. But all that changes when one person's wishes dominate the other's. Speak up, even at the risk of conflict, and voice your opinions, likes, and dislikes. Your partner will respect you for it. In time, you will find a new comfort zone.

Tools for Change

The universe invites you to use creativity and communication as your tools for change this year. Both can be invaluable assets to set and achieve goals and initiate positive career and health benefits.

Your creative energy is outside the norm—innovative and imaginative. Ideas are your strength, and you have an uncanny ability to spot emerging trends. You also can detach yourself from a problem just enough to look at it with a fresh eye that sparks unique solutions. A key part of the equation is intuition, which continues to grow as your inner voice becomes stronger.

Your sixth sense is equally valuable in communication, an area where you can expand and refine your already superb skills. Words—written and spoken—are a powerful tool for you now. If you would like to master the art of public speaking, take a class or find a coach who can help you develop this talent. You could be an exceptional motivational speaker or writer, and use your tools for change to empower others to do the same. In the process, you will gain self-knowledge and might be surprised where your conclusions lead you.

As you assess and reassess your career life you will discover that your goals are in the process of change. What was important a few years ago no longer is, and you clearly see the value of embracing new directions and new potentials. But you should resist change for the sake of change, tempting though it may be. Gather information, plan, and set goals before you take action. An informed decision is the best one.

Your health can benefit from a similar approach. If your lifestyle is less than optimum, you have the willpower within you to initiate positive change. Exercise, a more nutritious diet, rest, and relaxation will help you achieve your goal of a healthier and more vital you.

Affirmation for the Year

When I inspire others, I do the same for myself.

The Year Ahead for Libra

Jupiter in Sagittarius, your solar Third House, encourages you to express your thoughts through the written and spoken word. If you've ever wanted to write a novel, the time is right to create a product of your mind. Or, record your impressions and perceptions in a journal. Public speaking is another avenue that can make the most of your air sign's communication talent. Take a class or join a club to polish your presentation skills, or learn more about a subject that's always interested you. With your ability to see the big picture, you can build on your reputation as an idea person. Unleash your imagination and impress people with your vision and innovative solutions. Also try to schedule periodic long weekends away to unwind and re-center yourself, body and soul. You might want to plan a big holiday celebration this year because Jupiter enters Capricorn, your solar Fourth House of home and family, December 18. Decorate your place to the max and turn it into a family reunion.

Friends and groups continue to be in focus as Saturn advances in Leo, your solar Eleventh House. New people will enrich your life and among them could be a soul mate, someone who becomes a lifelong friend or mate. You'll also widen your circle with many acquaintances, some of whom can become valuable career and personal networking contacts. Carefully consider the time commitment if you're asked to take on a leadership role in a club or organization. Despite good intentions, you could end up doing far more than your share of the work. You'll also want to keep your home in top shape so you're set for everything from impromptu get-togethers with friends to hosting meetings and social events. But this Saturn transit has another emphasis: Take time to think about your goals and what you hope to achieve in the next few years. Dream big and take action to realize your ambitions. Saturn moves on to Virgo on September 2 to begin its two-year transit of your solar Twelfth House. Put yourself higher on your priority list during this period of self-renewal, when at times you'll enjoy your own company more than others.

Your work life may be unsettled with Uranus traveling in Pisces, your solar Sixth House. Although workplace changes are possible—even needed and hoped for—that's not the most likely scenario. You're in a transition phase, a sort of limbo, without much action. Frustration rises as a result and with it a more or less constant level of ongoing tension. That makes it vital to take time for yourself every day. Try for an hour and settle for thirty minutes when necessary. Personal time is just as important to your health as sleep, a nutritious diet, and moderate exercise.

Neptune, now in its tenth year in Aquarius, your solar Fifth House, continues to accent your social life and stimulate interest in creative endeavors. That could inspire you to get involved in a charitable organization or fund-raising effort for the arts, as well as to pursue your own talents. You might even decide to turn a hobby into a second income. Romance is irresistible with Neptune influencing your love life, and you have a certain something—a charismatic aura—that attracts admirers. If you're a parent, promote open communication with your children and encourage them to share their challenges and successes. You also might want to get to know their friends and participate in their school or sports activities, but only if you're one of many involved parents.

Words are power with both Jupiter and Pluto in Sagittarius, your solar Third House, an influence that sharpens your thinking. The planetary duo also boosts your determination and willpower, and once you set a goal, little can deter you from it. Intuition is another strength, and you have the ability to see what others miss—grasping the details as well as the big picture. This energy is likely to attract important people into your orbit. Cultivate them because these valuable contacts will pay off in the next few years.

This year's eclipses in Virgo and Pisces, your solar Twelfth and Sixth Houses, focus on health and well-being, work, and service. Strive for a balance of all three as one can enhance the others. Try meditation or yoga, and schedule regular checkups.

If you were born between September 22 and October 3, Saturn contacts your Sun after it enters Virgo, September 2. Although Libra is the universal sign of partnership, time alone, preferably at home, will appeal to you during this transit as Saturn encourages you to enjoy your own company. Explore your inner self, your life, and your spiritual and intuitive sides. What you learn will help free you from the past and spark new insights into your place in the wider world.

Saturn also could trigger curiosity about your roots and prompt anything from family discussions to genealogical research to the desire to preserve your family history for future generations. What you discover might amaze you—it will fill in the gaps and give you insights into your personality, motivations, and talents. Key dates: October 13, November 30, and December 6 and 19.

If you were born between October 4 and 12, Uranus in Pisces, your solar Sixth House, has you feeling restless. As this freedom urge comes alive, your thoughts will turn to a situation, person, or circumstance. But think before you act. Change for the sake of change probably won't fulfill your needs and could leave you wondering why you acted in haste. That's because this transit is not so much about external change (which may be the ultimate result) as it is about personal change. You could assert your independence, for example, by changing yourself through diet, exercise, and an overall healthier lifestyle. Or step outside yourself and view the "offending" situation or person from another perspective to promote self-understanding. You also will gain knowledge about yourself, your needs and desires on a subconscious level, and a year from now you will be more confident and have a clearer personal direction. Key dates: January 22, February 7, March 4 and 31, April 27, June 8, September 4, October 8, and November 25.

If you were born between October 11 and 16, Neptune activates your inner voice and opens the pathways to sense how others feel. This can be a real asset in business and personal affairs, but you should take an important precaution. Because your channels are open, you can pick up unwanted energy, which, in turn, can drain your own. Learn techniques that can help you be selective in what you absorb. This also is a highly creative phase, and whatever you create—ideas or tangible products—will inspire you on many levels, including your spirituality. Your faith in yourself and the universe will touch nearly every area of your life. You can experience the ultimate in romance this year with your partner or in a dating relationship. If you're still searching for your one and only, enjoy every special moment, but hold off on commitment until you're sure you're in love and not just the idea of love. Key dates: January 20 and 26, February 9, April 5, May 6 and 13, June 26, August 12, September 23, November 23, and December 20.

If you were born between October 11 and 23, Saturn in Leo contacts your Sun from your solar Eleventh House. You'll experience the many facets of friendship, reunite with people from the past, and possibly meet a soul mate who will become a lifelong friend. Some friends may disappoint you when, for the first time, you see them as they are, not as you wish them to be. Consider it a lesson learned and move forward without regrets. But you should be somewhat cautious of anyone who comes on too strong because the person behind the charming words could be someone entirely different. If you're actively involved in a club or organization, the group might try to flatter you in hopes your ego will be stronger than your common sense. Don't bite unless you're ready for a challenge and willing to give a major endeavor your all. Be aware that it will be a tough job and you might be unsuccessful. Overall, though, the first eight months of the year (Saturn enters Virgo September 2) bring you the opportunity to fine-tune your leadership skills and learn more about group dynamics. Key Dates: January 20, February 10, March 22, April 19, May 9, July 1 and 30, August 13 and 20.

If you were born between October 19 and 23, deep thinking is the norm rather than the exception, and because you can tune out your environment, concentration is at its best. This helps you quickly and easily absorb information, analyze it, and reach a conclusion—a real plus if you're a student or want to master a subject or skill. But Pluto's intensity could bring so much focus that it will be tough to let go and move on. If you find yourself obsessed with an idea, event, or situation, ease up and turn your thoughts elsewhere. The same applies to worries. Take action. Seek answers. Resolve the matter. Key dates: February 19, March 18, April 8, May 12, September 19, November 5, and December 10.

Libra/January

Planetary Hotspots

Your love life is prone to ups and downs as the Sun, Venus, and Mercury contact Saturn, Jupiter, Neptune, and Pluto the last two weeks of January. You'll cherish the romantic moments, but if you're single, listen to the doubts raised by your inner voice. It's also possible a friend could disappoint you and another might need your help. If you're a parent, your children will need extra care and understanding. Get more involved in their lives—meet their friends.

Wellness and Keeping Fit

Set your creativity and imagination free as you greet the new year. Take a class to learn or perfect decorating techniques or hobby skills. Then produce a tangible work of art such as a room redo, a family scrapbook, or a home office. Mars in Sagittarius through January 15 sparks great ideas, and concrete results are the most satisfying.

Love and Life Connections

Family relationships are at their best the first week of January, when the Sun, Mercury, and Venus in Capricorn, your domestic sign, promote communication. This is also a terrific period to entertain friends, so consider hosting a get-together to return all those holiday invitations. Include a few neighbors in the group, especially if you're searching for romance. And now is the time to give in if a matchmaking relative wants to set you up.

Finance and Success

Although time at home is more appealing the first week of the year, the January 3 Full Moon in Cancer, your career sign, makes work a wise choice. Otherwise it'll be tough to catch up and you could miss an opportunity to showcase your talents for all the right people. Take the initiative to shine whenever and wherever you can.

Rewarding Days

1, 4, 5, 6, 9, 10, 12, 15, 19, 24, 27, 31

Challenging Days

3, 8, 11, 16, 18, 20, 22, 23, 26

Libra/February

Planetary Hotspots

Gear up for challenges in your work life, primarily because Mercury turns retrograde in your solar Sixth House, February 13. Decisions and plans will be in flux and it will be tough to make headway on, much less complete, projects. Do the best you can, but resist the temptation to push others. Even with your usual tactful approach, you're likely to meet resistance. Offset it by taking the lead. Promote teamwork.

Wellness and Keeping Fit

Take extra precautions to prevent a cold or the flu. But if either one catches you by surprise, stay home, sleep, and rest. Otherwise, the symptoms could linger into mid-March. Also take a few minutes in early January to schedule routine medical checkups.

Love and Life Connections

If you're still wavering about a close relationship, an exact alignment of Saturn and Neptune and the February 2 Full Moon in Leo could bring you closer to a decision. If you want to romance your partner or find someone new, the New Moon in Aquarius, February 17, enhances your powers of attraction. Turn on the charm as Venus enters Aries, your partnership sign, February 20, followed by Mars, which dashes into the same sign February 25. This influence is one of the best of the year for couples in love.

Finance and Success

Although frustration is more the norm than the exception in your work life, tension begins to ease several days after the Sun enters Pisces on February 18. That's mostly due to your efforts to promote communication and to help others begin to move past obstacles and resolve their differences. Finances are status quo.

Rewarding Days

1, 6, 7, 9, 12, 15, 17, 20, 27

Challenging Days

3, 4, 5, 10, 11, 18, 19, 24, 25

Libra/March

Planetary Hotspots

Some personal and professional relationships continue to challenge you this month although you'll be comfortable with the final outcome. Resolution may even give you a newfound sense of freedom and independence. If it's the right choice—which only you can know—walk away from a friendship, dating relationship, or a club or organization that no longer fulfills your needs or goals. Leave regrets behind and move forward.

Wellness and Keeping Fit

This month's lunar and solar eclipses in Virgo and Pisces encourage you to assess your lifestyle. If it's not as healthy as it should be, get motivated and reverse the trend. Start slowly, ease into new habits, and aim for lifelong health and well-being.

Love and Life Connections

Take the initiative to clear up recent minor mix-ups and misunderstandings after Mercury turns direct March 7. People will be receptive. If you're part of a couple, take advantage of favorable Venus contacts March 8–9. Dash out of town for a long weekend of love, while some singles commit to a lifetime of togetherness.

Finance and Success

A work-related opportunity could come your way the week of the March 19 New Moon in Pisces. Seize it only if you're sure you can meet the deadline because too much optimism and financial potential could prompt you to act prematurely. Ask questions. Get the details. Either way, you enter a positive financial phase March 17, when Venus enters your solar Eighth House of joint resources. This promising influence bodes well for an increase in family funds in the following four weeks.

Rewarding Days

1, 5, 6, 7, 10, 11, 13, 15, 16, 19, 20, 24

Challenging Days

2, 8, 9, 14, 18, 22, 25, 28

Libra/April

Planetary Hotspots

Get set for a hectic and fast-paced six weeks at work that gets started the first few days of the month and accelerates when Mars enters Pisces, your sign of daily work, April 6. Besides a heavy workload, you'll encounter difficult people as tension rises and peaks at month's end. Stay on the sidelines as much as possible and let others fight their own battles. Also try to avoid travel and legal matters the last week of April.

Wellness and Keeping Fit

Stress can get the best of you with this month's heavy work demands. That makes it all the more important to set aside at least thirty minutes a day for you. Meditate, walk, read, daydream, and push away any thoughts of your to-do list and people who attempt to trigger your hot buttons.

Love and Life Connections

People are drawn to you even more than usual, thanks to the Sun and Mercury in your solar Seventh House of relationships. Schedule important talks and appointments for the week of the April 17 New Moon in Aries, and feel free to ask for favors if you need them. On a personal level, love and partnership are at their best, and some singles get engaged or tie the knot.

Finance and Success

Unexpected expenses could pop up in early April when difficult planetary alignments also caution against investments, loans, and major purchases. You can use the same energy to take charge of your finances, rework budgets, and cut spending. Seek knowledge on your own or consult a professional after the Sun enters Taurus, your sign of joint resources, April 20.

Rewarding Days

3, 4, 9, 11, 16, 17, 19, 22, 29, 30

Challenging Days

13, 15, 18, 20, 21, 27

Libra/May

Planetary Hotspots

Finances are in focus as the May 2 Full Moon and May 16 New Moon direct your attention to money matters. As was true early last month, you should avoid major financial decisions and actions, including loans and investments. You also should check your and your partner's (and even your children's) credit reports for errors and protect all financial information from prying eyes. Be sure insurance coverage is up to date.

Wellness and Keeping Fit

Stick to the stress-relief program you began last month (or get started if you didn't), which will continue to offset the effects of fast-paced days. Also give some thought to a weekend away or vacation time, if not this month, then in June. Explore potential destinations as Mercury travels in Gemini from May 11–27.

Love and Life Connections

Love sizzles as Mars stirs passions during its six-week trip through Aries, which begins May 15, and has you at your most impulsive in matters of the heart. That's great for spontaneous TLC with your partner, but stop short if you even think about eloping. The fiery planet also can spark impatience, so go easy on yourself and others, especially loved ones.

Finance and Success

Your star rises May 8, when Venus arrives in Cancer, your solar Tenth House of career and status. It's followed by Mercury, which enters the same sign May 28. It's a safe bet you'll be even more of an attention-getter and enjoy being among the favored few. Take it one step further and do some subtle self-promotion to reinforce your position. Action taken now can lead to significant gains in June and July.

Rewarding Days

3, 4, 8, 11, 13, 14, 15, 17, 21, 22, 29

Challenging Days

5, 9, 12, 18, 19, 20, 25, 28, 30

Libra/June

Planetary Hotspots

Life is mostly as you like it this month, with opportunities to socialize, succeed, and romance your partner. You can expect a few bumps along the way after Mercury turns retrograde June 15, but June's major hotspot occurs at month's end. It's one you experienced earlier this year—a relationship issue triggered by Saturn and Neptune in exact alignment. The issue may involve the same person or people or someone new who's a friend or romantic interest, or a group in which you're involved. Whatever the issue is, you can and should resolve it now because it will be thirty-five years before this contact reoccurs.

Wellness and Keeping Fit

Fresh scenery is a great way to recharge before your career moves into high gear later this month and next. So go ahead and talk yourself into a vacation—even a short one—the second week of June. Make it a family trip, one with friends, or a romantic getaway designed for two. You might even be able to tack on few extra days for play if business takes you out of town.

Love and Life Connections

Love is almost anywhere you look for it, as Mars in Aries continues to energize your solar Seventh House of close relationships through June 23. Invite romance into your life, especially in mid-June; if you're single, the most likely location may be out of town or while socializing with friends after Venus enters Leo on June 5.

Finance and Success

You continue to come to the attention of important people. But with Mercury retrograde the last two weeks, you're unlikely to realize concrete gains until July. Nevertheless, people are watching, so turn in an impressive performance day after day.

Rewarding Days

1, 5, 6, 7, 10, 13, 14, 16, 17, 18, 23, 27, 29

Challenging Days

2, 3, 8, 12, 19, 20, 21, 24, 26

Libra/July

Planetary Hotspots

Let caution prevail no matter how promising an investment or financial deal sounds or what someone close to you advises. With Mars in Taurus, your sign of joint resources, contacting Saturn and Neptune, the same applies to loans and major purchases, which may have easy-to-miss hidden clauses. You'll also want to carefully check credentials before consulting a professional.

Wellness and Keeping Fit

Take advantage of the July 30 Full Moon in Capricorn, your domestic sign, to enjoy a few days off at home. Complete unfinished projects, clean closets and storage spaces, and generally give your place a breath of fresh air. Be careful, though, if you work with tools or climb a ladder.

Love and Life Connections

You'll enjoy your usual active social life the first two weeks of July, when Venus is in Leo, your friendship sign. Once your ruling planet enters the hidden realms of your solar Twelfth House on July 14, however, you'll be content with quiet evenings at home with your partner and close friends.

Finance and Success

Set your sights high this month. The July 4 New Moon in Cancer spotlights your career and offers you many opportunities to shine. Expect things to develop quickly after Mercury in Cancer turns direct July 9. Even if you're not searching for a new position or promotion, be alert for the chance to develop networking contacts after the Sun advances into Leo on July 22. They could come in handy as soon as next month, when knowing the right people can put you in the right place at the right time.

Rewarding Days

1, 7, 8, 9 11, 13, 14, 15, 17, 20, 21, 25, 30

Challenging Days

2, 3, 6, 10, 12, 16, 18, 19, 23, 24, 31

Libra/August

Planetary Hotspots

With the Sun, Mercury, and Venus joining Saturn in Leo at the New Moon in the same sign August 12, the focus is on friendship and group activities. You could be tapped to head up a club or organization or become more involved in one where you can widen your circle. Be a little cautious, though. Although this stellar lineup has the power to connect you with powerful people, all may not be exactly as it seems. Look beneath the surface, ask questions, resist pressure and ego strokes, and make an informed decision.

Wellness and Keeping Fit

Welcome a somewhat slower pace later this month as the Sun and Venus head into Virgo, your solar Twelfth House of self-renewal, and turn the focus on yourself for a change. Try for at least a day off to indulge yourself with a massage, facial, or pedicure, and a leisurely lunch with your best friend.

Love and Life Connections

You'll have more than enough contact with others this month to satisfy even a people-person like you. Among them could be a new romantic interest, an instant magnetic attraction that makes your heart zing. Enjoy it to the max, but don't lock yourself in just yet. What appears to be love could be only an infatuation. You'll know within a few months if it's the real thing.

Finance and Success

You'll be busy playing catch-up the week of the August 28 Full Moon in Pisces, your solar Sixth House of daily work. Expect last-minute projects, changes, and plenty to keep you busy into the first week of September. A confidential talk opens up possibilities for the future. Follow through.

Rewarding Days

3, 7, 9, 10, 11, 12, 16, 17, 18, 22, 26, 30, 31

Challenging Days

2, 6, 8, 13, 15, 20, 21, 23, 27, 28

Libra/September

Planetary Hotspots

Saturn enters Virgo, your solar Twelfth House of well-being, September 2. You'll enjoy more time to yourself in the next two years, as well as at home, as this influence encourages you to look within. It's an ideal period to resolve regrets and long-term issues so you're ready for a fresh start when Saturn moves on to your sign.

Wellness and Keeping Fit

Remind yourself the week of the September 11 New Moon in Virgo to schedule a routine checkup if you haven't done that yet this year. You'll also want to take precautions this month to help avoid a cold or the flu, either of which is easy to catch as the season shifts from summer to fall.

Love and Life Connections

Jump-start your social life as Venus resumes direct motion in Leo, your friendship sign, September 8. It's a cinch that you'll be right back in the swing, with Mercury in your sign from September 5–26, and the Sun arriving there September 22. Plan a romantic holiday with your mate at home or away around the time of the September 26 Full Moon in Aries, your partnership sign. Be alert that week if you're looking for love, when some singles discuss taking a relationship to the next level.

Finance and Success

Energetic Mars charges into Cancer, your career sign, September 28, to launch a busy and pressure-packed period that extends into November. Early this month, you can expect some tension when difficult people stir the pot at work. Steer clear of no-win situations.

Rewarding Days

5, 6, 7, 8, 9, 11, 12, 13, 14, 18, 22, 27

Challenging Days

2, 3, 10, 16, 17, 19, 21, 24, 26, 28

Libra/October

Planetary Hotspots

The New Moon in Libra on October 11 boosts confidence and motivates you to move forward with personal plans. Rather than dash, however, consider them a work in progress because Mercury turns retrograde in Scorpio the same day and returns to your sign October 23. Let your thoughts drift and explore ideas and options through month's end.

Wellness and Keeping Fit

Take an occasional time-out to enjoy your own company after Venus, your ruler, enters Virgo on October 8. Relax at a day spa one day and curl up with a best seller on another as you tune out the world and tune in your own thoughts and desires.

Love and Life Connections

You'll meet some fascinating people in your personal and professional life, thanks to Jupiter in exact alignment with Uranus and Neptune. Listen, talk, and be alert for a promising opportunity, as well as the sizzle of instant attraction at month's end. If you're part of a couple, put the rest of your life on hold for a romantic evening or weekend of love and togetherness.

Finance and Success

You should postpone major financial decisions and purchases until November. With Mercury retrograde in your solar Second House of personal resources, you could make a mistake based on incorrect information. If an appliance or other purchase is a must, consider an extended warranty and be sure to read the fine print. Give yourself—or your family—a financial checkup at the October 26 Full Moon in Taurus, your sign of joint resources. Look at debt, ways to cut costs, and insurance. Implement needed changes next month.

Rewarding Days

3, 4, 5, 6, 10, 11, 12, 16, 20, 21, 26, 30

Challenging Days

9, 15, 17, 19, 22, 23, 24, 25, 28, 29

Libra/November

Planetary Hotspots

Progress slows in the world at large as Mars turns retrograde in Cancer on November 15. You'll feel the strongest effect in your career life, where frustration rises as projects are delayed and decisions put on hold. Your best choice is to accept the inevitable reality and let matters unfold in their own time. If a new position is your goal, it's OK to send out résumés, but don't expect much to develop until at least February.

Wellness and Keeping Fit

A relaxing weekend getaway would be a welcome and much-needed break in the midst of the hectic holiday season. Manage it if you can around the time of the November 24 Full Moon in Gemini, your travel sign. If that's impossible, do an online search for potential winter vacation destinations to satisfy the urge for new horizons.

Love and Life Connections

Step into November 8 with a smile and all the confidence and charm heralded by Venus' arrival in your sign. Your powers of attraction are at their best into December, so make the most of this time to welcome your heart's desire. You'll also be popularity-plus at social gatherings and delight in magical romantic moments with your partner.

Finance and Success

Money matters benefit from the November 19 New Moon in Scorpio, your solar Second House of personal resources. You could earn a raise or receive a gift, but be cautious about investments and advice from a friend. If a deal sounds too good to be true, it probably is.

Rewarding Days

1, 2, 7, 8, 9, 12, 15, 20, 25, 26, 28

Challenging Days

5, 6, 11, 13, 18, 19, 21, 23, 24

Libra/December

Planetary Hotspots

Home life is in the spotlight as Jupiter enters Capricorn on December 18, followed by the Sun and Mercury within a few days. That's a great reason to host a holiday get-together before year's end. You'll want to do more of the same as 2008 unfolds and Jupiter progresses in its year-long transit of your solar Fourth House. Besides being your favorite and happiest location next year, you might get the urge to redecorate or remodel your home. Get started next spring; in the meantime, tour model homes for the latest trends and techniques.

Wellness and Keeping Fit

Pamper yourself during the first few days of December as Venus wraps up its annual visit to your sign. Update your look with a makeover, haircut, or new hairstyle, and treat yourself to a facial or massage. Top it off with new party clothes.

Love and Life Connections

You'll be on the same wavelength with most everyone this month, but some will frustrate you to the max. Try to steer clear of controlling people and those who refuse to listen to reason. Despite your outstanding powers of persuasion, it'll be tough to change anyone's mind. Family relationships are uplifting and inspirational at month's end, so you'll want to spend as much time as possible with those you love.

Finance and Success

Cross your fingers for extra cash, a bonus, or a windfall mid-month. With Venus in Scorpio from December 5–29, the boost may be one of several, including some terrific and coveted gifts. You'll get the most for your holiday dollars the second week of the month.

Rewarding Days

4, 5, 8, 12, 14, 16, 18, 19, 25, 26, 31

Challenging Days

2, 3, 6, 9, 10, 17, 22, 23, 27, 30

Libra Action Table

These dates reflect the best—but not the only—times for success and ease in these activities, according to your Sun sign.

	JAN	FEB	MAR	APR	MAY	JUN	JUL	AUG	SEPT	OCT	NOV	DEC
Move	1-3				6, 7							22-31
Start a class	15, 16								18, 19			
Join a club				24, 25	21, 22			16-17				
Ask for a raise		8, 9			29, 30		23					6, 7
Look for work	30, 31	9	19, 26		11		13, 17-19			2, 3	19	
Get pro advice	23, 24			11-18								18, 19
Get a loan			21, 22	27-30	2, 7		5, 17, 18					
See a doctor	8				11				11		5, 19	
Start a diet			17, 18	14, 15	11, 12		4, 5	28, 29				
End relationship				15, 16	13, 14	9, 10			26, 27			
Buy clothes	15-24		15, 16	11, 12							16	14
Get a makeover	10			29, 30		23			12, 13			3, 4
New romance	19-26		15-16	11, 12					22		16	14
Vacation	28, 29			12-20	21-27				30	1	24, 25	

SCORPIO

The Scorpion
October 23 to November 22

♏

Element:	Water
Quality:	Fixed
Polarity:	Yin/Feminine
Planetary Ruler:	Pluto (Mars)
Meditation:	I can surrender my feelings
Gemstone:	Topaz
Power Stones:	Obsidian, amber, citrine, garnet, pearl
Key Phrase:	I create
Glyph:	Scorpion's tail
Anatomy:	Reproductive system
Color:	Burgundy, black
Animal:	Reptiles, scorpions, birds of prey
Myths/Legends:	The Phoenix, Hades and Persephone, Shiva
House:	Eighth
Opposite Sign:	Taurus
Flower:	Chrysanthemum
Key Word:	Intensity

Your Ego's Strengths and Weaknesses

Success in any endeavor is directly linked to your incredible determination. You plow ahead, ignoring obstacles that others consider insurmountable. To you, any goal can be achieved when you set your mind to it.

You have a mysterious aura, a magnetic charisma that attracts people. But few penetrate your unwavering gaze, set in the classic poker face that appears calm even when you're seething inside. When you do express your views, you need few words to say it all.

Intense and focused, Pluto, your ruling planet, gives you tremendous willpower matched by an equal level of endurance. You can drive yourself relentlessly, stopping only when exhaustion sets in. Although that makes you highly productive, it can affect your health over time.

You are shrewd, intuitive, and creative. Combined, these talents often give you the edge because you're usually a step ahead everyone else. You also watch and wait, and act only when the time is right—and to your advantage.

People trust you and thus tell you their deepest thoughts and secrets. You rarely repeat what you hear because you're honorable and ethical, and have a profound respect for any information shared in confidence.

Hobbies and other leisure activities are excellent avenues for your creative energy. Using it regularly promotes relaxation and centering and provides an outlet for your often internalized emotions. This also helps free your inner voice, which is an excellent guide if you welcome and listen to it.

Your greatest gift is the power to transform. On a practical level, you can take what appears to be junk and create something new and useful. On a personal level, you constantly reinvent yourself to better your position in the world. In this sense you're adaptable, but only when you want to be.

You have the ability to amass a fortune, although you might be just as content with a comfortable lifestyle. Financially conservative, you take calculated risks and know how to use money to make money. Yet, few people, and possibly not even your partner, know your net worth. In money matters, as in most of life, you are secretive and protective.

Shining Your Love Light

Underneath your steely exterior is a soft, sensitive, warm heart that craves a stable and long-lasting partnership. Because you take relationships seriously, you're highly selective and willing to wait for the love of your life, someone to share the depths of your soul.

However, it takes quite awhile for you to reach a level of trust before you feel secure with anyone. Until then, you're reluctant to put yourself in a vulnerable position by expressing your emotions. Be careful! If you wait too long to open your heart, your lover may decide to move on.

You're loyal and protective of your mate, but also prone to jealousy because you can't imagine life without the one you love. More often than not, such feelings are based on insecurity rather than reality, so try not to jump to conclusions.

You delight in attentive, romantic moments and treating the man or woman of your dreams like royalty. Your passionate sensuality is in a class of its own!

You're a planner whereas Aries is pure action, and although this sign can be too spontaneous for you, you'll enjoy the sparks. In Taurus, your opposite sign, you could find a sensual soul mate who's just as possessive as you. Gemini's curiosity mirrors your own in a lighthearted way, but you might struggle coping with this sign's flirtatious nature.

Cancer might be too nurturing and overly protective for you even though your sensitivity and emotions are on a par. You're attracted to Leo, a sign that's far more outgoing than yours, but this sign's need for attention could drain your energy. You appreciate supportive Virgo's practicality and loyalty, so this can be a successful match if you maintain open communication.

You understand a fellow Scorpio better than anyone else in the universe, which gives you an advantage if you're both willing to compromise. You can see the world with Sagittarius, but might find it tough to feel totally secure with this adventuresome sign. You're drawn to Capricorn's ambitious nature, levelheaded approach to life, and practical advice, but Aquarius may be too independent and detached. You experience romance at its finest with Pisces, another sensitive, creative water sign with deep emotions.

Making Your Place in the World

Few can match your pace and passion in the work world. You give every task your all—and then some. Highly industrious, you have above-average potential to gain through performance- and incentive-based raises and bonuses. You are always thorough, but also have a knack for spotting short cuts that can increase productivity.

You readily accept responsibility and remain cool under pressure. These traits, plus your leadership ability, make you a prime candidate for management. If that's your goal, you ambitiously pursue promotions in your quest to reach the top tier of your career.

You are happiest when you can take charge and initiate action. Although impatient at times, you also understand that persistence is necessary to achieve long-term goals. It's also a safe bet that you can outlast the competition and weather difficult situations far better than most to get what you want.

Scientific research, the healing professions, counseling, and the pharmaceutical industry might appeal to you as career choices. In the financial field, you could excel as an investment banker, stockbroker, insurance adjuster or investigator, mortgage officer, tax or treasury agent, or collections specialist.

Some Scorpios are excellent detectives, coroners, morticians, and butchers. If interested in the arts, you could succeed as a performer or producer. Your powers of transformation might lead you to a career in salvage, home renovations, or recycling. You could also be an effective surgeon, military strategist, or emergency medical technician.

Putting Your Best Foot Forward

You are both determined and stubborn, the upside and downside of one of your key personality traits. The difference between the two is a fine line. Go one way and you're productive; go the other way, however, and you're marking time—at best. Being aware of this difference is the first step toward increasing your success quotient.

Your willpower is closely aligned with your equally phenomenal determination. Like a steamroller, you pursue a goal and let nothing block your momentum. This positive quality becomes less so, though, when focus turns to tunnel vision. Then it's difficult to see how your actions affect the end result. Broaden your view and you just might end up at a better place.

Once focused, you can push yourself relentlessly, unwilling to pause until a job is finished. This may fulfill your desire for achievement, but at what cost? Ease up and strive for a balanced lifestyle.

The same applies to your relationships. You can push others as hard as you push yourself. Not a good idea! Build support instead. Empower others and share the load through teamwork.

Then there's your flip side—stubbornness. There are times when you absolutely refuse to budge—for anything, any reason, or anyone. This, too, is linked to tunnel vision, and once your mind is set, rightly or wrongly, you're unwilling to change it.

Change is the operative word— you resist it unless you're the instigator. You are a master, however, at transformation—change on a global scale. This unique talent benefits people, places, and things when you have a free hand to implement sweeping change. But that's not always possible, nor desirable. Learn to accept small changes as progress toward the greater goal of transformation. Doing so will also help build your support network.

With this approach, you can transform stubbornness into determination and come full circle to realize your full potential. Listen along the way. Seek advice, opinions, and ideas with a mind open to new horizons and fresh insights.

Tools for Change

You have so much going for you this year, it's phenomenal. Although home life is a mystery, yet inspirational, money can provide security. Love and creativity are insightful, and your career life is fulfilling. You will experience all of these and gain from what your senses can see, touch, and feel, as well as whatever your sixth sense nudges into awareness.

Money boosts self-esteem as it validates your career success in concrete terms. If you have been reluctant in the past, now is the time to congratulate yourself for your achievements with a symbolic, yet tangible, reward. You deserve it.

You may find it difficult to connect with your family on an everyday, practical level. Yet you will sense their support and feel a spiritual connection that's as solid as the foundation of your home.

Creativity and love add sparkle to your life; both challenge you to stretch yourself and take a few risks. Embrace change, be spontaneous, eliminate preconceived ideas, let your imagination flow, and give the lighter side of life a prominent place on your agenda.

Learning is the common denominator for all these influences. You will gain through a winning combination of self-knowledge, friends, groups, loved ones, and information. Wherever you go and whatever you do in your daily life, welcome the chance to expand your horizons.

Affirmation for the Year

I find strength in change.

The Year Ahead for Scorpio

With lucky Jupiter in Sagittarius, your solar Second House, the odds are in your favor for a bigger bank balance. The challenge, however, is to hang onto the cash and end the year with more than you had in the beginning. That's because Jupiter can expand spending as well as income. Try to curb the urge to splurge, especially on credit. Then you're protected for leaner times and unexpected expenses because, despite your wishes and optimism, this influence won't last forever. Stash the cash and build a nest egg. You also should avoid obvious get-rich-quick schemes and be cautious with investments and anyone who promises a high return. You could win a lottery or contest prize this year, so take an occasional chance. But rising income is a more likely source of funds. Jupiter enters Capricorn on December 18. The shift to your solar Third House emphasizes communication and quick trips. Take a class next year for the fun of it, plan periodic weekend getaways, and consider getting involved in a neighborhood or community group.

Now in the final months of its two-year Leo transit, Saturn continues to highlight your career. You may have already experienced the potential gains offered by this placement, as well as long hours and expanding responsibilities. If you have yet to pursue a promotion or new position—or your sights are set on another step up—try to lock it in within the first four months of the year and don't hesitate to negotiate for a better salary and benefits package. Be confident and believe you deserve it! Saturn will enter Virgo, your solar Eleventh House of friendship, September 2. As you embark on this new phase, you may become involved (or more involved) in a club, organization, or another group of like-minded people. This is a great opportunity to widen your circle with new acquaintances and networking contacts.

Where Saturn demands hard work, Uranus in Pisces invites you to play. Now midway through its long transit of your solar Fifth House, Uranus accents exciting people and places, fun, and social events. Uranus is just your style this year—spontaneous, active, and independent. It enhances your spirit of adventure as it jazzes up your love life and encourages you to free your creative instincts at work and at play. Pause occasionally to listen to your inner voice because this intuitive planet stirs your sixth sense. A hunch could lead you to the right place at the right time to cash in on the future as well as a lucky win. But this is not the year for financial risk, no matter how promising an offer sounds.

Since 1998, when Neptune entered Aquarius, your solar Fourth House, your foundation has been shaky and solid, sometimes stable and at other times unsettled. The Fourth House represents home and family, as well as the symbolic foundation, or base, from which life evolves. It also represents the starting point for new endeavors. Nebulous Neptune can thus make it difficult to establish a new direction or get a new endeavor off on solid footing, in part because of your shifting interests. You may experience a similar effect with family relationships, where adult children or other relatives move in or out. But this transit also has an upside: creativity. Put it to work for you in home décor with the goal of creating the ideal sanctuary where you can retreat from the outer world. Do the same with your patio or garden.

Pluto is in the last year of its long trek through Sagittarius, your solar Second House of money. The dual influence of Jupiter in the same sign identifies this year as one of boom or bust. The outcome, which is more likely to be favorable, is largely dependent upon your choices and decisions. Shy away from risk because luck goes only so far, and be sure your property is adequately covered by insurance. Pay off debt, rather than incur more, and opt for a lower mortgage payment if you purchase a home.

This year's eclipses are in Virgo and Pisces, your solar Eleventh and Fifth Houses. That's a plus for your social life and is almost guaranteed to bring new people into your life. Among them could be an intriguing romantic interest.

If you were born between October 23 and November 2, you benefit from Saturn after it enters Virgo on September 2. Reconnect with friends and visit relatives you were too busy to see in the past few years. Get better acquainted with neighbors. Consider hosting a holiday open house to see them all, especially if you want to show off a newly redecorated home. Also set aside time to reflect on what you achieved while Saturn was in Leo. Now is a good time to set new goals. Put them in writing and review them every few months to help stay on track. You might want to join a professional organization to help further your aims and polish your public speaking skills, or take an active role in a neighborhood or community group where you can make a difference. But be careful about the commitments you make. You could end up doing far more than your share of the work as people look to you for solutions and depend on you to create order out of chaos for a major project or fund-raising effort. You might enjoy the challenge initially, but it soon will wear thin. Do what's right for you and what you want to do rather than give in to pressure from other people. Key dates: October 13, November 30, and December 6 and 19.

If you were born between November 3 and 11, Uranus in Pisces invites you to view yourself from a new perspective. No one would disagree that you're comfortable with change—when it's your idea! This year it will be just that, as well as easy and enjoyable. But change is unlikely to happen on its own. The magic formula is you, your determination and willpower. Set plans in motion to achieve whatever you want to change your personal or professional life. Uranus's solar Fifth House transit has also committed Scorpios in the mood for the most romantic of moments. If you're single and searching for someone special, you could feel the zing of love at first sight and delight in a whirlwind romance. A new hobby—or perfecting a skill—is a great way to satisfy your creative instincts. You might even stumble upon a new invention as you transform junk into something useful. Some Scorpios will welcome an addition to the family this year; others will learn much about life through the eyes of their children. Key dates: January 22, February 7, March 4 and 31, April 27, June 8, September 4, October 8, and November 25.

If you were born between November 10 and 14, Neptune in Aquarius contacting your Sun from your solar Fourth House signals everything from confusion to inspiration. You'll experience both and at times feel like you're drifting through life. Yet through Neptune's mists will emerge a clearer view of yourself, your place in the world and the important relationships in your life. Spirituality is another theme linked to Neptune, which encourages you to listen to your inner voice and decipher its intuitive messages. This year isn't the best for property deals because you could end up with costly hidden problems. If a home purchase is a "must," make it contingent upon a full inspection. Also regularly check your home and major appliances for leaks, and, if you live in a flood-prone area, cover yourself with insurance. Key dates: January 20 and 26, February 9, April 5, May 6 and 13, June 26, August 12, September 23, November 23, and December 20.

If you were born between November 10 and 22, Saturn contacts your Sun from Leo, your solar Tenth House of career. This is a pinnacle, a time when past efforts and experience pay off. Like much of life, this transit is all about what you make of it. You can either sit back or dive in and enhance your reputation and career. But be prepared to take on extra duties without being asked, and to promote your skills and talents with decision-makers. It's equally important to live up to your promises; if you take on a project, be sure you can complete it and deliver superb results that single you out for recognition. But be especially cautious about whom you trust this summer. Someone—a co-worker or supervisor—could have less than your best interests in mind, so keep personal matters to yourself, document information, and generally cover your bases. Oddly enough, it could be your creative ideas and innovative thinking that spark a jealous streak in someone. But don't let that stop you from using all your know-how to impress those who count. Key Dates: January 20, February 10, March 22, April 19, May 9, July 1 and 30, August 13 and 20.

If you were born between November 18 and 22, Pluto in Sagittarius empowers you to take bold steps and gives you easy access to your considerable inner strength and willpower. It can help you transform yourself, inside or out, through diet, moderate exercise, and positive self-programming. As a result, you'll feel terrific about yourself, and with increased confidence will come the realization that you are your most valuable possession. Pluto also can give you the incentive and determination to realign personal finances and spending habits. Focus on security and building a fortune, dollar by dollar, for your retirement years. Key dates: February 19, March 18, April 8, May 12, September 19, November 5, and December 10.

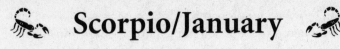

Scorpio/January

Planetary Hotspots

Plan ahead. With three planets joining Neptune in Aquarius and contacting Saturn in Leo, you'll be stretched thin the last two weeks of January when domestic and career responsibilities demand equal attention. The catalyst could be weather or water damage to your home or the need for a major repair. Be alert and check your home daily for potential problems. If you want to begin a remodeling project or a home-based business, make a wise decision. Postpone it until the second half of the year.

Wellness and Keeping Fit

Launch the new year with a relaxing winter getaway the first week of January as the Full Moon in Cancer on January 3 spotlights your solar Ninth House of travel and learning. If time off is impossible, take a fun class to satisfy your creative urges. Learn a new hobby or master new skills.

Love and Life Connections

Family and other close relationships are both frustrating and uplifting, confusing and enlightening. Each is a learning experience in human nature and self-understanding if you go with the flow and let events unfold at their own pace. You'll be more inclined to entertain at home this month, with the Sun, Mercury, and Venus moving into Aquarius. But interest begins to shift to the outer world, socializing, and romance January 27, when Venus enters Pisces.

Finance and Success

You could be in line for a nice raise or bonus the second week of January as Mars wraps up its time in Sagittarius, your solar Second House of money. If interested in or offered a promotion, get all the facts. A step up may not be worth relocating for it. Be kind to your budget. Impulsive Mars also can trigger a spending spree.

Rewarding Days

2, 6, 8, 10, 12, 14, 17, 18, 22, 25, 30, 31

Challenging Days

1, 11, 13, 19, 20, 21, 23, 25, 26

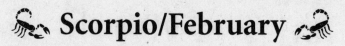

Scorpio/February

Planetary Hotspots

Work and family continue to compete for time as Saturn and Neptune move closer to their exact alignment at month's end. Between that influence and Mercury turning retrograde in Pisces on February 13, you'll have your hands full trying to juggle it all. You also can expect delays in the completion of domestic projects, financing, and property deals until mid-March.

Wellness and Keeping Fit

Walking is an excellent and relatively easy way to reduce stress and tone your body, and it's a lot more fun with a partner. Ask a neighbor to join you and get started while Mars is in Capricorn through February 24. Walk a neighborhood route or join a mall-walkers group and meet new people.

Love and Life Connections

Your love life benefits from Venus in Pisces and, if you're single, a magnetic attraction could spark a whirlwind romance in early February. Once the Sun arrives in Pisces on February 18, you'll have plenty of social invitations and be among the most popular party guests. Some outings could be pricey, however, so check costs before you go, and confirm dates, times, and places after Mercury turns retrograde.

Finance and Success

With the February 2 Full Moon in your solar Tenth House of career and status, you'll have a packed agenda the first half of the month. Give it your all because what you do now is directly linked to potential gains next month. Take time to cultivate relationships by socializing with co-workers after Venus enters Aries, your sign of daily work, February 20.

Rewarding Days

1, 6, 8, 9, 13, 14, 15, 18, 22, 26, 27

Challenging Days

3, 5, 7, 10, 16, 23, 28

Scorpio/March

Planetary Hotspots

Career frustrations are the norm the last week of March when Mars aligns with Jupiter, Saturn, and Neptune. Keep your cool and try to be flexible because the harder you push, the less progress you'll make. All will eventually come together with the help of an ally who might be the least likely supporter. You'll also want to gain family support beforehand, so they're willing to pick up the slack when necessary.

Wellness and Keeping Fit

Be careful around the house. With Mars and Mercury, which is retrograde through February 6, in your domestic sign, an accident can happen in a flash. Take precautions if you're on a ladder, working with tools, or in the kitchen. Need a repair? Call a professional.

Love and Life Connections

The March 5 Full Moon in Virgo lights up your solar Eleventh House of friendship, and the New Moon in Pisces on March 19 does the same for your love life. That's a terrific influence to fill your calendar with social events. Expect even more after Venus enters Taurus, your partnership sign, March 17, followed by Mercury entering Pisces the next day. Romance is pure delight the last few days of the month, when some singles get engaged and others fall in love at first sight.

Finance and Success

A raise, job offer, or promotion could be yours the first full week of March. Be a little cautious, though, if you're contemplating a major change or step up because career matters are this month's hotspot. If possible, hold off until April, when you'll have a better idea of what's involved and what you want.

Rewarding Days

4, 10, 12, 13, 15, 17, 21, 26, 27, 30

Challenging Days

8, 9, 14, 16, 18, 22, 23, 28, 29

Scorpio/April

Planetary Hotspots

If you're a parent you'll discover—or be reminded—just how expensive kids can be. The same applies to your social life and other leisure-time activities. Save by cutting costs where possible and opting for free or low-cost events. Fun and togetherness, not the price tag, is what's important.

Wellness and Keeping Fit

The Aries Sun encourages you to give yourself a lifestyle checkup, as well as to schedule routine medical appointments. If you want to lose a few pounds, get started at the April 2 Full Moon in Libra and you could see initial results by the New Moon in Aries on April 17. Complement a more nutritious diet with an exercise program, but go easy at first. Overdoing it can trigger sprains and strains.

Love and Life Connections

Although April gets off to a rocky start as Venus clashes with Saturn and Neptune, it's merely a blip in an otherwise upbeat month for close relationships. You'll want to devote as many evening and weekend hours as possible to loved ones, as well as more than a few romantic ones with your partner. Expand your focus to include social events with business contacts after the Sun, your career planet, enters Taurus on April 20. With Mercury in Aries from April 10–26, you'll also have many opportunities to get to know co-workers and develop a solid friendship with a few.

Finance and Success

After more than a few career frustrations in recent months, momentum builds as Saturn in Leo turns direct April 19. You'll reap the benefits within a few days, thanks to Mercury's positive planetary contacts that could put more money in your paycheck, especially with Venus in Gemini, your sign of joint resources, after April 10.

Rewarding Days

4, 9, 10, 11, 14, 16, 17, 22, 26, 29

Challenging Days

5, 6, 13, 15, 18, 21, 27, 28

Scorpio/May

Planetary Hotspots

Relationships give you a few challenges this month. Although the tension is primarily work-related, job stress can affect personal and family ties. Pleasing the boss the second week of May will be tough, but far easier if you follow rules, procedures, guidelines, and directives. You might even learn a things about yourself and human nature, both of which can benefit you in the long run. Keep this thought: it's OK to change your mind.

Wellness and Keeping Fit

Start searching for a vacation destination when Venus enters Cancer, your travel sign, May 8. Although even a few days off might be impossible this month, you can get things started for June or July. In the meantime do the next best thing. Take a couple of weekend day trips to re-center yourself, body and soul.

Love and Life Connections

The May 2 Full Moon in Scorpio could trigger temporary stress and strain in a close personal relationship when ideas, needs, and desires clash. Open the lines of communication and try to view things from the other person's perspective. With a little compromise you'll be ready for a fresh start at the New Moon in Taurus, your partnership sign, May 16.

Finance and Success

Expect a fast pace and a heavier work load after Mars enters Aries, your sign of daily work, May 15. Longer hours are possible and deadlines are many in the next six weeks. But it's well worth the effort because your chance to shine arrives in June. An unexpected expense could pop up this month, but finances are mostly status quo. Be prepared, though, to resist the temptation of easy credit.

Rewarding Days

1, 4, 6, 7, 11, 15, 19, 21, 23, 29

Challenging Days

5, 9, 10, 12, 16, 18, 25, 30

Scorpio/June

Planetary Hotspots

June is mostly uneventful until the last few days, when Saturn and Neptune form their final exact alignment across your solar Tenth-Fourth House axis. This brings the domestic, career, and relationship issues you experienced earlier this year almost to an end. Resolve any lingering concerns, but think twice before you cut ties. With Mercury traveling retrograde after June 14, you could regret the decision and find it impossible to undo. Think long term, rather than what might satisfy your immediate needs.

Wellness and Keeping Fit

Welcome summer with the incentive to get in better shape. You can do it if you set your mind to it and tap into the high energy of Mars in Aries, your solar Sixth House of health. Walk, ride a bike, skate, or join a gym. You'll get the side benefit of reduced stress during this high-powered time at work.

Love and Life Connections

Although the fast pace at work limits leisure time this month, that's all the more reason to set aside a few evenings to socialize with friends. If nothing else, plan a weekend away to reconnect with pals or your partner. A chance encounter mid-month could spark a whirlwind romance, but if you feel the zing with a co-worker, get better acquainted after hours.

Finance and Success

June has all the potential to boost your bank account, thanks to the June 1 Full Moon in Sagittarius and the New Moon in Gemini on June 15. A sizable raise or bonus is possible for you or your mate, along with a promotion. You also could benefit from an inheritance or gift from a relative.

Rewarding Days

1, 5, 7, 10, 13, 14, 15, 16, 17, 18, 23, 25, 29

Challenging Days

2, 3, 6, 11, 12, 19, 20, 24, 26

Scorpio/July

Planetary Hotspots

Expect some personal and professional challenges at month's end when Mars in Taurus, your sign of close relationships, aligns with Saturn and Neptune. Although it would be easy and natural to absolve yourself of any responsibility, conflict usually takes two. Consider it an opportunity to view yourself through the eyes of others as well as to learn when to back down and compromise.

Wellness and Keeping Fit

Try for at least a weekend getaway, if not an entire week, to relax and unwind as the July 4 New Moon in Cancer motivates you to go in search of new horizons. Or take a mental journey. Take a fun class to learn or perfect a hobby or do-it-yourself skills.

Love and Life Connections

Social Venus arrives in Virgo, your solar Eleventh House of friendship, July 14. Make the most of it because once Venus turns retrograde July 27, you'll have fewer opportunities to see friends and get acquainted with new people. Fill the gap with work-related get-togethers and group activities such as a club, organization, or volunteer effort—any of which could connect you with a new romantic interest who might be your long-anticipated soul mate.

Finance and Success

Career activities begin to pick up July 22, when the Sun arrives in Leo. Creativity counts and can set you apart from the crowd, as can an emphasis on teamwork and sharing the credit. But take care not to upstage the boss or anyone who might further your career, which moves into high gear in August.

Rewarding Days

1, 4, 5, 8, 9, 13, 14, 15, 17, 22, 25, 27, 28

Challenging Days

2, 3, 6, 10, 12, 16, 19, 23, 24, 31

Scorpio/August

Planetary Hotspots

Plan ahead to put most everything but your career on hold mid-month. An incredible array of planetary lineups in your solar Tenth House could propel you into the lofty realm of star-studded status. If only it were all that simple! Landing where you want to be with money to match will require finesse, knowledge, willpower, and determination, all of which you possess, plus aligning yourself with the right people. Take nothing at face value. Ask questions, get the details, and be sure you're well-informed about the potential downside as well as the upside.

Wellness and Keeping Fit

With so much going on in your career life this month, it's even more important to find time for yourself and moderate exercise. If not before, get motivated the week of the August 28 Full Moon in Pisces, when you can convince a friend to join you. Start slowly if you're out of shape and resist the temptation to overdo it.

Love and Life Connections

This month's people contacts run the gamut from positive to negative to challenging, rewarding, and uplifting. At times it could be difficult to know who has your best interests in mind, so be even more cautious than usual about whom you trust. Use your intuition. In matters of the heart, this is not the month to commit because Venus is still retrograde.

Finance and Success

Personal and joint finances benefit from positive planetary contacts and Mars in Gemini after August 6, but this upbeat influence can prompt you to take certain risks you would normally avoid. Protect your resources.

Rewarding Days

1, 3, 7, 9, 10, 11, 12, 18, 19, 23, 30, 31

Challenging Days

2, 6, 8, 13, 15, 20, 21, 28, 29

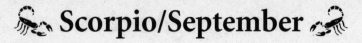

Scorpio/September

Planetary Hotspots

Don't jump to conclusions when Saturn enters Virgo, your solar Eleventh House of friendship and group activities, September 2. The friendship challenges you'll experience early this month are related to difficult planetary contacts from the Sun and Mercury in the same sign. In fact, you'll have many opportunities during the next two years with Saturn in Virgo to form lasting friendships and among them possibly find a soul mate. This month, though, you should put your interests first and let go of a relationship if that's the right choice for you.

Wellness and Keeping Fit

The Full Moon in Aries on September 26 highlights health and wellness. It's one of the best of the year if you want to lose a few pounds. Also schedule a routine checkup if you haven't had one yet this year.

Love and Life Connections

The September 11 New Moon in Virgo breathes fresh energy into your social life and encourages you to widen your circle of friendship. Get involved in a club, organization, or community group, or volunteer your skills for a good cause. You also can expect an increase in romantic opportunities after Venus, your partnership planet, turns direct September 8.

Finance and Success

Mars in Gemini, your solar Eighth House of joint resources, through September 28, has the potential to increase your bank account, but an unexpected expense is also likely. Be conservative with investments and don't loan money to friends or relatives. It will be a long time, if ever, before it's returned.

Rewarding Days

1, 6, 7, 8, 10, 13, 14, 15, 20, 27

Challenging Days

2, 3, 11, 16, 17, 19, 24, 26, 28

Scorpio/October

Planetary Hotspots

Expect minor frustrations after Mercury turns retrograde in Scorpio on October 11, and slips back into Libra on October 23, the same date the Sun arrives in your sign. The planetary influences will primarily affect personal plans, although you'll want to choose your words with care to help prevent misunderstandings. You also should postpone new personal endeavors until next month's New Moon in your sign.

Wellness and Keeping Fit

Tune in to your inner voice through meditation or quiet time this month, especially around the New Moon in Libra, October 11, and after retrograde Mercury returns to Libra. You'll gain fresh insights into life, love, and family as you deepen your spiritual connection with the universe.

Love and Life Connections

Your social life gets a lift October 8, when Venus enters Virgo, your friendship sign. You might reconnect with a pal you haven't seen in years, but tread carefully if you encounter a former love interest. Focus on why you parted ways and remember that people rarely change. The October 26 Full Moon in Taurus, your partnership sign, is ideal for love and togetherness, and some singles launch a whirlwind romance or discuss plans for the future.

Finance and Success

Jupiter in Sagittarius, your solar Second House of personal resources, links its lucky energy with Uranus and Neptune this month. You could luck into a win or windfall or receive news of a possible gift from a family member. But take care. The same influence could prompt you to spend big bucks on credit. Postpone major financial decisions until next month, when Mercury turns direct.

Rewarding Days

3, 4, 6, 7, 10, 12, 14, 17, 18, 21, 26, 30

Challenging Days

2, 5, 9, 15, 19, 22, 24, 28, 29

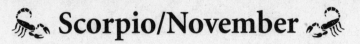

Scorpio/November

Planetary Hotspots

Information is tough to come by after Mars turns retrograde in Cancer, your solar Ninth House, November 15. The red planet can also trigger travel delays and cancellations through the end of January, when it turns direct. As the ruler of Aries, your solar Sixth House of daily work, you can expect periodic slowdowns on the job, when projects lose momentum and decisions are postponed.

Wellness and Keeping Fit

Dream big, set high goals, and be ready to launch new personal endeavors at the November 9 New Moon in Scorpio, the symbolic beginning of your new solar year. It's also a terrific time to pamper yourself. Indulge in the royal treatment at a day spa, or treat yourself to a coveted item.

Love and Life Connections

See friends early this month as Venus wraps up its time in Virgo, your friendship sign. Once the love planet enters Libra on November 8, you'll want to partially step out of the social scene until next month. If you're part of a couple, this could be one of the most romantic times of the year. Plan evenings and weekends designed for two as love and togetherness kindle passions.

Finance and Success

Let the November 24 Full Moon in Gemini, your sign of joint resources, prompt you (and your partner) to take a close look at finances. If you have debt, create a plan to eliminate it, as well as to increase savings and retirement funds. Also review current company benefits and shop for insurance to compare rates. But wait until Mars turns direct the end of January before you switch policies or change benefits.

Rewarding Days

1, 3, 4, 8, 9, 10, 13, 15, 18, 22, 26, 28

Challenging Days

5, 6, 11, 16, 19, 21, 23, 24, 29, 30

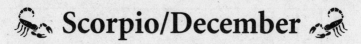

Scorpio/December

Planetary Hotspots

Communication, travel, and learning come into focus as Jupiter begins its year-long trip through Capricorn, your solar Third House, December 18. If you're interested, check out classes for pleasure or profit, as well as winter or spring vacation options. If you plan to travel around the time of the December 24 Full Moon in Cancer, remember that retrograde Mars in the same sign can trigger anything from delays to lost luggage.

Wellness and Keeping Fit

Give some thought to your goals for 2008 after Mercury enters Capricorn on December 20. But rather than latch onto the first few ideas that enter your mind, take your time and zero in on what would bring you the most personal happiness. Journaling can help guide you to the jackpot.

Love and Life Connections

December 5 is your day! Venus arrives in Scorpio, bringing with it all the magnetic charm and charisma your sign is noted for. Keep it flowing, along with your social and love life, all the way through December 29, when Venus moves on to Sagittarius. A chance encounter could spark a sudden attraction mid-month, when spontaneity increases the passion for couples in love.

Finance and Success

Your natural financial know-how comes in handy this month. Where other people might be tempted to stretch their budgets with easy credit, you have more restraint. Even so, it might be tough to resist. Access your strong willpower and tell yourself to walk away, because retrograde Mars slips back into Gemini, your solar Eighth House of joint resources, December 31. You be glad you did when few bills arrive in January.

Rewarding Days

4, 5, 7, 11, 12, 14, 16, 19, 21, 25, 29

Challenging Days

2, 3, 6, 9, 10, 13, 17, 22, 23, 30

Scorpio Action Table

These dates reflect the best—but not the only—times for success and ease in these activities, according to your Sun sign.

	JAN	FEB	MAR	APR	MAY	JUN	JUL	AUG	SEPT	OCT	NOV	DEC
Move	4-27		10-16	11, 12							16	
Start a class	5-13, 18			10	7			23, 24	20, 21		13, 14	
Join a club		7, 8		26, 27			17, 18	24-31	1-3, 10, 11			
Ask for a raise			12					22	18			
Look for work	23, 24			11-18, 25	21, 22			13				17-19
Get pro advice			21, 22		15, 16		9					
Get a loan				19, 20	21-27		12		30	1	25	
See a doctor	22			12-18, 30		9, 10			13	10		3, 4
Start a diet				15, 16	13, 14				27, 28			
End relationship					15	11, 12	9		28, 29			
Buy clothes	29-31	18, 19	18		11, 12						18, 19	15
Get a makeover		8, 9			29, 30						8	5-7
New romance	30, 31	2-10	18		11, 12						18, 19	15, 16
Vacation	30, 31		25, 26		19, 20	22-30	13-22				26, 27	

SAGITTARIUS

The Archer
November 22 to December 22

♐

Element:	Fire
Quality:	Mutable
Polarity:	Yang/Masculine
Planetary Ruler:	Jupiter
Meditation:	I can take time to explore my soul
Gemstone:	Turquoise
Power Stones:	Lapis lazuli, azurite, sodalite
Key Phrase:	I understand
Glyph:	Archer's arrow
Anatomy:	Hips, thighs, sciatic nerve
Color:	Royal blue, purple
Animal:	Fleet-footed animals
Myths/Legends:	Athena, Chiron
House:	Ninth
Opposite Sign:	Gemini
Flower:	Narcissus
Key Word:	Optimism

Your Ego's Strengths and Shortcomings

As the adventurer of the zodiac, you're the modern-day equivalent of some of the world's great explorers—Lewis and Clark, Marco Polo, Leif Eriksson, Ponce de León, Amelia Earhart, James Cook, and Magellan. Like these people, your quest is knowledge, truth, and new horizons.

Most Sagittarians love to travel and consider every vacation an opportunity to explore another corner of the globe. The universe of the mind also attracts you, and you're a natural learner who views each experience as an addition to your vast storehouse of knowledge. You're intrigued by everything from museum exhibits to ethnic cuisine to the latest self-help best seller that can satisfy your need to understand what motivates you and what holds you back.

With expansive Jupiter as your ruling planet, you're an enthusiastic, outgoing positive thinker who sees the big picture. But at times you can be overly optimistic and ignore the realities of a situation when a less idealistic outlook would be in your best interests. Accomplishing that can be a challenge because Jupiter's luck-factor comes to your rescue time and time again. Yet even this benefic planet has its downside: it can compound a problem rather than lessen it, so don't count on it as your never-fail guardian angel.

Physical activity comes naturally and is an important part of your well-being. It also helps tame the impulsiveness and impatience of your restless sign, which can be quick to anger. Yet it is this fiery spirit that adds zest to the friendly, confident, upbeat nature that boosts your popularity.

Generous and sincere, you nevertheless can push your honest, ethical, truth-seeking ways beyond appropriate limits. Try to remember that people are more receptive to a tactful, diplomatic approach that leaves them feeling good about themselves, even when a candid opinion or constructive criticism is merited. The bonus is you will have gained another supporter. After all, you never know who might be your next lucky charm!

Shining Your Love Light

Playing the field is your style and you can fall in and out of love in a heartbeat. The thrill of the chase appeals to your active nature and you can be relentless in your pursuit of a potential romantic interest who catches your eye. All that dating experience helps you zero in on the qualities you value most in a mate.

When you're ready to settle down, which might be later than most of your peers, intellectual compatibility and a sense of humor are traits you seek. Your ideal match is also likely to be open-minded, curious, and lively—and even might be more of a flirt than you!

Gemini, your opposite sign, is a strong draw. You keep each other guessing because no two days—or hours—are exactly the same.

You're naturally attracted to the fire signs—Aries, Leo, and fellow Sagittarians—who share your passions and need for excitement. Aries can be a bit too impulsive even for you, though, and Leo's need for attention can be draining. You'll enjoy the spontaneity of another Sagittarius, but coordinating schedules and keeping track of each other could be a major challenge.

Although Taurus can bring financial security, this sign could be too slow and possessive for your freewheeling lifestyle. Cancer is supportive, but might "smother" you with caring. With Virgo you have a mental connection, although it can be tough to blend your big-picture outlook with this sign's detail-oriented perspective.

Libra's grace and charm delight you, and you're in sync with your appreciation for justice and fairness, but indecisiveness can test your patience. Scorpio's allure can mesmerize you, although jealousy can be an issue. You can lighten Capricorn's serious outlook and will appreciate this sign's stability if not the cautious nature. Aquarius is even more independent than you are and can be mentally stimulating, albeit aloof. Pisces is inspiring, spiritual, and creative, but sensitive and moody.

Making Your Place in the World

You're a hard worker, efficient and organized once you find your career niche and a job that satisfies you mentally and emotionally. You need the freedom to structure your daily work as well as the time to complete each task thoroughly.

Although not necessarily driven to reach the top of your profession, you are goal-oriented and expect your skills and talents to be rewarded financially. You won't sacrifice your principles to get ahead, and value performance above politics. That can work both ways career-wise. Sometimes who you know can trump what you know.

You might be drawn to a legal career as an attorney, paralegal or mediator, or in the travel industry as a pilot, flight attendant, cruise director, or tour guide. In communications, you could excel in publishing, public relations, or advertising, or as an agent or writer.

Some Sagittarians are drawn to transportation careers, to enjoy the freedom that accompanies a job as a mail carrier, delivery person, or taxi, limo, or truck driver. Your desire to learn and teach could motivate you to pursue education as a profession, and your strong faith and spirituality might inspire a religious life. Coaching and other athletic careers, sales, and foreign affairs are other fields that could maximize your talents.

Putting Your Best Foot Forward

Truth and justice are colored with shades of gray—not limited to black or white, right or wrong, yes or no. Reality is perception; what some people see as finite fact, others view as part fact, part fancy.

As a Sagittarius you are the ultimate truth-seeker. Yet what you perceive as the truth may or may not be the final word. Do yourself a favor and live up to your sign's potential to be a broad-minded, visionary freethinker. Besides adding more information to your vast knowledge bank, you'll learn to appreciate the nuances that surround issues, questions, and solutions.

Listening is equally important. Do you ever tune out people based solely on first impressions? Do you do the same with those you don't respect or like based on what may be limited information? If you do, you're human! But you're also doing yourself a disservice. After all, you never know who might become your best friend, your partner, or a valuable career contact.

Listening also will encourage you to become more sensitive to other people's opinions. Even though you disagree with someone's thoughts, his or her perception of reality and truth is just as valid as yours. Tolerance and an open mind can get you further than standing firm on what you believe, but may not be the undiluted truth.

As you expand your views and learn to listen before you speak you're likely to develop a more tactful approach. Sagittarius is a sign well known for its bluntness. Although it's your style to state the facts as you perceive them, taking a softer approach that most people prefer is a far easier way to win friends and influence people and to convince them to see things your way.

So add some fluff, be sensitive to feelings, and color your words with a little gray. The more tactful you are, the more expansive your views will become, and vice versa.

Tools for Change

You are your best tool for change this year, as the universe guides you toward personal growth and self-empowerment. You also can come to appreciate the value of patience and to complement initiative with follow-through.

You may have recently responded to the nudge to broaden your horizons in a practical way. If you have yet to make that leap, this year offers you another chance. Either way, now is the time to embrace the future by building a solid educational foundation for future expansion. Learn, grow, and invest your brainpower in classes or studies to better prepare for coming career opportunities.

In the process, you might be surprised to discover yourself welcoming new ideas and goals about your role in the world. These "mainstream" thoughts, although not free-spirited in a traditional Sagittarian sense, signal the start of a new adventure. Your challenge is to be true to your spirit while adding a new structure to your life.

As you embark on this journey, remember that you are the decision-maker, the one in charge of yourself and your future. Choices made now can bring well-deserved personal and professional rewards in the next few years.

The end result is directly linked to your willingness to initiate change and carry out a well-conceived plan. The best news is it will be fairly easy to accomplish once you set your mind to it. Inaction is the major hurdle, and distraction a secondary one.

Seize the day, get motivated, empower yourself, and take the initiative to become all that you can be. Then have the patience to finish what you start, thus allowing yourself blossom into a wiser, more knowledgeable you.

Affirmation for the Year

I believe in myself and I'm ready for a challenge.

The Year Ahead for Sagittarius

Optimism sets the pace for a fabulous year fueled by Jupiter in your sign. With this lucky streak going for you, 2007 is filled with potential as Jupiter boosts your charisma and energizes your zeal for new endeavors. Put this spirit of adventure to good use as you embark on your new twelve-year journey (Jupiter visits each sign every twelve years). But Jupiter also can promote misguided optimism and encourage you to look on the bright side when a realistic view would be more helpful. If in doubt when faced with a major decision, seek a second opinion from someone you respect and trust. Then merge those thoughts with your own. Because Jupiter is the planet of expansion, a nutritious diet and regular exercise are especially important this year if you want to avoid extra pounds. Get the year off to a healthy start with a program that works for you. Stick with it! You'll feel and look great!

Saturn in Leo, your solar Ninth House, continues to spark a desire for travel and knowledge. You may have enrolled in school more than a year ago when Saturn entered Leo. If not, there's still time to take a few classes, study for advanced certification, or perfect a special skill. Any of these actions can boost your chances for career gains in the next several years. You also might enjoy a learning vacation, such as a sports camp, a cruise that features visits to historical sites, a gourmet cooking school, or a weeklong hobby- or craft-intensive clinic in a resort location. You'll also be motivated to learn and share your knowledge on a daily basis. Offer to teach a company training class, or organize an informal weekly session for co-workers. If you enjoy hands-on work, a do-it-yourself class can fine-tune your home-improvement skills. Distance learning via the Internet is another option to fulfill this year's information quest. What you learn during these final months with Saturn in Leo will be of practical use from September 2 on, when Saturn enters Virgo, your solar Tenth House of career. This new journey, one of hard work and responsibility, can net rewards and increased status for you in the wider world.

Uranus in Pisces continues to influence your solar Fourth House. This phase, which began in 2003, signals ongoing change in your home life, with the most obvious outcome being relocation or home improvements—even if you've done so recently. A relative or adult child could move in or out, as Uranus can trigger a change in family structure. You also can expect the unexpected: impromptu visitors, mechanical or electrical problems, or a surprise windfall. This placement also has the potential for changing relationships with neighbors, as well as neighborhood events that could prompt you to get involved in local politics.

Neptune's long transit through Aquarius (your solar Third House), which began in 1998, continues to enhance your intuition and creativity. Both are a real plus for problem-solving and provide a spark for your imagination. Even better, this sign-planet-house combination helps you successfully merge ideas that are innovative, yet practical, original and far-sighted. This is an asset in your daily life and career, as well as hobbies and other leisure-time activities. If you've ever wanted to write a novel or poetry, or create a work of art, give it a try this year. Listen to hunches and the subtle messages that emerge from your subconscious. You'll get new insights into how the past guides the present and the future.

You undoubtedly have experienced many changes since 1995, the year Pluto entered your sign. This year is the last of this powerful planet's long influence and one that ends much as it began: with the high hopes of Jupiter also in Sagittarius. Reflect on what you've accomplished and what you'd still like to do to complete this period of personal transformation to prepare for the new adventure set to begin in 2008.

This year's eclipses in Pisces and Virgo highlight your solar Fourth-Tenth House axis of home and family, and career. Change is possible—even likely for some Sagittarians—as you re-examine your place in the world and how to maximize your potential. You may relocate for a new job or promotion, establish a home, see an adult child move out, or take a more active role in a relative's life.

If you were born between November 22 and December 2, Saturn in Virgo challenges you to rise above the rest and reap rewards earned through hard work, attention to detail, and belief in yourself. Be aware that it could take until next year before you reach your next career goal. In the meantime, do all you can to showcase your know-how for decision-makers and networking contacts who can help further your aims. Snap up opportunities to take the lead and volunteer for extra assignments—within reason. Although your stamina may be subpar with this influence, it's all a part of learning patience, how to pace yourself, and how to work more efficiently. Master all three—or at least make significant progress—and you'll be that much closer to realizing your goal. If you're offered a promotion or new job during this period, ask pointed questions before you accept. Be sure you're fully aware of the responsibilities. Key dates: October 13, November 30, and December 6 and 19.

If you were born between December 3 and 11, Uranus in Pisces signals domestic and personal changes. A local or long-distance move is possible or you may decide to extensively remodel your current place. Much of this is due to your urge for freedom, independence, and change. Channel it well and after much thought; once you act, a reversal will be nearly impossible. This influence can be very uplifting if you direct the energy into positive personal change and a fresh start that can send you in exciting new directions. Enlightening thoughts and flashes of insight are part of the picture, and luck can have you in the right place at the right time to take advantage of a fantastic opportunity. Just be careful to get all the facts—the pluses and minuses—before you leap and avoid putting funds and property at risk. You also should review and update insurance coverage early in the year so you're protected in the event of the unexpected. Key dates: January 22, February 7, March 4 and 31, April 27, June 8, September 4, October 8, and November 25.

If you were born between December 9 and 14, Neptune in Aquarius has you in a highly creative phase, loaded with inspiration and the belief that almost anything is possible. Dream big! But be prepared to turn your dreams into an action plan designed to achieve concrete results. That's the tough part, especially early in the year. In later months, ideas will gel and you'll find it easier to set plans in motion as well as to pursue your passion. You'll also want to double-check facts and conclusions because Neptune can mask the truth and trigger confusion and wishful thinking. Talk with someone you trust and respect who will give you an objective opinion even if it isn't necessarily what you want to hear. You also have a real opportunity this year to access your intuition. In many ways, your sixth sense is linked to creativity—and the more you use both, the stronger both will become. Key dates: January 20 and 26, February 9, April 5, May 6 and 13, June 26, August 12, September 23, November 23, and December 20.

If you were born between December 10 and 22, you benefit from Saturn's steady energy. This sensible planet provides a good balance for your fiery enthusiasm and helps you turn clever ideas into practical results. It's also your turn to broaden your knowledge base as you seek to gain the wisdom offered by Saturn in Leo, your solar Ninth House. Although you'll want to absorb as much practical information as you can, this transit has another less obvious influence: learn all you can about yourself, your needs and desires, your strengths and weaknesses. Be honest with yourself. With this self-knowledge you'll be better prepared to define your career goals in order to take full advantage of Saturn's upcoming Virgo transit. With these forces reinforcing your confidence and faith in yourself, your talents, and your skills, you're prime for career gains. All of this is part of your 2007 learning curve and one you can master with minimal effort. Key Dates: January 20, February 10, March 22, April 19, May 9, July 1 and 30, August 13 and 20.

If you were born between December 17 and 22, Pluto in Sagittarius forms a powerful contact with your Sun as it concludes its long transit through your sign. You thus have the opportunity to benefit from all you've learned about relationships and self-empowerment since 1995, when Pluto entered Sagittarius. But you also could be tempted to overcommit yourself in your zeal to do it all. Try to broaden your perspective rather than succumb to tunnel vision; the closer you allow yourself to become to a situation, the more difficult it will be to see obvious solutions and alternatives. Do this and you'll have the determination and stamina to accomplish amazing things, including desired personal changes. If you want to get in shape or replace a bad habit with a healthy one, this is the year to do it. Although it won't be exactly effortless, willpower will strengthen your resolve. Key dates: February 19, March 18, April 8, May 12, September 19, November 5, and December 10.

Sagittarius/January

Planetary Hotspots

Your thoughts are both practical and creative, buoyed by optimism and enthusiasm. Yet it's also easy to lapse into wishful thinking or to become disillusioned when events differ from dreams as planets align with Neptune and Saturn in your solar Third and Ninth Houses of communication and knowledge. Pursue your vision with a realistic outlook and have faith in yourself and your abilities. On another level, be cautious about what and whom you believe. If it sounds to good to be true, it probably is.

Wellness and Keeping Fit

You know, more than many, that self-knowledge is power. Follow the lead of this month's Mars-Pluto-Saturn alignment in Sagittarius and Leo and make that one of your top goals for 2007. The more you learn about yourself, the better equipped you'll be to acquire wisdom and practical information.

Love and Life Connections

With Mars, your romance planet, in your sign, take the initiative to socialize and meet new people, and don't hesitate to get things started if someone catches your eye. Family life comes into focus at month's end, when Venus enters Pisces, your domestic sign, January 27. That's an equally positive influence for time with loved ones, cozy evenings with your partner, and entertaining at home.

Finance and Success

Finances grab your attention throughout the month, with the chance for a raise or small windfall. Keep that thought and use the Full and New Moons in Cancer and Capricorn, your money signs, to build a fatter bank account—especially after Mars enters Capricorn on January 16.

Rewarding Days

4, 5, 6, 10, 14, 15, 19, 24, 27

Challenging Days

1, 9, 13, 16, 20, 22, 29

Sagittarius/February

Planetary Hotspots

January's communication and knowledge theme is reinforced as Saturn in Leo and Neptune in Aquarius form an exact alignment under the Full and New Moons in the same signs. Continue to question facts and take little, if anything, at face value the first two weeks. But even after that you'll want to be cautious about matters related to travel, finances, legal issues, and education because Mercury turns retrograde in Pisces on February 13 and returns to Aquarius on February 26.

Wellness and Keeping Fit

Take a mental journey rather than a physical one to satisfy your quest for new horizons. It's a better choice with this month's planetary lineups and a terrific way to de-stress at the end of a long day. Browse the library or a bookstore, surf the Internet, or join a book discussion group.

Love and Life Connections

With the Sun, Mercury, and Venus in Pisces, your domestic sign, part of the month, you'll enjoy time at home and with loved ones. Think before you speak, though, and then choose your words with care. With Mercury retrograde the second half of the month, misunderstandings can spark disagreements and hurt feelings. Stir up some interest in socializing with friends and set aside lots of time to romance your partner after Venus enters Aries on February 20.

Finance and Success

Money continues to flow your way, thanks to energetic Mars in Capricorn, your solar Second House of personal resources. Keep tabs on your budget because this influence can prompt you to spend more than you save.

Rewarding Days

1, 6, 7, 8, 12, 13, 15, 17, 20, 22, 27

Challenging Days

3, 4, 5, 18, 19, 23, 24, 25

Sagittarius/March

Planetary Hotspots

Life flows along until month's end when Mars in Aquarius contacts Saturn and Neptune, as other planets did in January and February. This time, though, you'll find events easier to handle and even make progress, thanks to Jupiter in Sagittarius. Even so, frustration and confusion are likely, so think calm and be patient with yourself and others. This lineup is also accident-prone, so take care on the road, in the kitchen, and working with tools.

Wellness and Keeping Fit

Get your creative energy going this month on a hobby or artistic project that takes you away from daily stresses and strains. Better yet, let the March 19 New Moon in Pisces, your domestic sign, inspire you to begin thinking about a spring room or garden redo.

Love and Life Connections

Romantic opportunities multiply with Venus in Aries through March 16, and the Sun advancing into the same sign four days later. Positive planetary alignments the first full week of the month further increase the odds that you'll meet someone special. If you're part of a couple, home is the best romantic destination after Mercury, your partnership planet, enters Pisces on March 18. It's also a plus for family communication.

Finance and Success

With a little luck, which you have, the week following the March 3 Full Moon in Virgo, your career sign, can bring you to the attention of important people. Knowledge, expertise, and creativity are key factors, as is teamwork. Make networking a priority, especially if you travel on business.

Rewarding Days

1, 5, 6, 10, 12, 16, 17, 19, 20, 27

Challenging Days

2, 4, 8, 9, 18, 22, 23, 25, 28

Sagittarius/April

Planetary Hotspots

Let warmer temperatures motivate you to put domestic projects at the top of your list. Mercury in Pisces, your domestic sign, through April 9 is ideal for planning, and incentive rises as Mars enters the same sign April 6. Tackle your to-do list first and move on to bigger projects where you can use your imagination and creativity. But be smart and take safety precautions. They're a must because Mars also is noted for risk-taking, accidents, and overdoing it.

Wellness and Keeping Fit

With the Sun and Mercury in energetic Aries part of the month, the timing is ideal if you want to tone muscles before bathing-suit weather arrives. Join a gym or sports league, take a yoga class, learn an individual sport, or jump on your skates or bike. Start slowly and give you body a chance to catch up to your new vision of you.

Love and Life Connections

Your social life takes off, thanks to this month's New and Full Moons in Aries and Libra. Line up dates and outings with friends, and get set to welcome new people into your life. At month's end, Mercury in Aries aligns beautifully with several planets, which could trigger a new love interest, a vacation trip, or a romantic getaway. Even better, Venus is in Gemini, your partnership sign, after April 10.

Finance and Success

This month, the Sun, Mercury, and Venus visit Taurus, your sign of daily work. Together, they step up the pace and bring many satisfying, productive days. Use the planetary energy to strengthen workplace relationships, which can pay off as soon as this fall.

Rewarding Days

3, 9, 11, 12, 16, 17, 19, 24, 29, 30

Challenging Days

5, 6, 8, 13, 18, 20, 21, 27, 28

Sagittarius/May

Planetary Hotspots

Relationships are somewhat strained in early May as Mercury in Taurus clashes with several planets. Rather than view this as an obstacle, see it as an opportunity to better understand and appreciate other viewpoints. With that approach you'll learn and grow personally and professionally and even experience flashes of insight as new truths emerge.

Wellness and Keeping Fit

This month's May 2 Full Moon in Scorpio, your solar Twelfth House, accents wellness. Schedule a checkup and commit to a healthier lifestyle if you feel it's an area that needs improvement. Stock your kitchen with the first of summer's fresh bounty.

Love and Life Connections

Romance, togetherness, and social events fill many of your May evenings and weekends, with the Sun, Mercury, and Venus visiting Gemini, your partnership sign, and Mars arriving in Aries, your solar Fifth House of romance and recreation, May 15. The influence peaks around the time the Sun enters Gemini on May 22 when the spotlight is on new relationships and cozy, intimate, TLC-filled hours for couples.

Finance and Success

Look to the future if you're asked to take on extra responsibilities at work. It could be well worth the extra time and effort as the May 16 New Moon in Taurus highlights your work life. At the same time, be sure you're well aware of what's required and what you can expect in return. With Venus entering Cancer, your solar Eighth House of other people's money, May 8, followed by Mercury on May 28, you could benefit financially.

Rewarding Days

3, 4, 5, 8, 11, 13, 14, 15, 17, 21, 26, 31

Challenging Days

9, 10, 12, 16, 18, 20, 22, 25, 30

Sagittarius/June

Planetary Hotspots

Events and issues of the past several months culminate the end of June when Neptune and Saturn form an exact alignment in your solar Third and Ninth Houses. Wisdom will accompany disappointment, inspiration, and enlightenment, and you'll probably come to view the world with a different perspective. As before, though, be cautious with legal and financial matters, as well as travel and putting your faith in promises.

Wellness and Keeping Fit

Stick with the exercise program you began in March—or get moving if you didn't. Mars in Aries fuels incentive and helps you make it a daily habit. You'll be glad you did and appreciate the stress relief when the work pace picks up as Mars advances into Taurus, your sign of daily work, June 24.

Love and Life Connections

You're drawn to people as the June 15 New Moon in Gemini, your solar Seventh House, focuses your attention on relationships. This influence favors love, family ties, and close friendships, and some singles commit to lifetime togetherness. Although the accent is on personal relationships, the lunar energy also highlights business partnerships and professional consultations. This month's other planetary lineups, however, advise some caution with these alliances. Check credentials. Protect resources.

Finance and Success

The June 30 Full Moon in Capricorn, your solar Second House of personal resources, can boost your bank account, trigger an unexpected expense, or both. A conservative outlook is wise until you know the final outcome in early July, when you could receive a long-awaited check. Try the lottery the first half of June.

Rewarding Days

1, 5, 10, 13, 14, 16, 17, 18, 23, 27, 28, 29

Challenging Days

2, 8, 12, 19, 21, 24, 25, 26, 30

Sagittarius/July

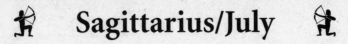

Planetary Hotspots

Mars in Taurus, your sign of daily work, signals a fast-paced month on the job. Steady progress and high productivity keep you on task the first three weeks. After that, however, you can expect some frustration and confusion when information is tough to come by and decisions are put on hold. Pushing won't help, so go with the flow, especially after Venus turns retrograde in Virgo, your career sign, July 27.

Wellness and Keeping Fit

Consider taking an extra few days around the first weekend of the month to visit out-of-town friends. Or, take a day trip with local pals. Either one satisfies your urge for new spaces and places while Venus, your friendship planet, is in Leo, your travel sign, July 1–3. The change of scenery will relax and recharge you for the busy month ahead.

Love and Life Connections

You'll probably be in touch with more people at a distance, including relatives, after the Sun enters Leo on July 22. Make a few calls around that time and you could become privy to some surprising and intriguing information.

Finance and Success

Finances begin to get back on track after Mercury turns direct in Cancer, one of your money signs, July 9. But that could be short-lived because Venus, which turns retrograde, is the universal money planet. That makes it wise to be conservative in money matters, which also are in focus at the June 30 Full Moon in Capricorn, your other money sign. If you're hoping for a raise it could be delayed until later in the year. In any case, this probably is not the month to ask for one.

Rewarding Days

7, 8, 9, 11, 13, 14, 17, 20, 21, 25, 26, 30

Challenging Days

2, 3, 6, 10, 12, 16, 19, 23, 24, 31

Sagittarius/August

Planetary Hotspots

Set your sights on new horizons as the Sun, Mercury, and Venus in Leo contact nearly every other planet in the Zodiac. The energy peaks at the August 12 New Moon, also in Leo. This powerful alignment could trigger plans for a fabulous trip, the start or completion of advanced schooling, a moving spiritual experience, or a publishing contract. Related events will continue to unfold into early October, when Venus, now retrograde, will complete its Leo transit. Dream big and make your wishes comes true!

Wellness and Keeping Fit

Take a break from life around the time of the August 28 Full Moon to reconnect with home and family. You'll enjoy time with both into early September. Even better, you'll have a chance to relax and recenter as you rediscover all the reasons you love those you do. Plus, your favorite people will appreciate the attention.

Love and Life Connections

Mars energizes your solar Seventh House of close relationships when it arrives in Gemini on August 7. The influence, which continues until the end of September, stirs passions for couples and brings some singles an exciting new romance. But resist the urge to push others who might prefer to take things at their own pace.

Finance and Success

Interest begins to shift toward your career life August 19, as Mercury enters Virgo, followed by the Sun four days later. You could be offered a terrific opportunity to shine that week. Consider it carefully—with a realistic view. Too much optimism could prompt you to take on more than you can accomplish in the allotted time. Ask for and listen carefully to the details. Then sleep on it.

Rewarding Days

1, 3, 7, 10, 11, 12, 16, 17, 24, 26, 30, 31

Challenging Days

2, 6, 8, 13, 15, 20, 21, 27, 28, 29

Sagittarius/September

Planetary Hotspots

A momentous event occurs September 2: Saturn enters Virgo, your solar Tenth House of career and status. This influence, which occurs only every twenty-eight years, is one to focus on and use to your advantage because it can deliver long-awaited rewards during the next two years. Take the challenge of this serious planet, which is a simple one. Live up to your job responsibilities and give them your all—even when it might be tempting to cut corners. Rise above the rest!

Wellness and Keeping Fit

Observation can teach you a lot about yourself and how you interact with others. Pause and reflect this month, whether the contact was easygoing and upbeat or one you'd rather not repeat. Then profit from it. Put the knowledge to work for you in future discussions to promote a positive outcome, which in turn reduces stress.

Love and Life Connections

September's love and life connections focus on friendship. Mercury's positive planetary contacts from Libra, your solar Eleventh House, September 5–26, signal fun- and laughter-filled evenings and days with pals and the potential to connect with new people, including networking contacts. A new romantic interest could enter your life, thanks to a friend, after love-planet Venus turns direct September 8.

Finance and Success

The heat is on this month as career demands rise, but amid the periodic challenges you'll find the chance to excel and catch the attention of important people. Communication and adaptability are key, as is quick thinking. Strive for positive gains the week of the September 11 New Moon in Virgo.

Rewarding Days

1, 7, 8, 9, 12, 13, 14, 18, 20, 22, 27

Challenging Days

2, 3, 11, 16, 17, 19, 23, 24, 26, 30

Sagittarius/October

Planetary Hotspots

Although life is hectic, you'll find much to cheer about while you dash from one thing to the next. Enjoy! But there's a potential downside to this month's Jupiter-Uranus-Neptune alignment that expands personal horizons. Try to narrow your focus and choose only the opportunities that can further your main mission—the new life direction that begins to emerge. Despite your wish to do it all, scattered energy yields only scattered results.

Wellness and Keeping Fit

Try to set aside fifteen to thirty minutes a day for quiet time to let your thoughts drift from one pleasant image to the next. This time alone will help free your inner voice, which speaks loudly, given the chance, thanks to Mercury in Scorpio, your solar Twelfth House of the unseen. The effect is enhanced after Mercury turns retrograde October 11. Listen closely for career insights.

Love and Life Connections

Friendship continues to give you an active social life, thanks to the New Moon in your solar Eleventh House. Make it a point to meet new people so you can widen your circle of contacts, one of whom could be your lucky charm. If you're involved in a group, club, or organization, you could be asked to accept a leadership role.

Finance and Success

You're an attention-getter, so prime yourself for success as Venus arrives in Virgo, your career sign, October 8. The influence peaks around the October 26 Full Moon in Taurus, your solar Sixth House of daily work. If you're ready for a new challenge, go for a promotion or send out résumés. Finances are also on the upswing with energetic Mars in Cancer, one of your money signs. Be ready with a list of accomplishments if it's time for your annual review.

Rewarding Days

4, 5, 6, 7, 10, 11, 12, 14, 16, 20, 21, 27

Challenging Days

2, 9, 15, 17, 19, 22, 23, 28, 29

Sagittarius/November

Planetary Hotspots

You'll want to monitor expenses and keep a close eye on your budget when Mars is retrograde in Cancer, your sign of joint resources, from November 15 until the end of January. This could—but doesn't have to—interfere with the holidays. Get creative and use your imagination to dream up ideal, yet inexpensive, gifts for all but the closest few on your list. If possible, put major financial decisions, including investments, benefits, and insurance, on hold until February.

Wellness and Keeping Fit

You'll probably want and need more time alone this month, which features the November 9 New Moon in Scorpio, your solar Twelfth House of self-renewal. It's also good for another reason: more rest and a slower pace can help prevent a cold or the flu. So try to reserve some evenings and weekends for yourself in the midst of the busy social season.

Love and Life Connections

You'll have plenty of invitations to fill your calendar, with Mercury in Libra, your friendship sign, through November 10, and Venus' arrival there November 8. Choose the best of the best and don't hesitate to decline what doesn't interest you. You might want to make an exception the second and last weekends of the month, however. Either or both could spark a new friendship, job contact, or love relationship. Romance your partner around the time of the November 24 Full Moon in Gemini, your partnership sign.

Finance and Success

Surround yourself with positive energy November 1–7, as Venus completes its trip through Virgo, your career sign. It will help you attract the same in return and be a good defense against difficult people who may try to block progress.

Rewarding Days

2, 7, 8, 10, 12, 13, 17, 20, 21, 25, 26, 28

Challenging Days

3, 5, 6, 11, 18, 19, 23, 24, 30

Sagittarius/December

Planetary Hotspots

Set your sights on a bigger bank account a year from now. The potential is there as of December 18, when Jupiter, your ruler, enters Capricorn, your solar Second House of personal resources. The odds favor increased income in 2008, but expansive Jupiter also can prompt you to spend. Plan now to pay yourself first. Stash cash in savings, pay off any debt, and live within your budget to get the most from this lucky influence. Unfortunately, it won't last forever!

Wellness and Keeping Fit

Treat yourself to a day of TLC in honor of the December 9 New Moon in your sign. Schedule yourself for the royal treatment at a day spa that week or weekend and tune out the outer world and your to-do list. After all, you deserve it!

Love and Life Connections

The first weekend of December is the most social of the month, as Venus aligns with Jupiter and Pluto. See friends, accept a party invitation, or host a get-together. If you're single, be alert for someone intriguing or ask a friend to introduce you to a potential romantic interest. Chances are, you'll click. If you're part of a couple, plan a cozy New Year's Eve for two and celebrate love as passionate Mars slips back into Gemini, your partnership sign.

Finance and Success

The work pace slows somewhat as Saturn turns retrograde December 19 in Virgo, your career sign. This is an excellent time to reflect upon what you accomplished in 2007, and to begin to shape your goals for 2008. Try not to be too disappointed if an expected year-end bonus is less than you had hoped for. That's possible because Mars is still retrograde. Think positive! You can make up the difference next year and then some!

Rewarding Days

4, 5, 7, 12, 14, 18, 19, 21, 25, 26

Challenging Days

2, 3, 6, 8, 9, 17, 22, 23, 30

Sagittarius Action Table

These dates reflect the best—but not the only—times for success and ease in these activities, according to your Sun sign.

	JAN	FEB	MAR	APR	MAY	JUN	JUL	AUG	SEPT	OCT	NOV	DEC
Move	30, 31	2-10	18-20		11, 12						18, 19	
Start a class	20-26			29, 30	26, 27			16, 17	12, 13, 23-26		6, 7	3, 4
Join a club				29, 30	26, 27			16, 17	12, 13, 23-26		6, 7	3, 4
Ask for a raise	2, 3, 17, 18				7					17	14	11, 12
Look for work	8		21, 22	26-30	15, 16		17, 18	24-31	1-3		3-5	
Get pro advice	29		23	19, 20	17, 21, 22		11, 12			1		
Get a loan	28-30	8	25, 26		15, 19		13, 14					
See a doctor		8, 9	21, 22	30	15, 16, 30						9	
Start a diet					15					26, 27		
End relationship						13	11, 12		30	28, 29	24, 25	
Buy clothes	23, 24	25		11-18		9, 10			27			18, 19
Get a makeover	15, 16		11			28			18		11, 12	9
New romance	23, 24			15-17		9, 10	7		27			19
Vacation				24, 25	21, 22			5-18	8, 9	5, 6		

CAPRICORN

The Goat
December 22 to January 19

♑

Element:	Earth
Quality:	Cardinal
Polarity:	Yin/Feminine
Planetary Ruler:	Saturn
Meditation:	I know the strength of my soul
Gemstone:	Garnet
Power Stones:	Peridot, diamond, quartz, black obsidian, onyx
Key Phrase:	I use
Glyph:	Head of goat
Anatomy:	Skeleton, knees, skin
Color:	Black, forest green
Animal:	Goats, thick-shelled animals
Myths/Legends:	Chronos, Vesta, Pan
House:	Tenth
Opposite Sign:	Cancer
Flower:	Carnation
Key Word:	Ambitious

Your Ego's Strengths and Shortcomings

Ambitious Capricorn's guiding lights are the past and the future. You think and plan long-term. Each important decision and action is weighed according to your experience, its potential long-term effects, and whether it will help you build a stronger foundation for future gains.

Yet with serious Saturn as your ruler, you can be overly cautious at times. Try to scale back to a less conservative level. Learn to take an occasional well-calculated risk to realize your lofty, but realistic, dreams. It's simply a matter of adjusting to a new comfort zone. Start small and move on from there.

You're organized, patient, and methodical. These qualities, along with your strong sense of responsibility and conscientious approach, are terrific assets as you climb the ladder of career and life success. You expend extra energy to get where you're going, in part because one of your greatest—and usually unfounded—fears is failure.

You view most everything from a practical standpoint and prefer a more traditional lifestyle. You're also thrifty and will scrimp and save to create a financially secure future. But you also understand that perception is reality and, therefore, spend what's necessary—within reason—to present the right image. Status is important to you because it's the outward representation of your many achievements.

A catch phrase often associated with Capricorn is "old when young, and young when old." That description sums up the instinctive mature wisdom and common sense you rely on daily. There is much that you just seem to "know" and you excel at correlating past experiences to current situations. In a sense, since you begin life ahead of the game with a vast storehouse of knowledge, you can take things a bit easier in later years when your peers are still learning life lessons you mastered in your younger years.

Age forty represents a symbolic turning point for many Capricorns who realize their greatest successes from then on. To others it might appear to be a meteoric rise, but you know better. You planned every step of the way!

Shining Your Love Light

You want the security and stability of a loving relationship and a supportive partner who can help you achieve your ambitions.

Although outsiders seldom see your emotional side, commitment gives you the confidence necessary to open up and share your feelings and sensuality.

You give each potential love interest your all and prefer to date one person at a time in your search for a kind and considerate, caring and nurturing partner. Once you do, you pledge your heart for a lifetime and take your family responsibilities seriously.

Many Capricorns settle down later in life, only after their careers are well under way. Others link hearts with someone who is significantly older or younger.

You're in tune with the earthy energy of Taurus, Virgo, and fellow Capricorns. All are practical and conservative and share your desire for stability. Taurus, however, could be too possessive for you, and Virgo too detail-oriented and critical. You have the most in common with another Capricorn, but you might have to schedule time to be together.

Your opposite sign, Cancer, might be the best match, and can bring out your softer side. But your mate might not understand your need for regular time alone.

Aries could be too much of a risk-taker for you, even though this sign encourages you to play. Gemini's energy is light and flirtatious, but the changeable nature of those born under this sign can challenge your security needs. Romance can be pure delight with Leo, but might require too much attention.

Although Libra can be indecisive and extravagant, status is important to both of you. Life with passionate, magnetic Scorpio appeals to your sensual side although it can be tough to find a workable compromise. Sagittarius is likely to be too free-spirited for your tastes, but you'll enjoy the adventure.

Aquarian spontaneity and independence can keep you guessing, but this sign might make a better friend than lover. Pisces' sensitive nature could be difficult to understand even though this one's imagination and creativity attract you.

Making Your Place in the World

Worldly success is a driving force in your life and, more often than not, career matters occupy your first and last thoughts of the day. Achievement is closely linked to your overall happiness and how you measure your path through life, which is slow but steady, and carefully outlined.

You excel as a leader and in management or supervisory positions. Although you expect a lot from people, you instinctively understand how to motivate them. You take a similar approach with superiors, forming relationships that can further your aims, sometimes many years in the future.

In your day-to-day work life you need the freedom to work on your own and fully take charge of a project or assignment. An excellent and efficient multitasker, variety and mental stimulation maximize your talents. You also work best with short bursts of intense energy and concentration that can yield ingenious ideas and solutions.

You might be attracted to the construction industry in a hands-on job or as a contractor, engineer, or architect. You could excel in watch- or clock-making or repair, as a geologist, or historian. If a medical career appeals to you, you might enjoy work as an osteopath, chiropractor, or orthopedic surgeon. Politics, government service, tailoring, and archaeology are other options.

Corporate life is a natural fit for many Capricorns who are executives and administrators in a wide spectrum of fields from the arts to manufacturing to the computer industry. Your exceptional organizational skills and practical creativity can lead you to career heights with a paycheck to match.

Putting Your Best Foot Forward

Your sign is associated with ambition and leadership, and almost all Capricorns discover this side of themselves sooner or later. Even before you do though, an objective observer can spot your natural take-charge attitude.

This quality pervades nearly every area of your life, from leisure-time pursuits to education to your family and career. Whether the scale is large or small, personal or professional, your analytical brain sizes up the situation and sets things in motion. But when possible you prefer to take the time to develop a solid plan so you know exactly where you're going.

This marvelous ability contributes greatly to your success, but it also can be your downfall.

You have a talent for organization, analysis, planning, and implementation, and thus can do by instinct what others need time to learn and process. That can frustrate you and make it easy to quickly slip into the "I'll do it myself" mode, rather than make the effort to mentor others so they can benefit from your strengths.

No, you don't have to do it all yourself! Learn to share the load—and the credit—and feel the satisfaction that comes from being a true leader and mentor to many, which is part of your life mission.

You're quick to take charge in any situation where you feel confident and doing so builds more confidence. That can prompt people to label you as "bossy" or even "dictatorial." In reality it's your people skills that are under fire, not your ability, because everyone appreciates competence.

Next time, pause before you dive in and begin issuing "orders" to get everyone organized, on the same page, and moving forward. Chances are, a potential leader will emerge from the crowd, and you can cast your yourself in a supportive role.

Use the same technique with friends and family. Although tough on you as a parent, sometimes the best choice is to let children learn the hard way—just as you did. And no doubt your partner is capable of doing many things, given the opportunity, and also will appreciate your willingness to share the load. Let friends plan the next get-together. Show up and have a great time!

Tools for Change

In many ways, this is a year of both completion and preparation. Your life view will continue to evolve as you focus on short- and long-term goals, what you really want and value, and how best to achieve your desires.

Although you'll want to—and should—seek input from those you respect, the process is primarily an internal one as you strive for greater self-understanding. More than usual, you'll enjoy time alone to think, plan, reflect, and dream. Keep in mind, though, that you could become so comfortable with your own company that it would be easy to cut yourself off from friends and loved ones. Strive for balance!

If you've never experimented with meditation, now would be a great time to give it a try. Besides being a helpful way to access your subconscious, it's an excellent relaxation tool that can strip away the stresses and strains of your hectic life.

You'll also want to listen to your inner voice even if you've never considered yourself intuitive. All that could change this year! Start small and learn to trust the messages you receive. They'll offer practical guidance as well as insights into your big-picture life questions as you get ready for a new and exciting chapter.

Affirmation for the Year

I understand myself.

The Year Ahead for Capricorn

This is a year of consolidation and preparation as Jupiter comes full circle, poised to enter your sign in 2008. Now in Sagittarius, your solar Twelfth House of self-renewal, Jupiter encourages you to look within. Let your thoughts first drift to 1995, when Jupiter was last in Sagittarius, the year you began this journey. In the intervening years you have learned much about yourself and how you respond to people, situations, and events. Now you can pull it all together and zero in on exactly what motivates you and what holds you back. With that knowledge you'll be ready to greet Jupiter on December 18 as it enters Capricorn and motivates you to embrace and pursue new personal directions. This year is also a lucky one in which you'll benefit from the protection of Jupiter's "guardian angel" position in your horoscope. In reality, this influence is part intuition and part good fortune; it can help you defy the odds to turn events in your favor, sometimes at the eleventh hour. But don't count on it 100 percent of the time because Jupiter can be as fickle as it is faithful and fortunate.

With Saturn now in the final stretch of its two-year Leo transit, you may have already felt the restrictive influence of this planet. However, Saturn's trip through your solar Eighth House of shared resources and other people's money can be an equally positive period, with increased income and other financial rewards. You're most likely to experience both sides of Saturn, so it's wise to save when the money flows. That way you'll have a nest egg when budgeting is tight. Because Saturn is the planet of experience and responsibility, this transit also encourages you to educate yourself about money management: investing, saving, spending, and debt. What you learn and the habits and attitudes you adopt will be tested seven, fourteen, twenty-one, and twenty-eight years from now as you measure your long-term financial progress. Saturn moves on to Virgo, your solar Ninth House of travel and knowledge, September 2. You might decide to return to school to complete your education or earn an advanced degree or certification. If you feel this is what you want to do, get the funding in place before Saturn enters Virgo. You may be eligible for a loan, scholarship, or tuition reimbursement.

The unexpected continues to be more the norm than the exception with Uranus in its fifth year in Pisces, your solar Third House of communication and daily activities. Some days are hectic, some calm, and Uranus keeps you guessing as to which will be which. This can be a challenge for your take-charge approach that includes leaving little to chance. Try to view this ongoing influence as an opportunity to discover the delights of life's more spontaneous moments. (Yes, they really can be fun!) Uranus also promotes change. Unexpected events are likely, but Uranus's major influence here relates to your thoughts and attitudes. Talk with people, open your mind to new information and viewpoints, and use your imagination in problem-solving and decision-making. With patience and faith, you can learn to trust your instincts. Combine intuition with your practical outlook to take your unique style of creative thinking to a new level.

Neptune continues its long transit through Aquarius, your solar Second House, the sign it entered in 1998. This mystical, visionary planet is also the master of illusion. It can inspire and disappoint you, spark confusion and clarity. All these factors continue to influence your personal finances this year, although on a subtle level to which you've by now become somewhat accustomed. You've also probably experienced the more apparent effects of Neptune here: money seems to disappear into thin air, but, more often than not, it also appears when you need it. Getting ahead is the challenge and one that can be overcome if you believe in yourself. As much as your solar Second House is about money, it's also about what you value. Put yourself at the top of the list! In many respects your earning power at this time is directly linked to the value you place on your skills and talents, so don't sell yourself short. Strive for a bank balance that reflects what you're worth—and then some.

Pluto concludes its twelve-year trip through Sagittarius this year. Known as the planet of transformation, Pluto's motto is "out with the old, in with the new." Its influence in your solar Twelfth House is primarily internal, nudging your subconscious into a more conscious state. This is a period of mental housecleaning as Pluto encourages you to free yourself from deep-seated concerns, worries, and fears, some of which may inhibit you from reaching your full potential. You'll want to complete the transformation process this year so you feel confident and empowered when Pluto enters your sign in 2008.

This year's eclipses in Pisces and Virgo, your solar Third and Ninth Houses, spotlight learning, travel, and spirituality. Learn all you can about yourself and the world around you, and stretch your mind with new information.

If you were born between December 22 and January 1, Saturn will be favorably aligned with your Sun after it enters Virgo on September 2. Exercise your mind by returning to school for fun or profit. If formal education would benefit your career, what you learn in the next two years will pay off when Saturn enters Libra in 2009. Enroll in school or, if time and family responsibilities are an issue, consider distance-learning via the Internet. If your motivation is curiosity and a thirst for knowledge, take a class to learn do-it-yourself or hobby skills, or study a new language and plan to visit that country in 2008 or 2009. This transit also emphasizes travel, so you might enjoy a vacation trip to historical sites, museums or ancient ruins, or a weeklong seminar in a resort location. Key dates: October 13, November 30, and December 6 and 19.

If you were born between January 1 and 9, Uranus in Pisces stimulates your mind, curiosity, and sense of adventure. With it comes an independent streak that motivates you to seek opportunities to express your individuality. But choose wisely and pursue only the best available prospects—despite the strong temptation to try to do it all. Be especially cautious if money is involved. Independence isn't worth the risk, particularly when you can find other, nonbusiness outlets to satisfy the freedom urge. Turn your innovative mind loose in a creative project such as writing, sculpting, furniture refinishing, woodworking, or building a better mousetrap. Or, take a class to learn a new hobby or more about a subject that piques your interest. Your sixth sense is no small part of the personal and professional equation this year. The more you listen to your inner voice, the stronger it will become; how-to books or a class can speed progress. Key dates: January 22, February 7, March 4 and 31, April 27, June 8, September 4, October 8, and November 25.

If you were born between January 7 and 19, Saturn in Leo contacts your Sun from your solar Eighth House of shared resources, with an emphasis on debt. Start by adding up your (or your and your partner's) net worth. Then take a close look at debt. Although Capricorns dislike owing money, circumstances sometimes make it a necessity. If that's your situation, or even if you have a small amount of debt, Saturn can give you the determination you need to pay off what you owe or to make a sizable dent in it before September 2, when Saturn enters Virgo. Establish a budget, get in the habit of paying by cash or debit card instead of credit, and watch the monthly balances drop. If your finances are in great shape, learn more about investments and how to put your money to work for you. Either way, this transit highlights the importance of saving and building assets for the long term. Key Dates: January 20, February 10, March 22, April 19, May 9, July 1 and 30, August 13 and 20.

If you were born between January 8 and 13, this year you'll question your role in life and your priorities and how to merge them to get the best of both. Begin by identifying what's important to you beyond the basics of food, clothing, and shelter. Money? A loving relationship? Friendship? Worldly success? Security? Family? Don't be surprised if this is a slow journey rather than a quick trip to an easy answer, as well as a greater challenge than you expect. That's OK. Drift with Neptune, which may take you in a completely different direction day by day, month by month, to year's end when you'll have a clearer idea of what you want. You also should pay close attention to money matters even if you're among the most financially conservative of your sign. With Neptune active in your solar Second House of personal resources, it would be easy to misplace a bill, overlook a payment, or incur a penalty. The same is true of contracts, which might contain misleading or hidden clauses. Read the fine print. Also safeguard credit card and other financial information from prying eyes. Key dates: January 20 and 26, February 9, April 5, May 6 and 13, June 26, August 12, September 23, November 23, and December 20.

If you were born between January 15 and 19, Pluto speaks through your inner voice as it connects with your Sun from Sagittarius, your solar Twelfth House. You may sense events before they manifest, and also feel you're gearing up for big changes in the next few years. You are. What you may notice most, however, is an inner strength beyond what you've previously experienced. This strength is accompanied by the determination and willpower to succeed on a personal level in almost anything. You might choose to get in shape, resolve old issues, or get more involved in helping others through a favorite cause. Key dates: February 19, March 18, April 8, May 12, September 19, November 5, and December 10.

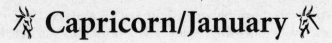

Capricorn/January

Planetary Hotspots

Although finances are up and down, you're more likely to end the month in positive territory. Nevertheless, you'll want to emphasize common sense even though yours is one of the most practical, financially savvy, and security-conscious signs. Think before you spend, avoid anything that sounds too good to be true or promises a guaranteed return. Protect valuables. You also might want to take a look inside the nearly forgotten boxes in the attic and closets. Inside one could be hidden treasure, such as an heirloom or collectible that's worth big bucks.

Wellness and Keeping Fit

Take thirty minutes or an hour, or whatever time you need, to unwind each evening before bedtime. Otherwise getting a restful night's sleep could be tough as Mars travels in Sagittarius, your solar Twelfth House, through January 16.

Love and Life Connections

The January 3 Full Moon in Cancer shines brightly on the close relationships in your life. Take a few evenings and weekends off this month to devote yourself to partner and family. They'll appreciate the time and attention, and you'll be reminded of all the reasons why you love the ones you love. The lunar energy sparks commitment for some Capricorns who are ready to take a dating relationship to the next level.

Finance and Success

More than ever, success is directly linked to you and your goals and ambitions. Use the first part of the month to decide what you want to achieve in the next twelve months. Then launch your plans at the January 18 New Moon in Capricorn, the symbolic start of your new Solar Year.

Rewarding Days

2, 7, 8, 10, 12, 14, 17, 18, 21, 25, 31

Challenging Days

1, 9, 11, 16, 23, 26, 28, 30

Capricorn/February

Planetary Hotspots

Money matters claim your attention again this month with the New and Full Moons in your solar Second and Eighth Houses of money. Last month's cautions remain in effect, especially in the first ten days of February and again at month's end. You'll also want to use the lunar energy to give yourself (and your family) a financial checkup. Shop around. Compare interest rates and get updated insurance quotes. If debt is an issue, develop a plan to cut costs and use the savings to pay down balances.

Wellness and Keeping Fit

Do something wonderful for yourself while Mars is in your sign through February 25. Schedule a spa day, get a massage, have a leisurely meal with a friend or your partner at an upscale restaurant, or spend the day at your favorite museum. You deserve it!

Love and Life Connections

Mix-ups and misunderstandings are possible, even likely, after Mercury turns retrograde in Pisces, your communication sign, February 13. Keep that in mind and steer clear of assumptions. Information received in early February could change by month's end, so leave your options open, especially with finances and work projects.

Finance and Success

Meetings, mail, paperwork, and talks can eat up precious time as Mercury travels in Pisces, your solar Third House of communications, February 2–25. That's enough in itself to put you behind schedule, but the effect is compounded when Mercury switches direction February 13. Be aware that decisions made during that time can be reversed in March. On the upside, a review of previous work can reveal errors and needed updates.

Rewarding Days

6, 8, 9, 13, 14, 17, 22, 26, 27

Challenging Days

3, 5, 10, 16, 19, 21, 24, 25

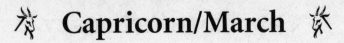

Capricorn/March

Planetary Hotspots

Look within when obstacles and frustrations arise this month as the intuitive Pisces Sun connects with Jupiter and Pluto in your solar Twelfth House of the unseen. You can readily access your inner strength and willpower, as well as your sixth sense. Combine them with your knowledge and experience. The result can lead you to practical solutions. Remember that faith in yourself and in the universe is as important now as is what's tangible.

Wellness and Keeping Fit

Try to take a few days off just before the March 19 New Moon in Pisces. A long weekend at home or away helps ease tension and gives you the opportunity to reflect and renew. Or treat yourself and your partner to a few nights at a nearby upscale hotel or spa.

Love and Life Connections

The Sun arrives in Aries, your domestic sign, March 20, three days after Venus switches its focus from Aries to Taurus, your solar Fifth House of romance and pleasure. The dual influence is ideal for family time and entertaining at home, as well as romance and socializing with friends. Include them all in your March calendar, with an emphasis on home life the first part of the month, when hearts and minds are in sync. This time frame also favors other family-related activities, such as a reunion or introducing a serious romantic interest to loved ones. Month's end brings a new relationship to some.

Finance and Success

Finances become more predictable after Mercury turns direct in Aquarius, your solar Second House of personal resources, March 7. But at month's end there may be further developments related to events of the past two months or a domestic expense.

Rewarding Days

4, 6, 10, 12, 13, 17, 19, 21, 26, 27, 30

Challenging Days

2, 8, 9, 11, 16, 18, 22, 23, 29

Capricorn/April

Planetary Hotspots

You can expect a few communication challenges, primarily early and late in the month. Surprising news and last-minute developments are part of the picture, so be prepared to go with the flow rather than make snap decisions you'll later regret. You also should hire a professional for any mechanical problems that pop up, which will be less expensive in the long run. Be cautious on the road.

Wellness and Keeping Fit

If you feel lost at sea, writing can help clarify your thoughts. Start (or continue) a journal, adding to it every day. Or talk with and listen to someone you trust and respect who will give you helpful feedback, which may or may not be what you want to hear.

Love and Life Connections

You social life is in full swing this month, with the Sun, Venus, and Mercury in Taurus, your solar Fifth House of pleasure, romance and recreation at various times. Put work on hold evenings and weekends for your children, partner or date, and friends. If a close relationship hits a rough spot in early April, don't say anything you might regret; re-evaluate as the month draws to a close.

Finance and Success

April arrives with the April 2 Full Moon in Libra, your career sign, so be prepared for a fast-paced start to the month that can bring you to the attention of decision-makers. Your work life benefits from Venus in Gemini from April 11 on, and it's possible you could earn a perk. But it's wise to continue the recent policy of financial caution, especially with investments and major purchases.

Rewarding Days

2, 3, 4, 9, 10, 11, 16, 17, 19, 22, 26, 29, 30

Challenging Days

5, 6, 7, 8, 13, 18, 21, 27, 28

Capricorn/May

Planetary Hotspots

If you're a parent, you might have to juggle your budget to cover extra expenses or other activities. Your own recreational interests and evenings out could fall in the same category, so plan ahead and check costs before you go. Fun doesn't have to be expensive if you use your imagination.

Wellness and Keeping Fit

With summer fast approaching, take advantage of Mars, which enters Aries, your domestic sign, May 15. This energetic planet is just the fuel you need to plant a flower, vegetable, or herb garden in the yard or patio pots. It will re-center you and bring hours of enjoyment in the months ahead.

Love and Life Connections

May's New and Full Moons in your solar Fifth and Eleventh Houses light up your social life and invite romantic opportunities for couples and singles alike. With Venus in Cancer, your partnership sign, after May 7, and Mercury in the same sign the last four days of May, you'll delight in memorable hours with your mate and loved ones. You also can expect workplace relationships to be congenial, supportive, and at times pleasantly surprising. Teamwork is the way to go this month.

Finance and Success

Look for praise and a possible financial reward for your efforts and expertise. Mostly, you'll have the self-satisfaction of high productivity, as well as knowing that your clever, creative ideas and solutions are appreciated. Try to plan ahead, though, because meetings, talks or paperwork can eat up precious time this month.

Rewarding Days

1, 4, 5, 6, 7, 11, 15, 17, 19, 23, 24, 29

Challenging Days

12, 13, 16, 18, 20, 25, 30

Capricorn/June

Planetary Hotspots

Neptune and Saturn form their final exact alignment across your solar Second and Eighth Houses at month's end. That signals the culmination of matters that first came to your attention early in the year. But it may take into August to completely wrap things up, so be prepared to be patient. In the meantime, continue to be financially cautious.

Wellness and Keeping Fit

If your goal is a slimmer you, get started at the June 1 Full Moon in Sagittarius, your solar Twelfth House of well-being. You'll have the determination and discipline to see it through to conclusion with the help of this month's second Full Moon, June 30 in Capricorn.

Love and Life Connections

You'll feel closely connected to people this month, with Venus in Cancer, your solar Seventh House of relationships, through June 4 and the Sun in the same sign after June 19. This positive influence can benefit both personal and work relationships as it emphasizes mutual understanding and support. Even so, take nothing for granted. Mercury, also in Cancer, turns retrograde June 15, increasing the odds for misunderstandings and false assumptions. Your social life and your love life get a burst of energy June 24 when Mars enters Taurus, your romance sign. Give TLC to your partner or turn on the charm and attract someone new.

Finance and Success

Set your sights on success and tune in to all the promise of the New Moon in Gemini, your sign of daily work. Extra effort pays off, and you're well-placed to showcase your skills and talents for all the right people. But be aware of what's going on around you and behind the scenes. It's possible someone could try a power play.

Rewarding Days

4, 5, 7, 8, 10, 13, 14, 15, 16, 18, 23, 29

Challenging Days

2, 3, 9, 12, 19, 20, 22, 26

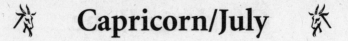

Capricorn/July

Planetary Hotspots

Life perks along this month, with one major exception: Venus turns retrograde in Virgo, your solar Ninth House, July 27. You may decide to put a trip on hold until September or October, but if you do travel, try to plan ahead for delays and cancellations and go with a carry-on rather than risk the chance of lost luggage. It'll also be tough at times to track down information, so start early and then be sure to confirm facts.

Wellness and Keeping Fit

Put yourself in the spotlight at the July 30 Full Moon in your sign and give yourself the gift of a day or two to do exactly as you please. This is also a terrific time to pamper yourself. Schedule a spa day, get a haircut or new hair style, and shop sales for career and casual clothes.

Love and Life Connections

The July 4 New Moon in Cancer focuses your attention on the close relationships in your life. Take the initiative to clear up any recent misunderstandings after Mercury, also in Cancer, turns direct July 9, and keep the lines of communication flowing all month. But if you're thinking about taking a relationship to the next level, it might be wise to postpone the decision until after Venus turns direct in September. Weddings are in the same category.

Finance and Success

Money matters benefit from Venus in Leo, your solar Eighth House of joint resources, July 1–13, but it's smart to continue June's cautious approach. An unexpected family or domestic expense could pop up at month's end. Your work life hums along and you could have an opportunity for a private talk that could lead to a step up later in the year.

Rewarding Days

1, 4, 5, 8, 9, 13, 14, 17, 21, 22, 27, 28

Challenging Days

2, 3, 6, 10, 12, 16, 19, 23, 24, 31

Capricorn/August

Planetary Hotspots

Cross your fingers for a windfall! The August 12 New Moon in Leo illuminates your solar Eighth House of money—but that's only the beginning. The Sun, Mercury, and Venus in Leo contact each other and nearly every other planet in the zodiac around the same time. Focus on attracting wealth, but keep your wits about you. If a contract or another legal document is involved, get expert advice before you proceed. Also be cautious about taking on major debt. The lottery is worth a chance, as is a contest.

Wellness and Keeping Fit

Mercury enters Virgo, your solar Ninth House, August 19, followed by the Sun four days later. That makes knowledge—not just information—your ally. Take it one step further and expand the quest to self-knowledge. Get in touch with your spiritual side and reinforce your faith in the many skills and talents that make you unique.

Love and Life Connections

Mercury clashes with several planets around the time of the August 28 Full Moon in Pisces, your communication sign. Screen calls that week, especially from relatives, including in-laws, and schedule visits for another date, if possible. Return the calls when you're calm and centered. Also try to avoid travel during this time frame, and drive with care.

Finance and Success

Work is just the way you like it—fast-paced—after Mars zips into Gemini, your sign of daily work, August 23. But you could be tempted to take on too much the week leading up to the August 28 Full Moon. Use your common sense and, if necessary, don't hesitate to ask for help. Others will be glad to pitch in.

Rewarding Days

1, 3, 5, 7, 9, 10, 11, 16, 17, 19, 23, 24, 26

Challenging Days

6, 8, 13, 15, 20, 21, 27, 28, 29

Capricorn/September

Planetary Hotspots

A major planetary shift occurs this month. Saturn begins its two-year tour of Virgo, your solar Ninth House of travel and learning, September 2. This is a very positive influence if you want to return to school to complete a degree, earn another, or study for advanced certification. Consider it. Or take a class for the fun of it to expand your knowledge of other cultures, which you also can do through travel. This month, however, isn't the best for a trip. If it's a must, try to schedule it during the last ten days of September.

Wellness and Keeping Fit

Do yourself a favor during what at times will be a pressure-packed month. Take a little time each day for yourself, even if that's a quick lunchtime walk. This will help you manage stress and give you a sense of freedom, which in turn will boost productivity.

Love and Life Connections

Family and work relationships are your main love and life connections this month. Some will test your patience and people skills, especially in early September, but others will satisfy and delight you. Set aside extra time the week of the September 26 Full Moon in Aries, your domestic sign, for family dinners, activities, and household projects.

Finance and Success

You're a rising star, thanks to Mercury's upbeat planetary alignments from Libra, your solar Tenth House of career and status. With Mars in Gemini, your sign of daily work, it's a picture-perfect setup for success, including the chance for a promotion or job offer. The money flow begins to gain momentum September 8, when Venus turns direct, but avoid major financial moves the third week of the month.

Rewarding Days

1, 5, 6, 7, 12, 13, 14, 15, 20, 27

Challenging Days

2, 3, 11, 16, 17, 19, 23, 24, 26

Capricorn/October

Planetary Hotspots

The outer world and a packed schedule keep you on the go all month. But take an occasional time-out to tune in to your inner voice. Within is where you'll find the messages—and insights—offered by a Jupiter-Uranus-Neptune lineup and your guardian angel. Listen to hunches and let this protective force guide you to the right place at the right time.

Wellness and Keeping Fit

October offers you a unique opportunity to experience the power of your mind. Now, more than ever, you can use it to create the reality you desire through positive thinking, willpower, and determination. Dream and let your thoughts drift until your vision is complete. Back it up with a plan.

Love and Life Connections

Social events and laid-back hours with friends accompany Mercury in Scorpio, your friendship sign. But plan ahead and confirm the details because Mercury turns retrograde October 11. You'll also want to devote time to loved ones, with Mars in Cancer, your solar Seventh House of close relationships, all month. Whether at a reunion or by chance, you could reconnect with a former love interest as the October 26 Full Moon in Taurus accents your solar Fifth House of romance.

Finance and Success

You're in your element as the October 11 New Moon in Libra, your career sign, continues to spotlight success. Again this month the planetary energy works in your favor if a step up or a new position is your goal. Finances benefit from Venus in Leo through October 7 and also from Neptune's switch to direct motion October 31 in Aquarius, your solar Second House of personal resources.

Rewarding Days

3, 4, 5, 7, 10, 11, 12, 14, 18, 26, 27, 30

Challenging Days

2, 9, 15, 17, 19, 22, 23, 24, 28, 29

Capricorn/November

Planetary Hotspots

Close relationships are unusually prone to ups and downs between the time Mars in Cancer, your solar Seventh House, turns retrograde November 15 and when it resumes direct motion the end of January. Family members may be more sensitive at times and need your reassurance. Also choose your words with care to help prevent misunderstandings, and think before you react because first impressions may be based more on assumption than fact.

Wellness and Keeping Fit

With the holidays comes the temptation to put a healthy lifestyle on hold. Tune in to the November 24 Full Moon in Gemini, your solar Sixth House of wellness, and keep that tendency in check with a workable compromise. Sample everything, but focus on the most nutritious foods, and try for regular moderate exercise.

Love and Life Connections

Your social life begins to take off as Mercury joins the Sun in Scorpio, your friendship sign, November 11. A week later, the New Moon, also in Scorpio, adds another burst of energy. Get things started early in the month before your calendar (and everyone else's) begins to fill up.

Finance and Success

Get set to make your mark during yet another month designed for success. Leading the way is Mercury in Libra, your solar Tenth House of career and status, November 1–10. Even better is the arrival of popularity-plus Venus in the same sign, November 8. You'll sail through some days, but others will require finesse and all your people skills in order to keep things on an even keel. Step up to the challenge and let others see you at your very best—even when egos clash.

Rewarding Days

3, 4, 8, 9, 10, 15, 22, 25, 26, 28

Challenging Days

5, 6, 11, 18, 19, 21, 23, 24, 27

Capricorn/December

Planetary Hotspots

Rev up for December 18! That's the date lucky Jupiter arrives in your sign, bringing with it all the optimism and enthusiasm this planet represents. Use the days leading up to this event to think about what you want to accomplish during its year-long influence, personally and professionally. Dream big, set high goals, and go for it! Luck is on your side!

Wellness and Keeping Fit

Think slim and trim and get off to a healthy start when Jupiter arrives in your sign. Otherwise, you could see some pounds creep on over the next twelve months. Jupiter is also the planet of expansion. Focus on personal growth and skip the expanded waistline.

Love and Life Connections

With Mars still retrograde in Cancer, those closest to you will continue to appreciate your caring, kind, and supportive approach. You'll also benefit if you listen more than you talk and welcome new insights into human nature. Friendship and socializing also continue this month, thanks to Venus in Scorpio from December 5–29. If you're single, a friend could be your link to love, but this is not the month for a new commitment. Wait until after Mars turns direct the end of January, and have fun in the meantime.

Finance and Success

A private talk or confidential information in the first two weeks of the month could signal an exciting career opportunity on the horizon. Keep the thought, but don't expect further developments until next year. The third week of December could bring a well-deserved year-end bonus when the Sun and Mercury join forces with lucky Jupiter in your sign.

Rewarding Days

4, 5, 7, 11, 12, 14, 16, 19, 25, 28, 29

Challenging Days

1, 2, 3, 6, 9, 13, 17, 22, 23, 30

Capricorn Action Table

These dates reflect the best—but not the only—times for success and ease in these activities, according to your Sun sign.

	JAN	FEB	MAR	APR	MAY	JUN	JUL	AUG	SEPT	OCT	NOV	DEC
Move	23, 24	20-28		11-19		9, 10			27			19
Start a class		2-9	18, 19			7					18, 19	
Join a club	12, 13	8, 9			29, 30						9, 10	5
Ask for a raise	14-19		15, 16	12							16	
Look for work	10, 11			20		13-15		16-17	12, 23-26			3, 4
Get pro advice	30, 31						13-19			3, 4, 30		
Get a loan				24, 25	21, 22				7	5	2	
See a doctor	15, 16		12	20	17	14, 28		22				10
Start a diet						13, 14	11, 12			1	24, 25	
End relationship	3						13		5	2-4	27	
Buy clothes			21, 22		15, 16							21
Get a makeover	2, 3			10	7					17		11
New romance			18-22	27-30	16						22, 23	19-21
Vacation	7-9						17-19	24-31	1-3	7, 8	3-5	28, 29

AQUARIUS

The Water Bearer
January 20 to February 20

♒

Element:	Air
Quality:	Fixed
Polarity:	Yang/Masculine
Planetary Ruler:	Uranus
Meditation:	I am a wellspring of creativity
Gemstone:	Amethyst
Power Stones:	Aquamarine, black pearl, chrysocolla
Key Phrase:	I know
Glyph:	Currents of energy
Anatomy:	Circulatory system, ankles
Color:	Iridescent blues, violet
Animal:	Exotic birds
Myths/Legends:	Ninhursag, John the Baptist, Deucalion
House:	Eleventh
Opposite Sign:	Leo
Flower:	Orchid
Key Word:	Unconventional

Your Ego's Strengths and Shortcomings

Independent Aquarius is the sign of contrasts. One day you're as traditional as a grandmother; the next you're ready to sign up for a trip to the Moon! This unpredictability is part of your charm and why you keep most everyone guessing and coming back for more.

A humanitarian at heart, you're the champion of equality and individual rights and accept people as they are. Your many friends, both male and female, come from all walks of life and those who reach your inner circle are unusual in some way—different and fascinating, just like you and your ruling planet, Uranus, which reflects your spontaneous, progressive, inventive nature.

Both stubborn and determined, depending upon the situation, you're also impatient and uncomfortable with change unless it's your idea. At times you initiate change for the sake of change just to keep life lively and interesting. But sometimes the status quo is a better choice, so analyze your motives before taking action. It's also to your benefit to view change initiated by others as an opportunity to work current trends to your advantage.

Aquarius is an air sign, so you're more comfortable with a mental connection than you are with an outwardly emotional one. And in an instant you can switch from fun-loving to detached to distant and even be as cold as your wintry sign. That makes it tough for others to understand you and can play havoc with close relationships. Share your thoughts and feelings, even on an intellectual level, if only so others won't feel they're lost in a void.

You also can be short-tempered when others don't listen to you. That's because you enjoy sharing your knowledge, especially when others ask for it. Try to be a bit more patient and, if necessary, try a different approach to explain what might be a difficult concept.

You're intuitive and often sense approaching trends and events, sometimes years in advance. Flashes of insight guide your life and signal important turning points that can take you in new directions. The more you listen, the stronger they can become.

Shining Your Love Light

Dating delights you and you enjoy lighthearted fun with each new romantic interest as you play the field. You can literally talk and think your way into and out of love, and open communication is a must in any long-lasting relationship.

You seek a mate who is both friend and lover, warm, generous, and outgoing. Although you're more comfortable intellectualizing your feelings, your partner may want romance at its emotional best. Find a balance that works for both of you.

You're noted for your independence, so it's vital that you and your partner reach an understanding about your need to develop and pursue your own interests and spend time with your many friends. Encourage the same in your mate and support each other in your path through life as you both grow as individuals.

Aries is as fun and spontaneous as you are, and you can motivate each other to excel. You and Taurus have determination in common, although your free-spirited nature could be a challenge for this possessive sign. Flirtatious Gemini's wit entertains you and you'll value the mental rapport.

Although warm and family-oriented, Cancer might "smother" you with caring. A match with Leo, your opposite sign, can be ideal if your mate doesn't require constant attention. Virgo shares your humanitarian outlook, but may be too analytical and dwell on details.

Libra, also an air sign, is sociable and charming and understands your emotions. The intensity and passion of Scorpio mesmerizes you, but jealousy can be an issue. You're in sync with independent Sagittarius, a sign that's also future-oriented.

Capricorn might be too traditional for you, but can help keep your feet on the ground. Love with another Aquarius can be fabulous, though you probably won't see much of each other. Pisces touches your heart, but might be too sensitive for your airy personality.

Making Your Place in the World

A calm, serene working environment appeals to you, and you consider co-workers part of your extended family. This can make it tough to move on even when doing so is in your best career interests. But your fondness for self-initiated change will eventually win out when you're ready for a new challenge.

Job and career satisfaction also are linked to the freedom to explore new ideas and methods and an atmosphere that promotes free-thinking and innovation. Teamwork is very important to you and you benefit most from unstructured, informal brainstorming.

Although not outwardly ambitious, you nevertheless have a deep-seated desire to get ahead in the world. Each promotion you gain is a surprise to some people because you seldom voice your ambitions even though you always have a long-term plan in place.

The world of science might appeal to you as you could excel as a meteorologist, neurologist, surgeon, inventor, radar technician or in the radiology field. A career as an electrician or electrical engineer, or in information technology or computer science might draw you, as could television, advertising, and public relations.

Your intuitive skills would be an asset if you're interested in becoming a detective, investigator, agent, or psychologist. Some Aquarians find success in the travel or space industry, and the nonprofit sector is another area where you could do well as a social worker or fundraising executive.

Putting Your Best Foot Forward

Aquarius is a future-oriented sign, and you're far-sighted and ahead of the times, aware of approaching trends long before others see the first glimmer of possibility. What you sense is part intuition, part inspiration, and part insight. Often it takes only a casual comment for your quick mind to make the leap into the future.

You also can be very goal oriented, a side of you others rarely see or fail to recognize. Here, too, you think long term and frequently measure your progress. When you're on track you can be patient, sometimes for years, knowing that every day brings you a step closer to your target. This can, of course, keep you well ahead of the competition. But to what end?

Ask yourself when you last enjoyed the moment and the little victories on your path to success. On a daily basis, are you focused on what you'll do this afternoon, tonight, tomorrow, this weekend, next month, next year, rather than this morning? When you successfully jump a hurdle, do you think only of the next one?

Trite but true: Stop and smell the roses. Enjoy the small things, the simple pleasures you can experience every day. The future will still be there, beckoning you and waiting for you to arrive.

Aquarius can be high-strung, which makes it even important to slow the pace and take time for yourself. De-stress. Put the day's cares and concerns—and the future—on hold for at least thirty minutes a day. Walk, work out, meditate, take a yoga class, get lost in a hobby, or do something else that will take your mind off everything but that moment in time. You'll feel better physically, mentally, and emotionally, and renew your determination to achieve all that you hope to in the future.

Tools for Change

This year brings you a wonderful opportunity to learn from others while they learn from you. Knowledge is your main tool for change, but relationships run a close second. The two are intertwined in many ways, with one interacting with the other as you strive for greater self-understanding.

Think about the people closest to you and those you regularly encounter in your professional life. What traits do you like about them? Dislike? Make a list of each. Then do the same for yourself.

What are your strengths and challenges? What would you like to change about yourself? Your life? Be honest. Unless you choose to share it, you're the only one who will ever see it.

Then compare your personal list to the others. Are there similarities? Chances are, you'll find several, and possibly many. Take note of the similarities, and then think about those people. How did they come into your life? What experiences have you shared? How did each of you react?

These are the people from whom you have the most to learn, and who likewise can benefit from your knowledge and experience. The factors you have in common are part of the reason you met and forged a relationship, whether that's a partnership or a friendship.

As you pursue your quest to maximize your strengths and minimize your challenges, you'll probably see the same happening in others. Even if you say nothing, they will learn through your example. But you never know. They might ask for your insights into their life quest. Freely share your knowledge even if it isn't at first well received. Plant seeds and watch them grow—along with yours!

Affirmation for the Year

I strive to be the best I can be.

The Year Ahead for Aquarius

You're set for a fabulous year of friendship, thanks to expansive Jupiter in Sagittarius, your solar Eleventh House. It's an ideal opportunity to connect with people, widen your circle, and fill your address book with exciting new personalities. The more people you meet and get to know, the greater the benefits; some will be your link to luck. A club or professional organization is an easy way to get acquainted with new people, or you might decide to get more involved in a group you've been associated with for some time. Either way, you're likely to be offered a leadership role, which can increase your visibility and networking power. This year could bring rewards for past efforts, such as an award, promotion, or raise. Jupiter also encourages you to review and update short- and long-term personal and professional goals. Be selective and narrow the list to your top priorities rather than give in when Jupiter urges you to do it all. After a whirlwind year, you'll be ready to take a breather when Jupiter moves on to Capricorn, your solar Twelfth House of self-renewal, December 18. Your social life will become temporarily less important and you'll enjoy having time to yourself for your own interests. It's also a time to look inward as you prepare to launch a new twelve-year period when Jupiter enters your sign in 2008.

Saturn is in the final months of its two-year trip through Leo, your solar Seventh House of close relationships. This is, above all, a growth opportunity—if you choose to make it one. Take note of your interactions with others and how they and you react in various situations. With this knowledge you can refine your approach to improve communication and thus strengthen ties. It's also an important learning experience as you begin a seven-year climb to what can be a career pinnacle. Supporters gained now may be just the people who help advance your aims in the future. Also use this period to address personal or business differences you consider to be unfinished business. Resolving these matters will free you to move on, whether or not you remain in touch. On another level, check credentials if you need to consult a professional, such as an accountant, realtor, or attorney. The same applies to a potential business partner. Saturn advances into Virgo, your solar Eighth House of shared resources, September 2. This can be a period of financial gain as well as one during which you should pay off debt, rather than incur more. You'll also want to think long term regarding investments and retirement income, even if your leisure years are far in the future.

With Uranus, your ruling planet, influencing your money, you have the power and the freedom to choose how you spend it, save it, earn it, and invest it. Wise choices made now will be to your benefit for many years to come. Moneymaking opportunities can pop up at the least expected moment as Uranus reaches the midpoint of Pisces, your solar Second House of personal resources. But take all factors into consideration before you jump because this quirky planet can just as easily trigger a loss. Unexpected expenses also are likely, so a conservative financial approach will help ensure you have funds available when needed. Save all you can, and learn to walk away when the urge to splurge takes hold. Budgeting is equally important—and you'll do yourself a favor if you can learn (or continue) to live within one.

Spirituality, intuition, and creativity are your guiding lights with Neptune in Aquarius. Now in the tenth of its fourteen-year transit of your solar First House, Neptune continues to broaden your perspective of the world around you. You may take a greater interest in those who are less fortunate as Neptune enhances your humanitarian spirit. But you're also in a highly sensitive and sympathetic period, so listen to your head as well as your heart and don't let others sway your thinking. Direct some of Neptune's energy into developing your creativity through a hobby, the arts, or a group that helps awaken your hidden talents. Intuition can give you the edge in many situations; nurturing your sixth sense—and listening to it— will enhance your spiritual connection with the universe and reinforce self-confidence. Have faith. Trust and believe in yourself.

With Pluto concluding its transit of Sagittarius, 2007 is the year to complete what you began in 1995, when Jupiter also was in Sagittarius. If you became involved with a special-interest group, club, or organization any time since 1995, your efforts culminate now, and you may take on a more visible and influential role. The same is true of your career. There is, however, a potential downside to this otherwise significant planetary influence: you could be subject to—or feel compelled to initiate—power plays. Guard against this because such manipulative behavior can have a detrimental effect on what you hope to achieve. Your intensely focused perspective could make it difficult to see what's obvious to those around you, so it might be wise to periodically ask a trusted friend for feedback.

This year's eclipses in Pisces and Virgo, your solar Second and Eighth Houses, reinforce the financial emphasis of Saturn and Uranus and encourage you to be financially conservative. Protect and increase your resources.

If you were born between January 20 and 30, Saturn in Virgo from September 2 on offers you a financial learning experience. Although that might sound like something you'd rather avoid, it can be positive depending upon the choices you make. Saturn in your solar Eighth House requires you take responsibility for money matters that involve other people, such as family funds, insurance, and investment and retirement accounts. Debt may be the most important of all. If you have credit card balances and other consumer debt, plan now to pay them off within a few years. Whether debt is or isn't an issue in your life, this is not the time to significantly expand your credit. The exception is a home mortgage, but only if you can get an affordable interest rate. You also should think carefully before entering into a financial partnership. On the upside, Saturn could reward you or your partner with increased income, or you could benefit from a family gift or legacy. Key dates: October 13, November 30, and December 6 and 19.

If you were born between January 30 and February 8, Uranus in Pisces triggers a restless feeling as it contacts your Sun. You're ready for a change, but identifying exactly what, where, and when is a challenge. The solution involves personal and financial resources. You may decide to satisfy this freedom urge by developing another income source, such as free-lance work or a second job. This could be a profitable and fulfilling move, but Uranus can be erratic, so earnings will likely fluctuate. You also could choose to focus on a skill or talent that, when taken to the next level of expertise, could result in career advancement. Another option is to turn the spotlight on yourself and take the plunge to get in shape as part of an ego-building makeover. Key dates: January 22, February 7,

March 4 and 31, April 27, June 8, September 4, October 8, and November 25.

If you were born between February 6 and 11, this year could be one of the most inspirational of your life as Neptune joins your Sun in Aquarius. The experience will be primarily internal as you get in touch with your spiritual self and your inner voice. Although at times you may feel as though you're aimlessly floating on a endless sea, what will emerge at the end of this cycle is a clearer understanding of yourself and your place in the world. On a practical level, however, you'll want to take a few precautions. Because you are more open to subtle vibrations, it's important to protect yourself from the negative energy generated by some people and places. You'll also be more susceptible to hard-luck stories, thus encouraging some people to play on your sympathies. Keep that in mind and protect your resources as your mystical journey unfolds. Key dates: January 20 and 26, February 9, April 5, May 6 and 13, June 26, August 12, September 23, November 23, and December 20.

If you were born between February 6 and 20, Saturn in Leo focuses on relationships—partner, family members, and close friends. You may cut ties or distance yourself from some, and grow closer to others. You might, for example, become even more committed to a romantic relationship, but purposely limit contact with friends you feel in some way limit personal growth. If you're involved in a serious dating relationship, you'll feel pushed to make a decision about the future before Saturn enters Virgo on September 2. Ultimately, you should do what's right for you, but if you fear commitment, examine the reasons why. A soul mate may enter life at this time. Instant rapport could herald his or her arrival, but the strongest link may be with someone you initially dislike. So keep your options—and your mind—open to the possibilities. You have much to learn from this person, and vice versa. Key dates: January 20, February 10, March 22, April 19, May 9, July 1 and 30, August 13 and 20.

If you were born between February 14 and 20, you're likely to connect with powerful people during this year of networking opportunities. With Pluto in Sagittarius, your solar Eleventh House of groups and friendship, you may encounter them through a club or organization, or through mutual friends or co-workers. You also can direct this dynamic energy into your career life, where you could move into a more influential position. Use the energy wisely and benevolently and initiate change with care. Although you have a vision that includes reinventing anything from daily procedures to a group's main mission, people will respond more favorably if they're part of the evolutionary process. Key dates: February 19, March 18, April 8, May 12, September 19, November 5, and December 10.

Aquarius/January

Planetary Hotspots

Relationships cover a broad spectrum, from confusion to inspiration to regret and optimism. Ultimately, though, you'll learn a great deal about yourself through the power of projection—seeing yourself reflected in the eyes and actions of others. Benefit from the learning experience as the Sun, Venus, and Mercury in your sign connect with several other planets, including Saturn in Leo, your solar Seventh House of relationships.

Wellness and Keeping Fit

This month's New Moon in Capricorn accents your solar Twelfth House of health. Let that motivate you to schedule a checkup if you haven't had one recently. Also give your lifestyle the once-over and take action to change whatever you think needs changing.

Love and Life Connections

You're in your element this month with Mars in Sagittarius energizing your solar Eleventh House of friendship through January 15. Include a co-worker in the group the second weekend, which is a positive time frame for networking. You're also well-prepared to attract a new romantic interest with Venus in your sign from January 3–26. Accept (or ask) a friend's offer to arrange a date and turn on the charm!

Finance and Success

The January 3 Full Moon in Cancer signals a fast-paced work week to launch the new year. Make completion a priority and give yourself a mid-month deadline to wrap things up. Money begins to move your direction January 27 as Venus enters Pisces, your sign of personal resources. Use the last few days of the month to share your financial wishes with the universe and think positive thoughts about what could be yours in February.

Rewarding Days

1, 5, 6, 10, 12, 14 15, 16, 19, 24, 28, 31

Challenging Days

3, 7, 13, 20, 23, 25, 26, 29

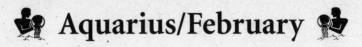

Aquarius/February

Planetary Hotspots

The New Moon in Aquarius on February 17 inspires new directions by encouraging you to focus on your needs and interests until month's end. Be flexible about personal decisions, which are likely to evolve into next month because retrograde Mercury returns to your sign on February 26. That's actually the universe working in your favor because events prior to that date will spark a change in your thinking.

Wellness and Keeping Fit

Mars charges into your sign February 25, bringing with it all the high energy and initiative this planet embodies. That can make it tough to "turn off" at bedtime. Do yourself a favor. Make it a policy the next six weeks to unwind and quiet your mind every evening, or at least for thirty to sixty minutes before you slip under the covers.

Love and Life Connections

Turn the spotlight on close relationships—partner, family and best friends—the week of the February 2 Full Moon in Leo. Open up communication, listen, and connect with their hopes, wishes, concerns, and desires. The lunar energy could also link you to a networking contact who may come in handy the end of February.

Finance and Success

Mercury spends part of its January retrograde period in Pisces, your solar Second House of personal resources. That makes it wise to pay bills early, check statements for errors as soon as they arrive, and confirm debit and credit amounts before you sign off. Also take precautions to protect financial information from prying eyes at work and when shopping.

Rewarding Days

1, 6, 7, 9, 12, 14, 15, 17, 20, 27

Challenging Days

4, 5, 10, 16, 19, 23, 25

Aquarius/March

Planetary Hotspots

Insights and inspiration are yours, thanks to Mars and Mercury in your sign. Have faith because what at first seems impossible can become reality with persistence and determination. Use your imagination, envision the future, and, most of all, talk with a close friend whose opinion you respect and trust. Present the facts and your feelings, and then take the good advice to heart.

Wellness and Keeping Fit

As much as Mars in your sign motivates you all month, it also can prompt you to take risks you'd otherwise avoid. Be careful, especially the second half of February, when an accident could happen in a flash. Let someone else climb the ladder and lift heavy boxes.

Love and Life Connections

Words are your specialty while Mercury is in your sign through March 17—after it turns direct March 7. Turn on the charm if someone catches your eye, and take the lead in meetings and presentations, especially mid-month. You'll also want to spend extra time with family and your partner after March 16 when Venus is in Taurus, your domestic sign. If you want to host a get-together, plan it for month's end, when Venus aligns with Uranus, your ruler.

Finance and Success

Finances benefit from Mercury as it advances into Pisces, your solar Second House of personal resources, March 18, the day before the New Moon in the same sign. It's a promising influence to attract money, but you could also be pressured to contribute to an organization or loan money to a friend. Do what's right for you and your bank account. Earlier in March, the Full Moon in Virgo spotlights joint resources. Study investment and retirement accounts, and implement a debt reduction plan, if necessary.

Rewarding Days

5, 6, 7, 10, 12, 15, 19, 20, 24, 27

Challenging Days

2, 3, 8, 9, 16, 18, 22, 23, 29

Aquarius/April

Planetary Hotspots

Family relationships present a few challenges in early April. Whatever the issue—it might be money—you have the power to be the mediator who can choose to promote calm discussion and solutions and guide others in that direction. At the same time, don't compromise your values or accept responsibility for what isn't yours.

Wellness and Keeping Fit

The pace picks up and is hectic at times this month with the April 12 New Moon in Aries, your solar Third House of daily life. That's the only reason you need to take a break the following weekend, when Mercury in the same sign favorably contacts several planets. Dash out of town for the weekend or take a day trip. Fresh scenery will relax and re-center you, and you'll appreciate fun- and laughter-filled hours.

Love and Life Connections

Once past the events early this month you'll experience some of the most rewarding times of the year with family. With the Sun, Mercury, and Venus in Taurus, you'll feel a special closeness to those you love and want to spend more time with them and at home. You'll be ready to socialize with friends after Venus enters Gemini, your sign of leisure, April 11. If you're searching for romance, you could connect with a soul mate at month's end, when couples rediscover all the reasons that brought them together.

Finance and Success

Mars dashes into Pisces, your solar Second House of personal resources, April 6. That boosts your moneymaking potential the next six weeks, but it does the same for spending. Plan now to end the period with more than you started with and resist the urge to splurge that pops up at month's end.

Rewarding Days

3, 8, 11, 12, 16, 17, 19, 22, 23, 26, 29, 30

Challenging Days

1, 5, 6, 13, 18, 21, 27, 28

Aquarius/May

Planetary Hotspots

May zips along with busy days filled with routine activities—work, play, and home. But be prepared for family stress and strain the first part of the month as the Sun and Mercury clash with Saturn, Uranus, and Neptune. Try to remember that current issues are more a matter of perspective, and not necessarily reality, so strive to understand their viewpoints. Accomplish that and welcome a fresh start at the May 16 New Moon in Taurus, your sign of home and family.

Wellness and Keeping Fit

Nurture your creativity all month. Try writing, an artistic endeavor, a new hobby, or home decorating. Or, put your inventive mind to work building a better mousetrap! What you do isn't as important as investing your imagination in a leisure-time pursuit guaranteed to help you relax.

Love and Life Connections

May is one of your best months of the year for romance and socializing. With at least one, and at times two, planets in Gemini, your solar Fifth House of pleasure and recreation, this month, you'll have plenty of opportunities for both, as well as quality time with your children, if you're a parent. Target the fourth week of May to surprise your partner with memorable TLC-filled moments. If you're single, get things started with someone who interests you, or ask a friend to arrange a date.

Finance and Success

Your work life is hectic the first week of May as the Full Moon in Scorpio, your career sign, steps up the pace. Keep cool under pressure even if you disagree with a decision-maker. You may not have all the facts, but it's equally likely someone else is misinformed. Cover your bases, just in case.

Rewarding Days

1, 8, 13, 14, 15, 17, 21, 22, 26, 29, 31

Challenging Days

3, 5, 9, 10, 12, 16, 18, 25, 30

Aquarius/June

Planetary Hotspots

June is mostly uneventful with life as usual up until the final days of the month. That's when Neptune and Saturn form their final exact alignment across your solar First and Seventh Houses. Relationship challenges that first emerged early in the year will resurface for resolution. Although this is not the best time for a new commitment, it is the time to put the past behind you to embrace the future.

Wellness and Keeping Fit

Summer calls for outdoor activities, so let the June 15 New Moon in Gemini, your recreation sign, motivate you to stretch your muscles. Swim, walk, skate, ride a bike, or take a class to learn a new sport. Your body will love you for it.

Love and Life Connections

The Full Moon in Sagittarius on June 1 lights up your solar Eleventh House of friendship, and the Sun in Gemini through June 19 accents romance and socializing. Fill your calendar with dates, events, and more—take the initiative to meet new people. Among them could be a soul mate who becomes a lifelong friend or romantic partner. You also could click with a neighbor or someone you meet at a community event as Mars travels in Aries through June 23.

Finance and Success

You'll have much to cheer about in your work life—recognition, productivity, and congenial co-workers. But you'll want to take a few precautions after Mercury in Cancer, your sign of daily work, turns retrograde June 15. Take time to confirm facts and information and double-check details. If in doubt, ask. Back up files if you use a computer.

Rewarding Days

1, 5, 6, 10, 13, 14, 16, 17, 18, 19, 23, 27, 29

Challenging Days

2, 4, 8, 11, 12, 20, 21, 24, 26

Aquarius/July

Planetary Hotspots

Be kind to your budget and try to save more than you spend. Venus turns retrograde in Virgo, your solar Eighth House of joint resources, July 27. About the same time you could have an unexpected domestic expense. If it involves a household repair, call an expert rather than attempt it yourself. Check credentials; if in doubt, get a second estimate even if it means a delay.

Wellness and Keeping Fit

Make a note to schedule routine health checkups at month's end, when the July 30 Full Moon in Capricorn accents your solar Twelfth House of wellness. The lunar energy also favors time for yourself to rest, relax, and renew your spirit. Take a day or weekend off and focus on your interests.

Love and Life Connections

Close relationships benefit from Venus in Leo, your solar Seventh House, through July 13, and the Sun's arrival in the same sign, July 22. But frustration can spark family tempers at month's end when Mars clashes with several planets. Strive for compromise and try to be flexible. The same applies to workplace relationships, where someone's true nature may suddenly emerge. Be cautious.

Finance and Success

The New Moon in Cancer on July 4 brings fresh energy and a fresh perspective to your work life. Make plans and get organized the first few days after the New Moon so you're set to go when Mercury, also in Cancer, turns direct July 9. Be prepared, though, for changes, updates, and reversed decisions as momentum resumes. Soon you'll be up to speed and possibly even headed for a bigger paycheck.

Rewarding Days

7, 8, 11, 13, 14, 15, 17, 21, 22, 25, 30

Challenging Days

2, 3, 6, 9, 10, 12, 16, 19, 23, 24, 31

Aquarius/August

Planetary Hotspots

A close relationship may reach a turning point this month. The Sun, Mercury, and Venus in Leo contact nearly every other planet around the August 12 New Moon, also in Leo. That makes communication as important as listening, compromise, and blending another perspective with your own. By far, though, the major factor is retrograde Venus, which can prompt premature decisions or a reluctance to commit. Either way, the wise choice—which is ultimately up to you—may be to postpone action until early October.

Wellness and Keeping Fit

Take advantage of Mars' last days in Taurus, your domestic sign, August 1–6. Shift into high gear and free your space of clutter and more, including all those things you haven't used, or even seen, in years. It will clear your mind as well as your surroundings and reinforce your independent spirit.

Love and Life Connections

Your social life gets a burst of energy as Mars enters Gemini on August 7. Line up lunch dates, outings, and other events with friends, including pals you haven't seen recently. Family ties are also in focus. You'll draw closer to some, but want to distance yourself from others. Take the initiative if you're motivated to resolve old issues with friends or relatives.

Finance and Success

The August 28 Full Moon in Pisces challenges you to take charge of your money. Analyze spending and savings habits, debt, and your budget, and find easy ways to cut costs. Friends and money are a poor mix this month. Think carefully about advice and don't hesitate to say no to a friend who asks for a loan or donation to a favorite cause. Separate checks are the way to go when socializing.

Rewarding Days

2, 3, 7, 11, 12, 16, 17, 19, 26, 30, 31

Challenging Days

4, 6, 8, 13, 15, 20, 27, 28, 29

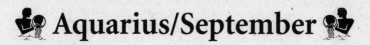

Aquarius/September

Planetary Hotspots
Saturn enters Virgo, your solar Eighth House of joint resources, September 2. You may need to tighten your budget during this two-year transit, but not necessarily. If you do, it can be a positive move if your goal is to increase savings and decrease debt. Reduced family income is also possible, so you should adopt a more financially conservative mindset to cover any extra expenses.

Wellness and Keeping Fit
Fresh scenery is a great stress reliever and one that can also change your perspective. A vacation or weekend trip can provide both for you. But if travel is impossible this month, you can find an alternative to take you away from the daily pressure. Try journaling, take a fun class, or browse the self-help section for books designed to help you maximize your potential.

Love and Life Connections
Mars in Gemini through September 28 energizes your social life, and relationships are generally more settled after Venus turns direct in Leo on September 8. However, events around September 21 can cause you to question a friendship or another relationship as Venus aligns with Neptune, and Mars with Pluto. What you discover may disappoint and disillusion you, but you'll also learn from it.

Finance and Success
Financial issues require attention in the days leading up to the September 11 New Moon in Virgo. Although related to Saturn, the events triggered by the Sun and Mercury in contact with several planets nevertheless reinforce the path to follow during Saturn's Virgo transit. Protect your resources and financial data, check your credit report, and do what's right for you even if it affects a friendship or close relationship.

Rewarding Days
1, 4, 7, 8, 9, 12, 13, 14, 22, 23, 27

Challenging Days
2, 3, 11, 16, 17, 19, 24, 26, 28, 30

Aquarius/October

Planetary Hotspots

Jupiter forms an exact alignment with Uranus and Neptune this month. This somewhat unusual configuration that links your solar First, Second, and Eleventh Houses signals opportunity and vision, but also the possibility of wishful thinking and even deception. Listen to all offers and proposals, but be skeptical of anything that involves a financial investment, comes with a guarantee, or sounds too good to be true. Get a second opinion if you need it.

Wellness and Keeping Fit

The October 26 Full Moon in Taurus makes home the comfiest place to be. Give yourself the gift of a relaxing weekend—or at least a day or afternoon—at home and do whatever pleases you. If you get a burst of energy, unleash your creativity and carve a masterpiece—a Halloween pumpkin!

Love and Life Connections

You're in sync with most everyone through October 7 as Venus wraps up its time in Leo, your relationship sign. Venus is an equally positive influence for business and personal contacts—people will be receptive and quick to grant favors. You'll also have many opportunities to see friends, with several planets in touch with Jupiter and Pluto in Sagittarius, your solar Eleventh House of friendship. Singles searching for love could be in luck the first week of the month.

Finance and Success

October is the first of several consecutive months with the potential for significant career gains. You'll make progress now with the help of Mercury in Scorpio, your solar Tenth House of career, through October 23, the date the Sun enters the same sign. But it may not be as much as you hope for because Mercury turns retrograde October 11. Stick with it. What you do now will pay off next month.

Rewarding Days

1, 4, 6, 7, 10, 11, 12, 14, 16, 20, 21, 27, 30

Challenging Days

2, 5, 9, 15, 17, 19, 22, 23, 24, 28, 29

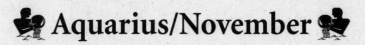

Aquarius/November

Planetary Hotspots

Workplace communication fluctuates and at times grinds to a halt between November 15 and the end of January as Mars travels retrograde in Cancer, your solar Sixth House of daily work. This can delay progress on some projects, but what may frustrate you the most is indecision. Besides interrupting your work flow, you'll have difficulty motivating others to take action. Be flexible and do the best you can.

Wellness and Keeping Fit

The Sixth House is also a health sector, so you'll want to take time each day to release the stress build-up associated with retrograde Mars. But don't overdo it if you exercise, because a strain or sprain is more likely now. You also may be more susceptible to a cold or the flu, so be aware and take precautions.

Love and Life Connections

Your social life picks up speed the week of the November 24 Full Moon in Gemini, your solar Fifth House of pleasure. That's a perfect match for the Sun's November 22 arrival in Sagittarius, your friendship sign. Since you'll want to see all your pals and get better acquainted with some co-workers, consider hosting an open house the fourth weekend of the month.

Finance and Success

A step up is possible this month, with the Sun, New Moon, and Mercury (after November 10) in Scorpio, your career sign. But don't be concerned if it doesn't quite come together before Mars turns retrograde. Try to be patient because you're definitely viewed as an up-and-comer. You also could find more in your paycheck this month, thanks to Venus in Virgo, one of your money signs, through November 17.

Rewarding Days

2, 7, 8, 9, 12, 15, 16, 17, 20, 22, 25, 28

Challenging Days

5, 6, 11, 14, 18, 19, 21, 23, 24, 30

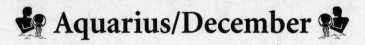

Aquarius/December

Planetary Hotspots

You love your many friends, but gift-giving can make this an expensive time of year. It's fine to scale back, whether out of necessity or because you have other financial priorities. The same applies to pricey social outings in which you may see little value as the Sun and Mercury in Sagittarius, your friendship sign, clash with Uranus and Saturn in your solar Second and Eighth Houses of money. Suggest an alternative or go elsewhere with pals who feel the same.

Wellness and Keeping Fit

A major planetary shift occurs this month. Jupiter enters Capricorn, your solar Twelfth House of self-renewal, December 18. Think of this year-long beneficial and lucky influence as a personal guardian angel who watches over you and helps guide you to the right place at the right time. You'll also feel a stronger spiritual connection with the universe, which will strengthen your inner resolve and intuition as you prepare for Jupiter's arrival in your sign in January 2009.

Love and Life Connections

You're in the social swing this month thanks to the December 9 New Moon in Sagittarius. Even better, the energy continues to flow into the new year because Venus enters Sagittarius on December 30. However, workplace relationships could be testy at month's end when the pressure is on to complete projects.

Finance and Success

You're one of the favored few, with Venus in Scorpio, your career sign, December 5–29. This fortunate influence also could bring you a year-end bonus the third week of the month, as well as some meaningful gifts the following week.

Rewarding Days

4, 5, 11, 12, 13, 16, 18, 19, 21, 25, 26

Challenging Days

2, 3, 6, 9, 17, 20, 22, 23, 30

Aquarius Action Table

These dates reflect the best—but not the only—times for success and ease in these activities, according to your Sun sign.

	JAN	FEB	MAR	APR	MAY	JUN	JUL	AUG	SEPT	OCT	NOV	DEC
Move			21, 22	27-30	6, 7, 15, 16					26, 27		
Start a class	23, 24			11-18								8, 9
Join a club	15, 16		10, 11						17-19		12	8-10
Ask for a raise	30, 31	9, 19			11			2			12	8-10
Look for work		9			29, 30	1	11-20				9-21	6, 7
Get pro advice			29	24, 25	21, 22					5	2, 29	
Get a loan	8		31	26	24		17, 18		11		5	28
See a doctor	17, 18, 31		28	10	13		13				14	11, 12
Start a diet	3, 4					30			5, 6	3, 4	26, 27	
End relationship		2					30	11	8		1, 29, 30	27
Buy clothes	23, 29		24	20, 21	17, 21, 22		12				25	
Get a makeover	19, 23, 24	16, 17	16	11, 12						21	16	14
New romance	[illegible], 27			19, 20	17	14, 15	12				25	
Vacation		7		29, 30	26, 27			16, 17	12, 23-26		6, 7	3, 4

PISCES

The Fish
February 19 to March 20

♓

Element:	Water
Quality:	Mutable
Polarity:	Yin/Feminine
Planetary Ruler:	Neptune
Meditation:	I successfully navigate the seas of my emotions
Gemstone:	Aquamarine
Power Stones:	Amethyst, bloodstone, tourmaline
Key Phrase:	I believe
Glyph:	Two fish, swimming in opposite directions
Anatomy:	Feet, lymphatic system
Color:	Sea green, violet
Animal:	Fish, sea mammals
Myths/Legends:	Aphrodite, Buddha, Jesus of Nazareth
House:	Twelfth
Opposite Sign:	Virgo
Flower:	Water lily
Key Word:	Transcendence

Your Ego's Strengths and Shortcomings

Pisces has the corner on creativity, which can manifest in many different ways, such as ideas, art, writing, crafts, or inspiring others to maximize their talents. Your special creative niche is undoubtedly one you capitalize on nearly every day, even if it's less tangible and you're unaware of it.

With Neptune as your ruling planet, you're sensitive, gentle, sympathetic, and compassionate, and your heart goes out to those in need. These traits, of course, increase your vulnerability and at times you sacrifice your needs for others. Sometimes a better choice is to let others learn the hard way and fight their own battles.

You're also intuitive—even psychic—and impressionable, and easily pick up subtle vibrations, as well as people's moods. Although this can work to your advantage, it's important to mentally surround yourself with a positive energy field to block the negative.

Like a chameleon, you can adapt to almost any situation or environment. This terrific talent allows you to "disappear" when you don't want to attract attention, and to respond perfectly in tune with the feelings and thoughts of others when it's to your advantage. Your empathetic nature comes in handy when socializing and networking because you instinctively say and do what others expect, want, and appreciate. You also have a mystical—almost magical—aura about you that attracts people.

Your strong faith and spirituality see you through tough times and situations. But even though you appear outwardly serene, you have a tendency to brood as your moods fluctuate. Time alone to meditate and dream can help you re-center, body and soul, so try to make it a habit at least every other day.

Idealistic and trusting, you strive to see the best in everyone and everything. That's an admirable quality that could help others. But it's also essential to keep things in perspective. No one is perfect, nor is any situation, so ask questions, take less for granted, and do what's right for you even if others try to sway you to follow another path.

Shining Your Love Light

You're an ultraromantic who knows intuitively how to treat a mate or a date with TLC. Romance is also vital to your well-being, so you can feel unfulfilled and lonely without someone to call your own.

It's as important to you to feel loved and appreciated as it is for you to express these emotions to your partner.

However, you should learn to protect your heart until you're sure of your romantic interest's feelings. Unlike some signs, love comes easily and quickly to you. But you also should not hesitate to move on when the attractions wanes, rather than try to hang on to a dating relationship without an obvious future—just to be with someone until a new love match walks into your life.

Your sensitive soul appreciates and understands fellow water signs Cancer and Scorpio. Cancer is caring and nurturing and can make you feel secure. Scorpio's intense magnetism can both unsettle you and stir your passions. Life with another Pisces can be pure romance, but you might need a business manager to keep you on track!

Aries can encourage your initiative, although you might view this sign's action-packed lifestyle as too fast and furious. A practical, sensual, and cautious Taurus could benefit from your faith in the universe. Gemini might be too changeable and outwardly unemotional for you. But you'll enjoy the mental stimulation.

Leo can fill your world with play and romance, although the dramatics can drain your energy. With Virgo, your opposite sign, you gain a mate who is practical and organized and can help you fulfill your dreams. Although charming, kind, and attentive, Libra tends to intellectualize emotions whereas you feel them.

Sagittarius, although spiritually like-minded, is a free spirit whose bluntness can hurt your sensitive heart. Capricorn provides structure and security, but this sign is uncomfortable with free emotional expression. Aquarian independence and aloofness is a mystery to you, but you can be fabulous friends.

Making Your Place in the World

For you, a pleasant—even upscale—working environment is essential for job happiness, satisfaction, and productivity. Encouragement and recognition are equally important. When too many of these necessary components are lacking, you quickly turn to the classifieds and Internet in search of a more promising position.

Although you're not averse to rising through the career ranks, it's not a critical factor in your life. What you need far more is the freedom to expand job responsibilities and skills. Switching tasks throughout the day also keeps things interesting.

Be cautious, though, about changing careers solely to pursue a new adventure. Chances are, there is no pot of gold at the end of the employment rainbow! When it's realistically time for a change, consider switching to a related career where you can apply your experience, skills, and talents in a different capacity.

You could excel in the arts as a performer, artist, dancer, or museum director. Stage and screen offer many other outlets for your creative talents, including set or costume designer, film editor, or theater manager. You also could find success as a photographer or creative writer.

If the health care industry appeals to you, you might consider a career as a physician, podiatrist, pharmacist, pharmacy technician, or nurse, or in related fields like physical therapy, massage therapy or homeopathy. A career in sales or the beverage, oil, or fishing industry might attract you. You also might enjoy the people contact of bartending or social work. If science interests you, a career as an oceanographer, biologist, or chemist could satisfy you.

Putting Your Best Foot Forward

The practical realities of life can escape you. You undoubtedly know this and might even rely on someone else to handle the day-to-day details. That's great if it works for both of you because it frees you to do what you do best.

Daily details, such as bill paying, are one thing, but life's big picture is entirely another. No one can do that for you.

Some Pisceans are content to drift through life, letting chance and the luck of the draw take them wherever they go. That approach has its merits. Your strong faith and belief that the universe will guide you is often rewarded. But not always. Imagine where you could go and what you could do if you set short- and long-term goals for finances, career, education, and more. Dream big! Dreams can become reality!

It's OK to start small if that's your comfort zone. If you lack confidence, look within and read self-help books to discover why. If you lack knowledge, read up on the subject, take a class, or consult a professional. Many resources are available if you look for them.

Then begin with simple goals for the day, week, or month, and measure your progress with a to-do list. Reward your successes and give yourself permission to try again, if necessary. In no time the rewards—the positives—will outweigh the negatives and you'll be ready for bigger and better things.

Move on to longer term goals. Start with a year, and then visualize where you'd like to be in five, ten, or twenty years. How do you get there? It's all in the planning. Write down short-term goals—the small steps—that can lead to strides and leaps to success at each of your target dates.

Tools for Change

Your work life and career offer the greatest tools for change this year. But not on their own. Your willingness to initiate or accept change can set you on a positive path to success.

It might be necessary to take a calculated risk to realize career gains, but you've become more comfortable with that concept in the past few years. It's also possible that you could be in the right place at the right time, so be alert for opportunities and follow through on them. Good fortune can arrive in many ways and in many different situations.

This year is also all about making your own luck. You can do that by giving your job your all. Showcase your talents, accept extra responsibilities, and be a team player. Network with other people who share your career interests, and get to know those who can open doors for you.

Self-promotion is also to your advantage. Learn this subtle art and take credit for your expertise and many accomplishments. Most of all, be sure the right people know about them. Supporting others is also important, but stretch yourself a little and get comfortable with the idea of putting your needs and your future first. It will pay off in dividends!

Affirmation for the Year

I believe in myself and my talents.

The Year Ahead for Pisces

Achievement! Recognition! Success! You're perfectly placed for all three and more as Jupiter travels in Sagittarius, your solar Tenth House of career and status. Set your sights on a step up, a promotion, or new job where you can maximize your skills and talents. Honors and awards are also possible, so this is the year to enter your work in a professional contest or take on the challenge of a company-sponsored competition. With lucky Jupiter on your side, the odds are in your favor. So many opportunities will come your way as the year progresses and your star rises that you'll be tempted to grab every one. But be selective. Otherwise you could get in over your head and dilute Jupiter's positive influence. Jupiter moves on to Capricorn, your solar Eleventh House, December 18. You may want to get involved in a club, organization, or special-interest group in 2008 to begin a new twelve-month phase that features friendship, networking, and a widening circle of acquaintances.

By now you've probably become accustomed to the heavy workload signified by Saturn in Leo and somewhat frustrated by an overall lack of appreciation. The tide is about to turn. This year you're poised to reap Saturn's rewards as this planet wraps up its two-year trip through your solar Sixth House. The outcome depends upon past efforts, what you've learned along the way, and, most importantly, the people you know. You still have plenty of time to fill in any missing pieces because gains are more likely this summer. Take good care of yourself along the way, as the Sixth House is also a health sector. Eat well, sleep, and try to exercise regularly. Your focus switches on September 2 when Saturn enters Virgo, your solar Seventh House of close relationships. Emphasize communication if you're in a committed relationship and work together to strengthen your bonds of love. Some singles will form a lasting partnership under this influence.

Life continues to deliver one surprise after the next with Uranus, planet of the unexpected, now halfway through its Pisces tour of your solar First House. You're a magnet for opportunities, some of which lead to greater self-understanding as you explore and experience different facets of yourself. Although Uranus' focus remains on you, this year it will shift slightly to include other people and different viewpoints, which will spark new insights into human nature, including your own. Put the knowledge to good use in business and personal relationships, and welcome the stimulating people who enter your life.

Neptune remains in Aquarius, the sign it entered in 1998. Placed in your solar Twelfth House, this mystical planet continues to encourage you to listen to and trust your inner voice. Intuition is strong and you sense the subtle vibrations others miss. Soul-soothing meditation can enhance this gift and is a terrific way to unwind. Give meditation a try if it's not already a part of your daily routine. You can benefit equally from sharing your talents with a good cause that appeals to your compassionate nature. However, don't feel obligated to help every friend and family member who asks for a handout of your time, money, and energy. Choose instead to guide them to other resources that can provide long-term solutions.

Pluto in its final year in Sagittarius empowers you to step into a more visible position. Although your sign is generally more comfortable on the sidelines, this is an opportunity not to be missed and one that will give you a tremendous sense of accomplishment. The journey you began in 1995, when Pluto entered your solar Tenth House, culminates now. Like Jupiter, however, Pluto can push you to try to do it all. Stop short at the first inkling you might be headed in that direction. Keeping an eye on the competition is also important because someone could try a power play. Make an effort to cultivate the support of decision-makers who can help tip things in your favor. Set your goals and rise to the top!

This year's four solar and lunar eclipses in Pisces and Virgo, your solar First and Seventh Houses, highlight personal and business relationships, with an emphasis on compromise and communication. If you're searching for love, this powerful energy could trigger a romantic commitment.

If you were born between February 19 and March 1, Saturn will contact your Sun after it enters Virgo, September 2. This transit, which occurs every twenty-eight years, can strain—but also strengthen—relationships. As is almost always true of taskmaster Saturn, the outcome is up to you and the choices you make. If you're part of a committed relationship, emphasize communication and learn all you can about each other's needs, desires, fears, hopes, and wishes. The more open you are, the more supportive you will become of each other as individuals and as a couple. If you're wavering about a dating relationship or feel pressured to commit, time apart could help you sort out your emotions. Follow your heart and do what's right for you, but if the thought of commitment in general is holding you back, try to decipher the root cause. Someone from the past could return to your life this year to complete unfinished business. Be sure to resolve the issues so you can move on. Otherwise, another reunion may occur seven or fourteen years from now. Key dates: October 13, November 30, and December 6 and 19.

If you were born between March 1 and 10, Uranus in Pisces sparks an independent streak as it directly contacts your Sun, and the mere thought of change motivates you to take action. Slow down! Carefully consider your options and opportunities, which will be numerous this year, including a chance encounter this spring that could trigger a career break. With quirky Uranus contacting your Sun, you never know who might be your lucky charm, so talk with even the most unlikely people. The urge to exercise your personal freedom is strongest of all. You can satisfy it by directing the energy into a positive outlet that expresses your individuality, such as a creative project or hobby. Or, use this motivational influence to change yourself, your image, your thinking, and your life outlook. Get healthy and get in shape. One caution applies: whatever major changes you make this year involving people, places, or things are likely to be permanent. Choose wisely! Key dates: January 22, February 7, March 4 and 31, April 27, June 8, September 4, October 8, and November 25.

If you were born between March 8 and 13, you'll cherish time alone in this otherwise "public" year as Neptune connects with your Sun from Aquarius, your solar Twelfth House of self-renewal. Try to make quiet time for yourself a part of every day, or at least several times a week, to re-center body and soul. Spend these precious hours lost in thought or meditation, or devote them to your favorite leisure-time activity. What's most important is to focus on yourself and your innermost needs during this spiritual period. You will learn more about yourself as the year unfolds, and dreams offer significant clues to self-understanding. Put pen and paper next to your bed to jot down notes you can refer to in the future. Some images may be prophetic. Key dates: January 20 and 26, February 9, April 5, May 6 and 13, June 26, August 12, September 23, November 23, and December 20.

If you were born between March 8 and 20, Saturn in Virgo through September 1 focuses your attention on work. You may be asked to take on added responsibilities, for which you're likely to feel underappreciated. Hang in there! Saturn is noted for rewarding those who are dependable and follow the "rules," and this year's planetary alignments could do so handsomely. Remember the long-term rewards on the days you feel overloaded and take things one step and task at a time. Attention to your health and well-being is even more important at this time because your energy level is likely to be lower than usual under this transit. Try not to push yourself too hard and make sleep your No. 1 priority to rejuvenate your body for long days. If you're not in the habit of daily exercise, you might want to change that. A daily walk can help ease tension and clear your mind. Most of all, stay focused on your goals and believe in yourself and your ability to achieve great things this year. Key Dates: January 20, February 10, March 22, April 19, May 9, July 1 and 30, August 13 and 20.

If you were born between March 16 and 20, you experience Pluto at its most passionate as the planet of transformation contacts your Sun from Sagittarius. You can reach the height of your career this year with the dual influence of Jupiter also in your solar Tenth House. Achieving your aims will require a careful balancing act, the right timing, and the support of influential people. You can do it! Showcase your know-how, skills, and talents at every opportunity, but take care not to step on toes. Also be alert to what others are doing because someone may try to manipulate you or a workplace situation or attempt a major power play. Cover your bases, be a team player, and don't get caught up in this potentially negative influence. Key dates: February 19, March 18, April 8, May 12, September 19, November 5, and December 10.

Pisces/January

Planetary Hotspots

Your inner voice is especially active this month, guiding you on a spiritual path of self-renewal. Listen closely to the messages, thoughts, and feelings as you prepare to symbolically emerge into the wider world when the Sun enters your sign next month. On another level, your sixth sense can be an asset in your work life, which will be bumpy at times.

Wellness and Keeping Fit

Give meditation or yoga a try (or renew your commitment). Both are excellent ways to calm your mind so your subconscious can release its hidden messages. Dreams are a likely outlet; put pen and paper next to your bed to record the images. Review them the next evening to prompt more.

Love and Life Connections

You're at the center of the social scene this month, thanks to four planets, plus the January 18 New Moon in Capricorn, your friendship sign. If you're searching for someone special, the first week of the new year could fulfill your wish. The January 3 New Moon in Cancer, your solar Fifth House of romance, activates the energy and a stellar Sun-Mercury-Uranus alignment could trigger the chance encounter that leads to love. Couples feel the sizzle!

Finance and Success

Your career life is fast-paced through January 15, as Mars wraps up its time in Sagittarius, your solar Tenth House of career. With it comes recognition and the chance to step up in the world. However, be cautious and aware of undercurrents at month's end, when work responsibilities multiply and competition is stiff. Not everyone is trustworthy. Be very selective about sharing information, even with those co-workers you consider to be friends.

Rewarding Days

2, 5, 8, 12, 14, 17, 18, 21, 25, 30, 31

Challenging Days

1, 6, 13, 15, 20, 23, 26

Pisces/February

Planetary Hotspots

Stops and starts define many of February's days, and just when you think life is back on track, another delay pops up. The main culprit is Mercury, which turns retrograde in your sign February 13. Expect confusion, misunderstandings, and misdirection, along with plans and projects in a state of flux. Also active this month is an exact alignment of Saturn in Leo and Neptune in Aquarius across your solar Sixth-Twelfth House axis of the seen and unseen. Previously hidden information will come to light, which could make you feel overloaded and underappreciated in your work life. Think positive!

Wellness and Keeping Fit

The Sixth and Twelfth Houses also are associated with health, so this is a good month to schedule routine medical appointments as well as to give yourself a lifestyle checkup. Ease into a new routine if diet and vitality aren't up to par. Your body will love you for it.

Love and Life Connections

Mars in Capricorn, your friendship sign, February 1–25 offers you many social opportunities. But with the Sun and New Moon in Aquarius, your solar Twelfth House of self-renewal, you'll also be content with your own company. Do a little of both. With Venus in your sign through February 19, you're at your most charming and ready for a sudden attraction. Take advantage of it!

Finance and Success

Your work life requires extra time and attention as the February 2 Full Moon in Leo, your sign of daily work, steps up the pressure to push matters to conclusion. Do all you can that week and the next, before Mercury turns retrograde. Promising career news accompanies a Mercury-Pluto alignment, but it will be month's end before you hear more, and March before you know the final outcome.

Rewarding Days

1, 6, 8, 9, 12, 14, 15, 17, 21, 22, 26, 27

Challenging Days

4, 5, 10, 11, 16, 19, 23, 25, 28

Pisces/March

Planetary Hotspots

A question of values arises this month as Mars clashes with Saturn and Neptune, and the Sun does the same with Pluto. Think carefully if you're asked to cut corners to speed a project to completion. With extra effort you can make that happen anyway—as long as you align yourself with the right people. Choose them carefully, and after much thought.

Wellness and Keeping Fit

Pamper yourself this month. A little self-indulgence can be a good thing, and if you need a reason, make it a celebration of the March 19 New Moon in your sign. Get a massage, a pedicure, or a facial, or whatever will relax you and make you smile—within reason! Treat yourself to new clothes for spring.

Love and Life Connections

The March 3 Full Moon in Virgo, your solar Seventh House of relationships, encourages you to reach out to others, especially loved ones. Make them the center of attention in early March and let them know how much they mean to you. You'll receive all that and more in return.

Finance and Success

You could see more money in your paycheck within the first two weeks of the month, thanks to Venus in Aries, your solar Second House of personal resources, through March 16. Recognition is almost a given, and a step up is possible as Venus aligns beautifully with Jupiter and Pluto in Sagittarius, your career sign. Just be sure you know the full extent of any added responsibilities before you agree to the extra load. Then enlist the support of co-workers. Teamwork works wonders and makes it easy on everyone.

Rewarding Days

4, 5, 6, 10, 13, 17, 20, 21, 25, 26, 27, 30

Challenging Days

1, 2, 8, 9, 11, 18, 22, 23, 29

Pisces/April

Planetary Hotspots

Personal and career frustrations occupy your time, energy, and thoughts the first 10 days of April. Try to remember it's tough to be objective when you're deeply involved in any situation; tunnel vision can take over and block input. Step back, gain a fresh perspective, and re-examine information and your approach. Then be patient. What seemed impossible will begin to come together by the third week of the month with the help of supportive people who want you to succeed.

Wellness and Keeping Fit

Mars charges into your sign April 4, bringing with it high energy and initiative. That's great! But overconfidence can get the best of you, and you'll be inclined to take risks you'd usually avoid. Slow down and think before you act, rather than tempt fate and an accident.

Love and Life Connections

Family relationships are especially satisfying after Venus enters Gemini, your domestic sign, April 11. You'll enjoy their company during laid-back evenings and weekends at home. The last weekend of the month is a good choice if you want to host a get-together for a few friends or co-workers.

Finance and Success

Like March, April offers the chance for recognition, increased earnings, and advancement, as Mercury in Aries, your sign of personal resources, forms positive contacts with planets in your solar Sixth House of daily work and solar Tenth House of career and status. Communication is a strength now, so step out with confidence and share all your great ideas the last two weeks of April. Make presentations, offer to teach a one-time company seminar, or arrange an informal weekly idea-exchange to promote brainstorming.

Rewarding Days

3, 4, 9, 10, 14, 16, 17, 19, 22, 23, 26, 29

Challenging Days

1, 5, 6, 12, 13, 15, 18, 20, 27, 28

Pisces/May

Planetary Hotspots

Frustration rises in early May as differences of opinion leave you wondering where to turn for solutions. You may or may not find the answers, mostly because others are unable to see the point or unwilling to change. This primarily impacts your work life, although tension also can affect personal relationships. Think positive. By the time of the May 16 New Moon in Taurus, your communication sign, all should return to normal.

Wellness and Keeping Fit

This month's focus on your communication sector makes it an ideal one to begin (or continue) daily journaling. Writing will help you work through issues and relieve stress, as well as explore your innermost desires in your quest for a deeper level of self-understanding.

Love and Life Connections

Family ties are in focus again this month, with Venus in Taurus the first week. Mercury travels in the same sign May 11–27, and is joined by the Sun on May 22. Enjoy life together and also promote communication. Listen closely to what your favorite people say. Chances are, they'll trigger new insights into current challenges, which will cause a shift in your personal views. Get out and about and socialize after Venus enters Cancer, your solar Fifth House of pleasure, May 8.

Finance and Success

Despite the communication challenges you experience on the job, May also brings an opportunity to showcase your skills and talents in a special project or activity. Even if you're unsure you're up to the task, take a chance and stretch yourself. With lucky Jupiter on your side and aligned with Mercury and Uranus, clever ideas can quickly set you apart from the crowd.

Rewarding Days

1, 3, 4, 6, 7, 11, 14, 15 19, 28, 29

Challenging Days

5, 9, 12, 16, 18, 20, 25, 30

Pisces/June

Planetary Hotspots

June brings job challenges at month's end, when Saturn and Neptune form their last exact alignment in Leo and Aquarius, your solar Sixth and Twelfth Houses of the seen and unseen. Communication is once again the main hurdle, and it will be tough to reach agreement on much of anything during that time frame and into early July. Nevertheless, stick with it because your vision will become clear when viewed through the words and actions of others.

Wellness and Keeping Fit

Take a break mid-month, even for a day, to enjoy the comforts of home. You can choose to be lazy, but you're more likely be motivated. Zip through your domestic to-do list and maybe even plant a summer flower or herb garden. What you do is less important than the brief step out of your hectic daily life.

Love and Life Connections

You'll be in the mood for summer fun, love, and socializing with Venus in Cancer, your solar Fifth House of recreation and romance, June 1–5, and the Sun there after June 19. Mercury is in Cancer all month, and turns retrograde June 15. Be sure to confirm dates, places, and times. If you're on the lookout for a new relationship, month's end could bring you face to face with someone intriguing. But it might take until mid-August before you actually get together to explore the possibilities.

Finance and Success

Career demands are at their peak the first week of the month as the June 1 Full Moon in Sagittarius spotlights your solar Tenth House of status. Look for potential rewards, including the chance for more money, the second week of June, when Mars in Aries, your sign of personal resources, aligns with Jupiter and Pluto in Sagittarius.

Rewarding Days

1, 5, 6, 7, 10, 13, 15, 16, 18, 23, 25, 29

Challenging Days

2, 3, 11, 12, 19, 21, 24, 26

Pisces/July

Planetary Hotspots

You'll feel the effects of Venus' retrograde cycle (July 27–September 8) more than many because this universal planet of relationships reverses direction in Virgo, your solar Seventh House of relationships. Rather than perceive it as a negative, however, consider it an opportunity to learn more about human nature and how you interact with others. It's also an excellent time for established couples to re-evaluate, reunite, and reaffirm their commitment. But this is not the time for a new union.

Wellness and Keeping Fit

With the July 4 New Moon in Cancer, your solar Fifth House of recreation, and Mercury turning direct in the same sign five days later, you can successfully launch an exercise program with a partner. Join a gym, take sports lessons, or find a neighbor who wants to walk and talk every morning or evening.

Love and Life Connections

The New Moon also fuels your social life, as does the July 30 Full Moon in Capricorn, your friendship sign. Fill the month with parties, outings, and get-togethers, and host one of your own soon after Mercury turns direct.

Finance and Success

Your job is satisfying as Venus travels in Leo, your sign of daily work, through July 13, and also after the Sun enters the same sign, July 22. However, workplace communication can become an issue at month's end when Mars clashes with Saturn and Neptune. Above all, keep your cool and say and do nothing you'll later regret. Distance yourself. Retreat to the sidelines when other people's tempers flare.

Rewarding Days

1, 4, 5, 7, 8, 9, 11, 13, 14, 15, 17, 22, 25, 27, 28

Challenging Days

2, 3, 6, 10, 12, 16, 18, 19, 23, 24, 26, 31

Pisces/August

Planetary Hotspots

Action centers in your solar Sixth House of daily work around the time of the August 12 New Moon in Leo. With the Sun, Mercury, and Venus in the same sign and in contact with nearly every other planet, you have a stellar opportunity to make your mark. Not all will be smooth, however, so you'll want to be on your toes and tuned in to the subtle vibrations. Use your intuition, let your creativity shine, follow through, and stay a few steps ahead of everyone else. Ask questions and take little, if anything, at face value. If a new job is your goal, send out resumes.

Wellness and Keeping Fit

Put Mars to work for you on the domestic scene after it enters Gemini, your solar Fourth House of home and family, August 7. Physical activity is a great stress reliever, so combine it with your imagination to redo a bedroom or bath in cool, calming colors. But know your limits and don't tackle what is beyond your skills. Put safety first, and balance enthusiasm with reality.

Love and Life Connections

Family relationships can be a bit rocky at times this months as first Venus, and then Mercury, both in your solar Seventh House, clash with Mars in Gemini. Let tempers cool before you talk things out. Willingly accept your share of the responsibility, learn from it, and move on with a smile.

Finance and Success

Career momentum begins to resume August 6 when Jupiter turns direct in your solar Tenth House. That's a definite plus for high visibility and this month's potential rise in status. But you may not see an immediate financial gain because Venus, one of your money planets, is still retrograde.

Rewarding Days

1, 3, 5, 9, 10, 11, 12, 16, 19, 23, 24, 30

Challenging Days

2, 6, 8, 13, 15, 20, 21, 28, 29

Pisces/September

Planetary Hotspots

A major planetary shift occurs September 2: Saturn enters Virgo, your solar Seventh House of close relationships. This two-year influence can be positive or negative, depending upon your approach, and ultimately will probably be both. You'll draw closer to some people, including friends, and distance yourself from others. Essentially, you'll strengthen ties with those who enrich your life and at least partially let go of those whose interests now differ from yours. If you decide to commit to a relationship and are 100 percent sure of your feelings, Saturn here can work like Super Glue, creating an unbreakable bond.

Wellness and Keeping Fit

Take time to think about all you have learned about people since Venus turned retrograde in July. New thoughts will begin to emerge as Venus resumes direct motion September 8 and proceeds to retrace its path. Take the initiative to clear up any misunderstandings, if only for your own peace of mind. Resolution brings closure.

Love and Life Connections

Once past a few communication challenges, primarily work-related, in early September, you can settle in and enjoy the positive people contact accented by the Virgo Sun through September 21. Start to line up your fall social schedule at month's end, when Mars enters Cancer, your solar Fifth House of pleasure.

Finance and Success

Finances benefit from Mercury in Libra, your sign of joint resources, September 5–27, and the Sun in the same sign after September 21. You, your partner, or both of you could earn a raise or bonus, or celebrate a small windfall. Stash it rather than spend it, and try not to give in to the lure of easy credit.

Rewarding Days

1, 5, 6, 7, 8, 13, 14, 15, 20, 22, 27

Challenging Days

2, 3, 4, 9, 11, 16, 17, 19, 24, 26

Pisces/October

Planetary Hotspots

The universe provides you with a brief break this month. Life perks along with only minor disruptions. There is one exception, however. Mercury turns retrograde in Scorpio, your solar Ninth House of travel and knowledge, October 11. Try to schedule any trips before then or after October 23 when Mercury retreats into Libra. You'll also want to double-check data and details to avoid what could be costly errors.

Wellness and Keeping Fit

Let the October 26 Full Moon in Taurus, your sign of quick trips, inspire a weekend getaway. Go somewhere nearby, or check into a local upscale hotel for a day or two. Either one will take you away from daily stress and renew your spirit.

Love and Life Connections

Togetherness and socializing get top billing this month, with Venus in Virgo after October 7, and Mars in Cancer, your sign of recreation and romance, all month. Stir the passion and surprise your one and only with TLC-filled evenings designed for two. Some singles meet a soul mate the first weekend of the month, which also accents friendship.

Finance and Success

Enjoy the recognition that comes your way the first weekend of October when Venus wraps up its time in Leo, your sign of daily work. Finances are in positive territory much of October, thanks to the New Moon in Libra, your solar Eighth House of joint resources. Again, this month you or your partner (or both) could luck into some extra cash. But safeguard financial information after retrograde Mercury enters Libra.

Rewarding Days

3, 4, 7, 8, 12, 13, 14, 17, 18, 30

Challenging Days

9, 15, 19, 22, 23, 28, 29

Pisces/November

Planetary Hotspots

Your social life slows somewhat beginning November 15 when Mars turns retrograde in Cancer, your recreation sign. The trend continues through the end of January. You'll be more or less content with that this month when the Full Moon in Gemini, your domestic sign, November 24, focuses your attention on home and family.

Wellness and Keeping Fit

Uranus turns direct in your sign, November 24, five days after the New Moon in Scorpio, your solar Ninth House of knowledge. Let the dual influence motivate you to take a mental journey in search of yourself, your desires, your motivations, and what holds you back. What you learn will be invaluable in the near future.

Love and Life Connections

You'll be drawn to people as Venus travels in Virgo through November 7. This is a delightful time for love and romance, as well as being with your favorite people. Be aware, though, that workplace conflict is possible. Stay away from controlling people and let others settle their own differences. Arrange a few dates with close friends at month's end, or invite them to your place for a casual dinner.

Finance and Success

Your star begins to rise November 22, when the Sun enters Sagittarius, your solar Tenth House of status and career. Look forward to more next month. Finances benefit from Venus in Libra, one of your money signs, beginning November 8, and you can easily clear up any recent mix-ups before then because Mercury turns direct the first day of the month.

Rewarding Days

2, 4, 7, 8, 9, 12, 18, 22, 26, 27, 28

Challenging Days

5, 6, 11, 19, 21, 23, 24, 29, 30

Pisces/December

Planetary Hotspots

December's big event surrounds lucky Jupiter. This expansive, upbeat planet enters Capricorn, your solar Eleventh House of friends and groups, December 18. Look forward to a year (Jupiter spends about twelve months in each sign) of social events, quiet times with your best pals, and opportunities to meet many new people. You also might want to get involved (or more involved) in a club or organization—a good cause, professional association, or social group.

Wellness and Keeping Fit

It's easy for extra pounds to creep on this time of year. Tap into Mars in Cancer, your solar Fifth House of recreation, and give yourself the gift of a gym membership or a yoga class. Or join the mall-walkers and window shop for holiday gifts as you zip along. Your body and mind will benefit from it.

Love and Life Connections

Take advantage of every opportunity this month to see friends. You'll have many events to attend, thanks to Jupiter's abundance, but a difficult contact between the Sun and Mars the end of December makes it wise to drive with care and socialize with a designated driver. This is not a time to take chances. Welcome 2008 with a small gathering at your place, safe and secure, as Mars retreats into Gemini, your domestic sign.

Finance and Success

You're in the spotlight this month, thanks to the Sun in Sagittarius, your career sign, through December 21, and Mercury there from December 1–19. The energy peaks at the December 9 New Moon in the same sign, when you can rise above the rest and possibly earn a promotion. Soon after, the odds favor a year-end bonus that will make you smile.

Rewarding Days

4, 5, 7, 11, 12, 14, 15, 16, 19, 25, 28

Challenging Days

1, 2, 3, 6, 8, 17, 22, 23, 30

Pisces Action Table

These dates reflect the best—but not the only—times for success and ease in these activities, according to your Sun sign.

	JAN	FEB	MAR	APR	MAY	JUN	JUL	AUG	SEPT	OCT	NOV	DEC
Move	28, 29	24, 25		15, 24, 30	17-27	13, 14			30	1	25	
Start a class			21, 22	27-30	1-9, 15, 16							
Join a club	2-13			9, 10	7			24, 25			14, 15	21-29
Ask for a raise	23, 24			16, 17				3	27			18, 19
Look for work	15, 16		12	24, 25	21, 22	18, 19		12, 13	18			9, 10
Get pro advice	8	5	30, 31	26			17, 18	24-31	1-4	8	5	
Get a loan	8	5	30, 31	26			17, 18	24-31	1-4	8	5	13-15
See a doctor	19, 23, 24		15, 16	12, 24, 25	21, 22			13		5	29	14
Start a diet		2					30		8, 9	5, 6	28-30	
End relationship	7, 8	3, 4	3						10	7, 8	4, 5	
Buy clothes	4, 30, 31		25, 26		19, 29, 30		13-14					
Get a makeover	28-31	8-10	18			7					18, 19	
New romance	30, 31		25, 26		11, 20, 29	2-4	13, 14			30		24, 25
Vacation		8-10			28-30		22, 23				8-21	5-7

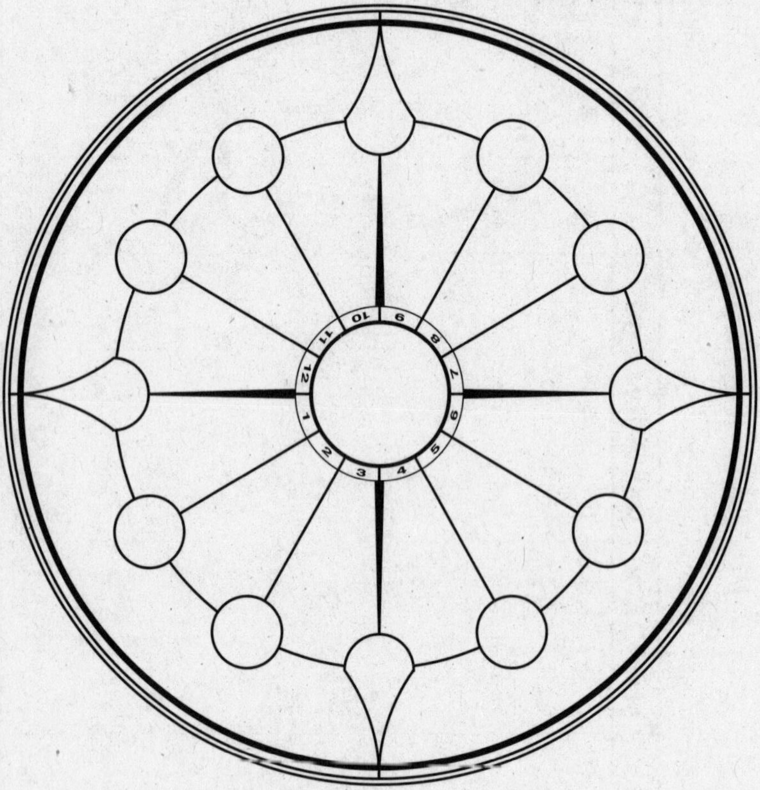
1
2
3
4
5
6
7
8
9
10
11
12

2007 SUN SIGN BOOK

Articles

Contributors

Nancy Bennett

Stephanie Clement

Alice DeVille

Sasha Fenton

Dorothy Kovach

Dorothy Oja

Leeda Alleyn Pacotti

Carole Schwalm

Inner Space

Home Remodeling Secrets

by Alice DeVille

What attracted you to your present home? Whether you are a homeowner or a renter, you made a very important decision in choosing your current residence. When you shopped for your home, what features or areas of the home were important to you—in other words, the "must haves?" Most homebuyers and renters place their critical eye on kitchens and bathrooms. Buyers like a home that boasts an updated, well-designed kitchen and impeccably clean bathrooms. Both renters and buyers look closely at storage options and closet space. If living space is too cramped, it is not going to satisfy residents. Garages house the car and often store overflow from the move.

People "buy up" or downsize every day due to changing housing needs. Individuals choosing less space and fewer trappings want easy access to their household goods, clothing, linens, and food items. Outdoor lovers want space like a balcony or deck that allows them to take in fresh breezes. Others want the largest possible master bedroom to fit a television, computer equipment, or reading area.

Rationale for Remodeling

Although the term remodeling is more closely affiliated with owning a home, many renters opt to personalize their space with minor makeovers. Renters should consult the lease and get their landlords' permission in writing before making improvements. Explore options for turning your home into the cozy retreat you desire. The tips here apply to a range of homes from a tiny efficiency apartment to a mega-sized McMansion. Hopefully they'll save you time and money on your projects. Finally, I share astrological insight from my work with clients who represent each Sun sign. These passages describe the type of projects they tackled and the end results, which may be relevant to your own needs. In astrology, the Fourth House is the department of life relating to the home you live in—everything you consider personal space and how you value or use it.

Remodeling Credentials

Before you begin any project where you will be hiring a contractor or a specialist who is going to work in your home, get at least three referrals and at least three estimates for the work. If there are noticeable price differences, find out why. After you have all your bids, check their credentials with the Better Business Bureau, local licensing boards, professional organizations, and past clients. Find out how long it takes them to start and finish a particular remodeling project. Take your time in the selection process if you don't have all the facts. Find out what materials will be used and check plans carefully if you are undertaking a large project. Misreading plans and blueprints runs up the price and creates major time delays.

Excellent sources for finding a renovation or home-remodeling company are local real estate companies, bankers, home-improvement outlets, and homeowners' associations. Ask for at least three recommendations and do the homework prescribed above.

I am a Realtor® affiliated with a large company that offers many step-saving services to our clients, including access to a directory of experts in every possible field affiliated with home maintenance: landscapers, painters, wallpaper hangers, roofers, junk haulers, etc. Our approved vendors must provide impeccable service to clients, respond immediately to any complaints, and honor their contracts.

Firms that do not live up to the standards do not receive further recommendations and are dropped from the list. I routinely offer the contact information of at least three companies to sellers, buyers, and renters. That way the resident decides whom to hire.

Experiencing Quality Living

Where do you spend the most time in your home? Your answer to this question could be the basis of your own remodeling project. If the space you describe is not meeting your needs or lacks the ambience you desire, start there. Space that has personal appeal for you makes a good case for a makeover. Why hang out in drab quarters when a little sprucing up can revitalize your psyche? The consumer trend in makeovers is bigger than ever. If your goal is to "get current," keep in mind that makeovers don't have to be extreme. Any place in your home with clutter or wasted space needs attention and is up for imaginative grabs in the remodeling world.

Maybe you have a favorite room in your home that could use some sparkle to make it more inviting or relaxing. Favorite spots experience wear and tear just like the carpet and become energy drains for inhabitants. Parents, children, partners, and singles want private, usable space. Don't have a pantry in your home? One of our Sun sign makeovers found an ingenious way to create one.

The Budget Factor

Unless you have a large sum of cash set aside for remodeling, tackle one area at a time. Multiple-room makeovers can take months (or years) to complete, especially if the job requires structural and electrical changes. Home-equity lines of credit or loans are a tax deductible way for you to finance up to $100,000 in improvements.

Your home is your castle and you want it to be as perfect as possible, not only while you live there, but when you decide to sell. I point this out because the typical person moves every six years. Even though the focus of this article is on your personal enjoyment and preferences in remodeling, I would be negligent if I did not point out that overimprovement in a transient neighborhood does not bring a much higher price for your home when you go to sell.

Today's homeowners put in updated kitchens and spa-like bathrooms. *Remodeling Magazine* reports (from the publication's "2004

Cost vs. Value" report) that owners can recoup nearly 93 percent of the cost of a kitchen remodel priced in the $15,000 range, an amount considered average for a minor remodeling project. The average bathroom remodel costs $10,000. For further information on pricing, appreciation, and amenities, consult professionals in your local real estate, remodeling, and construction market.

Unique and Chic

Where would you put your money if you were remodeling? Only you know what appeals to you emotionally and aesthetically. Here's how members of the Sun sign groups expressed their preferences.

Aries

This client moved into his first home with a garage. Now he had a place to store his prized vehicle, a BMW convertible, but he discovered his garage was dismal. His dark green chariot with a British tan interior deserved a better home. The garage had unfinished yellowed walls with spackle marks, a greasy stained floor, no shelves, rickety steps to his house entry, and a frighteningly squeaky door.

The Aries, whose Sun sign is known for having an interest in cars, tools, and machinery, hired a contractor specializing in garage makeovers. In less than a week, my client had the most artistic garage I have ever seen. Custom tri-color cabinets flanked the rear wall of the garage and completely hid all of his tools, cleaning and snow-removal equipment, pantry items, and car-care products. Frequently used tools were handily arranged between the tallest banks of cabinets on pegboard that rested above a workbench area. The side walls of the garage were finished and displayed artwork and citations. A new garage door and automatic opener replaced the tired model while new block steps to the entry were sturdy and functional. His garage floor looked like a dealer's showroom with attractive marbled black and white tile. As I stepped in to take a look, I couldn't resist asking, "How much do you want for the car?"

Taurus

Taurus is a sign that owns collectibles and wants the storage space to house them—especially my client who resides in a one-room efficiency. This man's 600-square-foot residence sits in the corner of a ten-story high-rise building, has light-filled windows on two sides, and plenty of wall space. His small kitchen did not have enough cabinets to fit his cookware, dishes, and pantry items, and his living room area was too small to display books and artwork.

After hiring a company known for its storage solutions, my client is smiling at the efficiency of his altered space. Next to his bank of cabinets, the installers built a six-foot-long by seven-foot-high bank of shelves perpendicular to the wall, creating a terrific room divider. On one side he stores glassware, dishes, canisters, and assorted kitchen items. The living room side of the divider attractively displays his books, knickknacks, photos, plants, and collections. Life is much more organized and this Taurus is happy with the end result.

Gemini

The Twin rents her condo and treasures the location for its easy access to shopping, entertainment, theaters, and restaurants. She travels frequently and does not need an excessive amount of space. Her frustration lies in coming home from business trips, opening her master bedroom closet door, and finding her wrinkled clothing strewn all over the floor. The closet has one flimsy shelf and a pole rod that falls down at times. She knows she can't alter the rented space drastically and sought a practical solution to keep her sanity.

After getting bids from closet organizers, she hired a firm that built a portable system that she can take with her when she relocates. The system includes shelves, drawers, and staggered poles that bear the weight of her clothing much better than the lone sagging rod. Now my Gemini client no longer passes up social engagements for a humdrum date with her ironing board.

Cancer

Cancer's love for working at home was a dream come true when she used part of a recent inheritance to build a custom office in her home. She had been feeling very crabby about cramped work quarters and a long commute. This Moon sign sketched her ideas, showed them to several space planners, and asked for estimates. My client had a bottom line budget figure for the job, something everyone should keep in mind when hiring a contractor.

One month after she signed the contract, my client was effortlessly conducting business in her new space. No walls had to be moved. The contractor upgraded existing wiring at the main box to building code. She added a few judiciously placed outlets and phone jacks. Cancer's makeover includes abundant work space, file cabinets, storage drawers, shelves, and a mail center. A soothing color scheme of cream, mauve, and sea green adds to her sense of security. Now she answers her office phone with a smile in her voice.

Leo

The Lion enjoys living in a "faux chateau," otherwise known as a "McMansion." The term is used especially for huge structures that are built on very small lots. In established neighborhoods where the older homes are much smaller, they tower above their neighbors.

Prosperity flows for this corporate head. My client bought a dated property and tore it down to build his beautiful dream home. He tells me the family stays home more than ever because the home has so many amenities to enjoy, including an indoor pool, two recreation rooms in the lower level, dual master baths, offices for both he and his spouse, and a state-of-the-art kitchen for entertaining. One Sunday a month, magnanimous Leo rolls out the red carpet and invites all the neighbors to brunch—and does all the cooking!

Virgo

Virgo must have been the model for the HGTV show, *Design on a Dime*. This frugal Sun sign looks for bargains in the home consumer arena, which can be a liability when poor workmanship is disguised as a "real deal." A Virgo client of mine found this out when looking to build a deck. He was ready to seal the deal, but had second thoughts. It seems his "bargain" contractor kept costs down by using inferior, untreated wood. Later, Virgo discovered that former customers claimed their decks became termite-infested a few years after construction and filed complaints against the "bargain" contractor.

My client hired another—more expensive—builder with a good reputation, and a pretty full schedule. My client waited patiently and was able to enjoy some late summer Sun on his deck. Next spring he plans to landscape the area and add Sun-loving plants.

Libra

Libra's laundry facility left something to be desired. It was unbalanced and left her feeling the same way. Adjacent to her kitchen was one of those stacked appliance closets with no storage room. The washer was too small to hold bedspreads or blankets and left soap scum after the rinse cycle. Lately, the dryer was behaving inefficiently. After cycling the same load of laundry three times, she threw in the towel. This solution-seeking Libra took a good hard look around her kitchen and decided that a lot of dead space could be converted to an efficient stand-alone laundry room. After consulting with contractors, my client selected a reputable firm.

Fast forward to the present and you see a smiling Libra showing off her dimpled cheeks and her brand-new, side-by-side laundry appliances with energy-saving features and whisper-quiet motors. Next to the washer is a laundry sink, something Libra had not seen since she lived with her parents. The contractor rerouted existing plumbing and carved out a longer, wider laundry alcove that has space-saving pocket doors (which slide or roll into the walls, unlike swinging hinged doors). Now she has cabinets and shelves above the appliances and a built-in drying rack for hand washables. This enterprising Libra shed the disjointed laundry facilities without compromising her kitchen and chased away the laundry day blues.

Scorpio

This sign put a high priority on his bath remodeling project. After being in his new home three months, he found the narrow shower-tub combination uncomfortable and dated. Also, the sink and toilet had functional, but unattractive, plumbing fixtures. The room seemed lopsided because all the fixtures were on one side and a long bare wall held only a towel rack that was too far away from the tub. A linen closet occupied space that would be ideal for a shower.

This Scorpio prefers a bathroom with a separate soaking tub along with a larger stall shower with dual shower heads and a seat. He found a contractor who had ideas to make this bathroom pop without draining all his cash. The tub stayed in the same place but was replaced with a larger, oval soaking unit. The linen closet was adjacent to the old bathtub so water could easily flow to the new, glass-enclosed shower with brass trim and fixtures. A free-standing linen armoire added a touch of class to the center wall of the bathroom. The contractor repositioned the towel bars and added new brass hardware to the sink. He put a partition between the toilet and the sink for more privacy and replaced a few bath tiles with decorative inlay to add pizzazz. My client is getting married in the spring. He says his new bathroom is like a visit to the spa.

Sagittarius

One of my favorite outdoor-loving signs, Sagittarius wanted a backyard pond to satisfy her craving to be more in touch with nature. She doesn't need to live near a lake or river to enjoy the sights and sounds of water. My client visited home-improvement stores to determine the system that best suited her location, budget, and local climate. After a feng shui inspection, a landscaper dug out the pond site so installation would be easier.

With fish in the pond, my client has to run her pump 24 hours a day, needs a nontoxic pond liner, and at least one foot of clear water below any ice on the surface. Her Taurus sister-in-law helped landscape the pond circumference with perennials, annuals, and grasses. A layer of flagstone between the plants and the pond edge adds an artistic touch. Nearby trees provide shade. My client can just add a bench and reserve a cozy spot to listen to the gently rippling water.

Capricorn

Capricorn wants to spruce up a tired kitchen without breaking the bank. Her cabinets are in terrific structural shape so she can minimize her cash outlay by refacing the surface and adding new hardware. She wants to create a more traditional look and add a glaze to give the lightened cabinets more cache. Water spots marred her lovely wood floors, but having them refinished made them look new again. The counter tops have seen better days, so Capricorn shops for a more durable surface and chooses a Silestone design. A fresh coat of paint complements the cabinets and counter tops. The local lighting center offers her a generous discount on a dining area light fixture and two pendulum lights to brighten her work surface.

Visitors can't believe the amazing transformation. Careful shopping saved $4,000, so her kitchen was well under budget. Next year my client plans to invest in new stainless steel appliances and add a center island with the same counter surface, but in a complementary darker wood shade. Knowing what she wants and setting priorities makes this organized Capricorn a model for planning home improvements. She added livability and aesthetics to her kitchen and has a room she enjoys. Kiss this cook, give her a golden apron, and treat her to dinner at her favorite restaurant. She's a winner!

Aquarius

Aquarius has been wanting to add a home-theater feature to his sprawling lower-level recreation room ever since he saw the models at the local design center show house. This gregarious host has an up-to-date DVD collection and access to newly released films. He consults media experts about installing his system and the desire for a screen that takes up an entire wall. He also talks to reputable contractors about adding soundproof walls and a beverage and food preparation center for serving snacks. He carefully calculates that he can accommodate theater seating for up to twelve guests.

Ordering, construction, and installation take nearly six weeks. Final cost was 11 percent above his estimated budget, not an uncommon difference. Part of this increase stems from changes in materials requested by my client. The final product is an entertainers delight. I was invited to the first screening of *Elizabethtown*. Crank up that old-fashioned popping machine and pass the popcorn.

Pisces

My Pisces client hated yard work, but wanted a lot large enough to house a swimming pool. His solution: buy a new home on a corner with an irregular lot line. All he had to do was add a lot of landscaping to the front and fence in the sides and back—a mandatory zoning requirement when a homeowner gets a permit to install a pool.

The entire job took about two months due to weather conditions, periodic county inspections, grading conditions, and the pool's design. Now my client steps out his sliding glass doors onto attractive natural stone pavers and colorful tile that surrounds his striking pool. Grassy, no-maintenance plants fill the corners inside the fence. Earthenware pots and cushioned storage bins add ambience and seating. This Pisces swears his abs are a lot flatter from swimming laps in the pool than they were from pushing his lawnmower.

Sun Sign Fashion
What the Cool Signs Wear

by Nancy Bennett

What sign has the most fashion savvy? What sign is a clothing slob? Who sets the trends when it comes to the zodiac and what colors and accessories work best for you? Before you head out shopping for that new outfit, take a look at what all the cool signs are wearing.

Aries

If you are an Aries, you like to be first to try new things—and that includes fashions. Trendsetting Aries loves to shop, but you need to watch your impulsive nature in order to spare your pocketbook. You have a closet full of clothes that were favorites one day and ready for the trash the next.

You like clothes that move freely and give you a sense of drama. You are picky about lending or borrowing clothes. Though you will shop thrift shops, it is usually to complement or mimic the latest fashion trend. You much prefer boutiques. Aries women like masculine clothes and have no trouble wearing a tie or a suit jacket with a full-length skirt. As far as colors go—intense is the word. Red or burgundy, jet black or Halloween orange. Think big and bold for your outfit. When considering jewelry, you want the real thing. Diamonds are an Aries' best friend!

Whatever you do, you dress for the part, like Aries singer Chaka Khan did in a January 2005 concert, changing from a classic black outfit into a classier red outfit to perform "My Funny Valentine."

Ram Accessories? Just check out Aries Elton John and his collection of glasses collection. Impressive? Who could forget Aries Alec Baldwin wearing that officer's suit in *The Hunt for Red October*, or Omar Sharif in his desert sheik attire?

Aries, you command a presence that makes people look twice. You never want to just blend in. Aries are the ones who make the world their runway!

Taurus

If you are a Taurus, you love natural fabrics and are prepared to pay top dollar for them. Linen shirts, hand-knit items, and woven skirts are staples in your wardrobe.

You may be inclined try your hand at sewing, for Taurus loves to create and takes joy in the process. Knitting Bulls? Taurus Uma Thurman was recently spotted buying twenty-six balls of casmerino wool, sixteen balls of yarn, needles, and a T-shirt emblazoned with a picture of a woman knitting in the nude.

You like familiar clothes and will wear your favorites to death. You detest trends, preferring classic styles. A royal Taurus, Queen Elizabeth II, looks equally good with her crown and jewels or in a hunting jacket and wellies (rubber boots). The queen takes a lot of heat from the press for wearing old, dated clothes. But they are classics, and you know, Taurus, that classics never go out of style!

For colors, of course, earth shades of beige and browns are good bets. But you will also look good in pale blue and other pastels. Emeralds and agates are good stones for you to wear. Scarves tie in as a good fashion accessory. As far as shoes go, forget about heels. You prefer sensible shoes with sensible soles.

Shopping with a Taurus can be time consuming as you demand perfection. If an item is beautiful and well made, you won't mind spending extra for quality—and it shows in what you wear.

Gemini

Geminis get bored quickly and want lots of choices. You are an individual when it comes to fashion. One day you'll be found in a pinstripe suit, the next in a fun, bright pink fur jacket.

Gemini Marilyn Monroe favored her capri pants and soft sweaters as much as she favored her designs from Jax, Ronetti, and Pucci. (Marilyn was buried in a green Pucci number.) To look great all the time when traveling, Marilyn would have several identical outfits so she never showed a wrinkle boarding or leaving a plane.

Comfort is a commodity you value as much as a Taurus does. Clothes can't be too tight or too rough. Make-up is minimal, as Gemini is always on the go. Your hair is probably easily maintained, no muss, no fuss, though you might add a purple streak in now and then just for fun.

Your best colors are yellow, turquoise, black, and violet. Indian tunic tops and long flowing skirts appeal to Gemini ladies, as well as caftans for men. If possible, you'd turn back time to the hippie era of the 1960s and early '70s, when clothes were flowing and colors were vibrant. Whatever you wear, folks are bound to look twice!

Cancer

If you are a Cancer, you have a great love for old and faithful things, even in clothes. The same old sweater you had ten years ago is still being cared for and worn on occasion. You will hang onto certain items for years hoping that the fashions will come back. Parachute pants, butterfly-sleeve sweaters, and grandfather's red flannel underwear all wait in boxes in your closet.

If you go out to buy the latest trend, first it must meet your comfort factor. Teal green, smoky gray, silver, and silvery blue are the shades you are most drawn to. Your hair is long and sometimes tied in place with a soft bow. Jewelry is long and loose and you love stones, especially green ones. Pearls always look good on you.

Not only do Crabs like their clothing comfortable, they really don't care what you think. In 2004, at the Emmy's, *Glamour* fashion editor Suze Yalof Schwartz complained that Meryl Streep "always wears clothes that are too big for her." Meryl Streep was once quoted as saying that "Expensive clothes are a waste of money."

Another Cancer, (Carly Simon of "You're So Vain" fame) says, "I've never really changed my style that much. I never thought about it. Early on I became attracted to capes—I think because I had a romantic nature, and I'd always wanted to be a spy . . ."

Both Carly and Meryl are quite the class acts. Typical Cancers, they know how to look for the world outside. Like it or lump it, the Cancer style sticks to you like a shell—a well-loved shell.

Leo

If your sign is the Lion, you love great clothes and aren't bothered by the price. You are a trendsetter and a go-getter. You don't mind fighting for that must-have outfit. Natural fabrics, especially from animal sources, are a purring success with Leo.

Dramatic Leos like to make an entrance. Orange and gold and royal red look gr-r-reat on you. You enjoy flowing elegant lines, and your clothes reflect this. You can still pull off a royal look in a business suit. Silk scarves or handkerchiefs are good accessories. Jewelry is fun, loud, and large. You like gold and you love to decorate your mane with barrettes or pins, or streak it with colorful dyes.

Leo Madonna is definitely a first with her fashions. Starting in the 1980s, she brought back fishnet stockings and reintroduced us to cone bras and wearing your underwear outside your clothes.

Leo also loves comfort. Madonna trusts Gucci to supply her with her favorite velvet jeans. When it comes to fashion Leo is something to roar about!

Virgo

You love natural colors like green, dark brown, beige, or even khaki. Your wardrobe contains classic lines and well-cared-for favorites. You can't stand clothes that restrict movement or your spirit.

You are cautious about new things. You hate to pay full price for anything, but you will eventually give in (but will complain all the way to the check-out) like Virgo Ingrid Bergman of *Casablanca* fame. Her daughter Isabella admitted that her mother was more than candid with some designers. "I think she offended several designers by saying their clothes were too expensive," said Isabella.

Like Ingrid, the clothes you buy are simple, tailored, and will last a lifetime. Not that you can't dress sexy! As Virgo Sophia Loren once quipped: "A woman's dress should be like a barbed-wire fence: serving its purpose without obstructing the view."

You like to have your hair neat and accessories minimal. One good stone in a great setting is a true Virgo style. Not one to shock, occasionally you will do something daring like wear a spaghetti tank with your jeans, showing off that body you keep as well groomed as your clothes. You can make anything look good if you want to.

When you move into a room, folks usually stop and stare. Don't worry, they're not thinking, "My God, is that the latest style?" it's, "Who is that classy dresser?"

Libra

As a Libra, you have a knack for combining the old and the very new for a tailored look. Your closet is full of fashions that work well together in scale. You like fashion and a good amount of your salary goes toward buying new trends. Because of this, you have a suitable outfit for every event, appointment, or social engagement.

Julie Andrews wore 124 different outfits for her 1967 role as Gertrude Lawrence, all with great style and impact (and even added coal dust to her face in *Mary Poppins* with the same class). Who can forget the string bikini? If Libra Bridget Bardot had not made an impact with it in Saint-Tropez (sometimes sans top!), an entire era of swimwear might not have reached the public beaches.

Your best colors are pink, pale green, and various shades of blue. Your friends often want your fashion input, and you will offer advice freely, and lend them just the eight accessories.

Everything must say symmetry for Libra. From head to toe and right to left, you must be on the same track. No single piercing or stripes with polka dots for you. Rules are important to Libra. You would never dream of wearing white past Labor Day! Sapphires can add luster your fashion look, as will the richness of rubies. Put it all together and Libra is balanced and ready for anything.

Scorpio

Let's face it. When it comes to fashion, if there is a rule breaker in the zodiac, it has to be Scorpio. Scorpion Katharine Hepburn, in true stinging fashion, told the press that "stockings were an invention of the devil." In the days when respectable women were wearing girdles and high heels, she wore slacks and sneakers. Once, when the movie brass took away her slacks (to force her to wear a skirt), she walked around the lot in her underwear until they returned them. Kate's pants became a symbol of independence for women, and soon everyone was wearing them.

If you are a Scorpio, you look great in deep red, maroon, chocolate brown, or black. You are aware of fashion changes and will adopt those that suit you best. You tend to dress for the occasion and swing from one extreme to another. Your power suit might hide some sizzling lingerie underneath, as scorpions are aware of their own sex appeal. Don't be surprised if you want to have an extensive collection of lacy underthings to complement your wardrobe.

Accessories either bore you to tears, or are hard to resist. Rubies and garnets fit the sensual Scorpio. If you can afford them, you have to have them! But for soft occasions, pearls and aquamarine stones are a delightful choice. Your hair might be long and luscious or short and spiky. You change it regularly, for you are a chameleon and you change clothes and looks to suit your mood. With makeup, you either paint on a full face or wear none at all. You delight in shocking people and keep them guessing at the real you. With all the choices in the fashion world, you never know what will sting you next!

Sagittarius

If one sign owns the monopoly on comfort it is Sagittarius. Most of the time you couldn't care less what the world thinks of how you dress. Like my Sagitarrius husband, if it's clean and cheap, he is living in it. Suits give you rashes and ties make you gag like Snoopy with a leash. Not that you can't look great dressed up, but most times you'd rather be in sweat pants and free beer T-shirts.

You still love bright colors—pinks, yellows, and lime—though dark blues, purples, and forest green are good choices for your conventional wardrobe. The hippie look and hemp fashions are good choices for you. You like to be outside, so hiking boots or good runners are always in reach. Sagittarius men like their hair scraggy and their beards long while the women like their hair wild and free.

Sagittarius Bette Midler has her own style from a peasant blouse slit on both sides from armpit to rib cage to multicolored petticoats and pantaloons, sequin-studded bikinis, red platform shoes, and miscrossed suspenders. The list goes on, and it seems that Archers can wear anything and get away with it. Another Sagittarius celebrity, sixty-plus Tina Turner, wears micro-minis and wild wigs.

Dress you up and you will take on the town, but at day's end, the suits are off and you will be found walking on a beach in a sarong or working in the garden with torn shorts, happy with who you are.

Capricorn

Practical Capricorn loves looking classy in classic looks. Capricorn won't be found in T-shirts and jeans (unless they are stylish and immaculate). The business suit was made for you and you delight in accessorizing it with the most modern gizmos. You were the first to wear digital watches and carry a color-coordinated cell phone.

Your jewelry is minimal, but classy. You prefer one pricey stone in a good setting to a dozen cheaper ones. Not that you don't like a bargain. Goats were born to shop. You can be counted on to find the designer items hidden in a bargain rack. You love your classics, as Capricorn David Bowie attests. While at Summer Stage in Central Park, David wore a lilac suit and the fab hand-painted T-shirt by Paris's Agnès B (one of his favorite designers) and his trusty Panama hat, originally bought in Chile in the Eighties.

Colors for Capricorn include lots of earthy browns, grays, dark green, and black. You take great care with your clothes and usually do your own mending. Your clothes must work for you.

Steady Capricorn occasionally should loosen that tie, sink into some comfortable loafers and designer sweats, and relax.

Aquarius

Water bearers don't like to be fashion followers, they like to create their own! Like Aquarian Farrah Fawcett with her feathered hair, you are still making waves. You're miles ahead of everyone else—the first to dye your hair blue and wear a mood ring. You also have a social conscience when it comes to clothes. No Third World labor goes into your gowns. No alligators die for your handbag. You can be seen in thrift shops or fair-trade stores looking for your wardrobe. When you find it, you will often alter it to create a unique outfit or pair it with something odd for a daring combination.

Best colors for water bearers are turquoise, aquamarine, white, and electric blue. Deep royal blue and purple are great to add depth to your work uniform. You will always try and find ways to push the boundaries with clothes you have to wear (Uniforms? Eww!), which can get you in trouble. Try as you might, you can't help adding that Snoopy pin or "Beam me up, Scotty" button to your business lapel.

You adore shoes and, though you need to have something that offers good ankle support, you are still drawn to those pretty snappy sandals and high-heeled boots. Make-up is your artist's palette. You use it often, in neat combinations for different outfits. Your hair is wild and often changing style. Forever changing, Aquarius likes to indulge in fantasy clothes and ethnic outfits. Luckily, you are a wise shopper, who makes the most of your fashion bucks.

Pisces

When I asked some Pisces friends their favorite outfit, they said "skin," as in not wearing anything! You love water and you probably swim or hot tub naked when you can.

If you are a Pisces you may like the freedom that certain clothes give you. You want nothing tight or constricting, so clothes like long flowing skirts and soft silk blouses appeal to you. You don't like to dress up, and get frustrated when social situations demand it. When you do find a suit for those special board meetings you eventually get used to it, and it becomes your uniform.

You look great in sea green, lavender or lilac, and other shades of purple. Though you don't take well to clothing, you do love jewelry. Moonstones are a great addition to a Pisces' wardrobe and white diamonds, as Pisces Elizabeth Taylor will attest, are indeed a fish's best friend. Pearls of all sorts, including naturally shaped pink ones are often found round your neck.

For footwear, fish prefer to be barefoot. When not able to do this, they often wear sandals or shoes that allow their feet to breathe. You like to draw attention to your toes with nail polish and anklets. At home, you prefer soft, flowing gowns or men's soft shirts to play in. You buy a lot of your wardrobe at the bargain stores and don't give a hoot who knows. Pisces is happiest with the fences high, the curtains drawn, and the fish within you free to swim through the day in nothing but your skin.

Dawn of the Global Citizen

2007 World Predictions

by Leeda Alleyn Pacotti

Many of us have wondered why we were born into these times. Those of us who are a bit older lived through the plastic and bombastic 1950s, experienced the spotlight turbulence of the 1960s (from the first protest music in 1965 through the fall of Saigon in 1975), and endured the mind-deadening staging of an American presidency. With the younger set, we shared two pointless wars in the Middle East, a brilliant president with an extraordinary penchant for a cigar, and a prayer-besotted American leader.

Nothing made a lot of sense. The cold war and flare-ups charged economies. Politicians espousing hate and promoting a strained sense of national distinctiveness grabbed headlines. The arts scene wavered and floundered. Even the escapes of music and film grated with lyrics and images equivalent to social putrefaction.

Deep in our aging souls echoed a simple refrain from *Hair*, a musty souvenir of hope that refused to be forgotten: "This is the dawning of the Age of Aquarius!" Like birds chasing into sunrise, we, too, eagerly and hungrily have soared toward that new beginning.

Nevertheless, we astrologers, metaphysicians, and psychics are only as good as our own personal maturity and become confused or disillusioned by the natural order of disintegration.

Although the experience of disintegration can be aching, even traumatic, its conclusion, in a moment and a whisper, transforms into that beginning we have waited so long to relish. The ashes of the past stir and a phoenix rises.

Behold! The Global Citizen

Since early 2004, Uranus and Neptune have been in mutual reception, sharing each other's natural signs, with Uranus adding individualization to the usually retiring Pisces and Neptune endowing sensitivity to aloof Aquarius. Each had the opportunity to prove its effects through a variety of unusual circumstances.

In late 2004, the unprecedented earthquake and consequent tsunami that inundated Indonesia, Sri Lanka, and the eastern Indian coastline, brought out the very best in us all. Donations of money, food, and goods poured into the area. Military resources throughout the world, despite the enclaves of terrorist training camps throughout southeast Asia, symbolically transformed battle equipment into ploughshares of hospitals, recovery teams, and reclamation. Transfixed by televised scenes of surging destruction, we wept in unison with death wails from those who submerged and never resurfaced. Every child became our child. The tremendous losses of the grieving clutched us, and our hearts poured out far deeper motivations than mere sympathies or empathies. The bewildering fear of shivering animals caused us to look anew into the soulful eyes of our beloved pets. An awareness changed us.

And the awareness lasted. Through the category 5 hurricanes that thrashed the southern United States and the horrific earthquake in Pakistan, we no longer cared if these people were foes or unknowns. We saw unimaginable suffering, pain, and emotional paralysis in faces distinctly human. Despite what we saw, we knew we would let no one needlessly die. At last, we realized we were all in this together.

Other signs, too, showed a change was being wrought within the collective psyche. People were on the move, forcing national barriers in their determination to be and live in other places. With the commingling of lifestyles, we learned that the contagions of old and new illnesses could not be limited to regions or continents. Those with illness came to places of health. Those in abject poverty went to countries of wealth. All desiring the golden key of knowledge sought out colleges and universities, where they would be appreciated.

With Uranus and Neptune in close proximity at the middle of Pisces and Aquarius, respectively, we can expect them to seal the deal of the archetypal global citizen. Nations throughout the world, much like the European Union, will be forced to create accessible border passage for neighboring national residents. No longer will freedom of movement be reserved strictly for diplomats, military, and commercial executives—or those who can buy their way out. Individuals left without homes or families because of catastrophe, cataclysm, or contagion will find no resentment behind the faces on the welcome wagon.

The Loss of National Identity

A telling portent of the Uranus and Neptune mutual reception is the citizen without borders. We found these individuals amassing in population groups, based on ideology rather than territory, the most striking example of which is the terrorist.

Contrary to popular opinion, terrorism did not start with this new century. An outgrowth of the cold war psychology of the late 1950s, we encountered terrorism in the espionage thriller, *The Manchurian Candidate*. Domestically, we saw it in violence groups on college campuses during the 1960s and 1970s. Political terrorism was a problem in Germany during the 1970s, and in England and Ireland for several decades. As with Al Qaeda, religious facades fooled no one; nor did exhortations to return to some nonexistent blood purity.

Even though the participants in terrorism groups may not recognize the basis of their rebellions, objectively they are a process of change and have an aim no different from the spread of multinational corporations or the swells of illegal immigration or guest workers. The truth is the rising educational level throughout the world prevents intellectual people from having blind allegiance to a piece of land.

People are realizing that they want to be in proximity to their intellectual counterparts, whether they relocate or travel. Like camaraderie on the Internet, they freely connect together through thought and communication. Consequently, individuals form radically disparate groups, stretched like vacuous nebulae, all over the face of the planet.

As a hallmark of the Age of Aquarius, nothing tangible can stop an idea. Proponents of a belief, a religion, an ideology, a philosophy, or a discipline will not be deterred from seeking those of similar ilk. Borders, walls, or coasts will be transgressed, until nations understand that their foundations do not rest on land mass, but on political constructs that allow ideas to flourish. As nations expand or fall during this century, the successful ones will be those that can absorb and cultivate the diversity of the global citizen.

The Economic Impact

During 2007, economics worldwide will regroup after the stringency of the previous year. With Saturn in trine to the conjunction of Jupiter and Pluto, necessity and practicality take the front seat in spending. People throughout the world have felt economically bereft, but they realize expenditures must cover the requirements of life first.

Expect primary purchases to be replacements of vehicles and major appliances, for models that now have energy-saving features. A close second will be expenditures to refurbish existing housing. On the home front, a resurgence of self-reliance demands more adult-education courses in sewing, basic automotive maintenance, meal preparation, domestic economics, and part-time business ventures to realize income from former hobbies.

With shifting job prospects, decreasing wages, and bankruptcy bailouts by corporations, seminars in estate and retirement planning are beyond the reach of most individuals. Their limited incomes help them only tread water.

After August, the common-sense attitude of Saturn moves into a square with Jupiter and Pluto. Rebelling against the limits of

Saturn, the expansive character of Jupiter amplifies the excessive qualities of Pluto. Such excesses are a backlash against the unremitting feelings of dispiriting poverty experienced the last three years.

People still have little to spend but they exhibit outrageous tastes, such as garish prints in clothing or wild fruit colors to repaint cars. Behaviors go to extremes, with more food, drink, and drug indulgence. Although wage earners and professionals are no better off than before, the attitude is let the good times roll, no matter who gets hurt.

With no money to throw around to keep up with the Joneses, the old game of one-upmanship strikes a familiar chord of superiority. Holiday spenders will still overdo it, but the braggadocio comes from who hit the best sale or who spent the least money. All in all, trash and fads characterize the most sought-after holiday purchases.

Nations in Focus

Although this is a year favoring personal renewal through individual effort, several nations come to the fore in world events.

China

With an extremely diverse population, China's government of twenty-five years has progressed into Capricorn, the realm of international image. Persistently and doggedly, China will continue to carve its niche in world markets and politics throughout the next two decades. With a population in the billions, the national leadership will propose new educational programs, particularly those involving studies abroad. Married women are the obvious recipients of this boon and many have clamored for greater international presence. During the year, the leadership precariously tips between contraries. The population wants greater legislative reform to strengthen marital rights, whereas the government is drawn to recognition through the arts and recreational pursuits. Internationally, the nation is seen as fiscally stable. However, the domestic coffers have been reduced by military expenditures and expensive fossil fuel contracts. International debt and partnerships are in dubious positions, as foreign debtors delay or outright ignore payments. During the spring, the northwestern sector of China is in the path of a partial solar eclipse. Problems along the borders of Kyrgyzstan and Tajikistan may turn into local skirmishes, causing some regional directors in the western Chinese provinces to lose their positions. Although little has been said about the potential of a bird flu epidemic, China has been hiding the numbers of those stricken or dead.

European Union

Starting with twelve nations in western Europe, the EU now boasts twenty-five members, extending into Scandinavia, the old Soviet Eastern Bloc, the Balkans, and partially into the Middle East, if Turkey's candidacy is accepted. With a beginning to the end of the militant squabbling of France and Germany, the EU was born with a built-in terror network. If terror cells strike throughout the European community, the member populations may fell that they just have had enough. Since establishment in 1993, Europe's peoples have kept a wary eye on the EU's authority, especially the combined Eurocorps, which has primarily participated in peacekeeping missions. Nothing, though, speaks like money, and the introduction of the Euro, as a common exchange unit, bolstered the EU's standing. Nonetheless, this year may see tests of terrorism throughout the European Union from isolated, but dedicated, strategic groups, which chafe under the mantle of homogeneity. This year will be a financially cautious one for the Union, which balances well the demands for military development and a response to an unexpected illness throughout the population. Problems, however, arise among the troops, whose loyalties are stretched between home nations and the encompassing territory of the Union. Early in the year, a bombing may be attempted during a meeting of the Council rather than the Parliament. Such a strike might be slated during an adjournment of the Council.

Kyrgyzstan

About the size of South Dakota, Kyrgyzstan lies due south of prosperous Kazakhstan, sandwiched delicately between communist China and U.S.-sympathetic Uzbekistan. Agriculturally based, this tiny nation is still organizing itself after the disruption of the Soviet Union. Its diverse society undermines recognition of a national identity. Economically, the country is poor—a condition that will persist for another twenty years, with few prospects for proximate trade partners. Worse, the national astrology shows corruption throughout the legislative bodies, which understand the country lies in the transport route of narcotics from the Asia to Europe. Owing to the slow national organization and pervasive drug movement, opium farming has crept into the agricultural base. Despite their poverty, the Kyrgyz people are proud and patriotic; the possibility of border skirmishes with local Chinese may be necessary to draw the line on drug trafficking. This year, the national leadership attends to legislative matters, especially questions arising over land and business ownership. The health of the general population is at risk, from a foreign-borne illness or a military campaign. Mistakenly, women are falsely accused as being carriers or conspirators.

Russia

Like China, a portion of south central Russia lies in the eclipse path. Near this path are former Soviet republics, which are still organizing themselves into viable nations. This year, the Russian Federation experiences a checkup from a Saturn opposition and will review whether attempts to regain world-power status is the correct course of action. This question is a primary and hot discussion in the Russian press and among the Soviet people, who are particularly ready for legislative actions that secure the national identity. The President, who is aware of and willing to deal with these matters, shares the broad vision of a Russian legacy. However, his efforts are complicated by influences from the criminal underworld, which has contributed heavily and secretly in loans to national coffers. The deep soul of the Russian people is stirring. The President can succeed in strengthening the national identity and image, if he propounds cultural imperatives, built over the centuries, which the public sees as the nation's virtues. Financially, the Federation can stabilize its economy by offering consultation in military matters or opening colleges to instruct in strategic planning and campaigns. Both possibilities keep military executives in top mental form and introduce fresh tactics to combat communication disruptions and terror strikes. Mining natural resources, leased on a short-term basis to foreign interests, will also keep the nation afloat domestically. For at least the next fourteen years, Russia will be wiser to curtail foreign trade and develop a self-reliant network of internal domestic trade. This land giant has never fully explored or developed its vast resources for its own sake. As long as the President and legislature attempt to force the nation onto the world stage, the more Russia will be denied an elusive recognition from outside its borders. It is time to structure and fortify a stable domestic foundation.

Tajikistan

To the south of Kyrgyzstan, lies Tajikistan, which also shares borders with Uzbekistan to the west, China to the east, and Afghanistan to the south. Civil war disrupted the country during the 1990s, which delayed its economic development. Further, this mountainous country has less than 7 percent agricultural land with only 1 percent of the total land cultivated. Everything mechanical and technological must be imported, but Tajikistan is abjectly poor. Much of its 7.2 million population is spread throughout the western portion of the country, leaving the eastern lands open to contend with China—an ongoing negotiation. Given the dearth of stability, the Tajik people have severe hurdles to overcome. The natal astrology of this country indicates both the legislative bodies and the presidency have a high turnover. The primary reason Tajikistan remains independent is the fierce hopes of its people. This year, the efforts of the President and the legislature are opposed by the people, who are ready to seek international recognition, which they believe will help solve domestic ills. However, the national debt is extremely high and any further funding from foreign interests will have too many strings attached. The national health is also in jeopardy, with a carrier coming from a foreign country. The Tajiki are a sturdy, resilient people. Although they may not experience a killer epidemic, illness will be protracted. One saving economic feature for Tajikistan is an undisclosed corrective health discipline, which other countries would welcome through training or purchase.

United States

In this pre-election year, the United States' presidency experiences the astrological effects of a lunar eclipse in early March and, portentously, a solar eclipse on September 11. In March, the President will launch a surprising health care plan that alienates the American public. Although seemingly well-thought-out, the plan is riddled with holes and unsupportable. The President believes he is in touch with the national psyche, but his information is tainted by undisclosed private interests. The September 11 eclipse will shock the dignity of the President's Office, if not the man himself. If there is an attempt on the President's life, he will survive. More likely, the President will experience a surprise reversal from military leadership, which has legislative and public support. Less thoughtful citizens will regard another September 11 event superstitiously, as a retribution. The denouement of the Bush Presidency is an isolated head of government just sitting out the days. During 2007, expect the President to occupy himself with quiet comforts, recreation, and escape in general. Problems will continue domestically, especially with turbulence in collecting on international loans. The public, which finds its petitions heard by legislative representatives, is aggravated by surprising proposals and developments in land ownership, health care, and, of course, oil. Altogether, this is a better year for the strong voice, energies, and preferences of the American public than for rallying attempts by a flagging president.

Mundane Natalogy

People's Republic of China, December 4, 1982, 00:00:00 AWST, Beijing

European Union, November 1, 1993, 00:00:00 CET, Brussels, Belgium

Kyrgyz Republic, May 5, 1993, 00:00:00 USZ4S, Biskek

Russian Federation, December 24, 1983, 00:00:00 BGT, Moscow

Republic of Takijikstan, November 6, 1994, 00:00:00 USZ4, Dushanbe

United States of America, March 4, 1789, 12:13:12 am LMT, New York City

Twenty-first Century Careers

by Stephanie Clement

When we think of career fields, we tend to think in linear fashion. First we consider what I will call the "subject" involved. Where professions are concerned, we recognize doctor, lawyer, teacher, and many others. We remember nursery rhymes like "the butcher, the baker, the candlestick maker."

When it comes to the actual choice of jobs, the actual work we may choose to do, we take a different approach. Here we consider the breadth of possibilities within a career field. The modern baker, for example, has a person who keeps the shop clean, a person who mixes the dough, someone to knead it, someone to make sure the ovens are working properly at the right temperature, etc. There is also a bookkeeper and someone skilled in sales and advertising. There may even be a delivery system and its staff. No longer do we only have the baker in a crisp white apron, a lawyer in a crisp three-piece suit, or a doctor in a crisp white coat. We have a few or many team members working together in many different capacities.

We are often encouraged to choose a career field early in childhood, and certainly in high school and college. At such an early age, true life purpose may not be clear. Certainly we are subject to pressures from family, teachers, and even peers concerning career goals. These pressures contribute to career decisions that may not sustain our interest and satisfaction, although for some people early career decisions carry them throughout their lives.

While the career field is the broadest consideration, it may turn out not to be the most compelling consideration. There are at least four other considerations that could take the forefront:

Education—The expense and time involved in obtaining college and advanced degrees plays into career decisions in a big way.

Technology—Electronic, medical, and manufacturing technologies themselves may be more interesting to you than the career field in which they are applied.

What you really like to do—Statistics indicate that most people change careers several times, unlike many of our parents, who had the same job their entire lives. Why do they change? Because they are not satisfied, whether it be layoffs, the work, the associates, or the money that causes the dissatisfaction.

Industry stability—Will the job still be there in ten years?

If you are considering a first career or if you are looking for the quintessential "best" career when you make your next job switch, you may want to collect as much information as possible before making your decision. You need to know yourself and your desires, and there are plenty of personality and aptitude tests out there to help you gain that understanding. In this article, you will see how exploration of two rapidly expanding career fields can encompass every Sun sign, either in the career field, or in actual work tasks.

First, let's look at this list of career fields compiled by the U.S. government. I found this list a bit strange, as it excludes many of the career names I would have expected. I have sorted the careers by Sun sign. (Please note: While Libra seems to be under-represented in this list, there are plenty of careers on the list that utilize the skills of Librans, such as necessary arbitration, the beauty industry, interior design and decoration, judges and justices, and warfare!)

Broad Career Fields

Aries

Steel manufacturing; construction; motor vehicle and auto parts manufacturing

Taurus

Arts, entertainment, and recreation; Banking; Securities, commodities, and other investments

Gemini

Radio and television broadcasting; broadcasting; educational services; advertising and public relations services; printing; telecommunications; postal service; truck transportation and warehousing; (autos) motor vehicle and parts manufacturing

Cancer

Social assistance; food manufacturing; agriculture, forestry, and fishing; child day care services; hotels and other accommodations; food services and drinking places; grocery stores

Leo

Motion picture and video industries; mining utilities; arts, entertainment, and recreation

Virgo

Food manufacturing; food services and drinking places; grocery stores; apparel manufacturing; clothing, accessory, and general merchandise stores; employment services; health services; textile mills and products.

Libra

No broad career fields provided.

Scorpio

Computer systems design and related services; insurance pharmaceutical and medicine manufacturing; software publishers

Sagittarius
Educational services; air transportation; legal professions; publishing, except software; wholesale trade

Capricorn
Construction; federal government, except the postal service; state and local government, except education and health; mining; utilities

Aquarius
Management, scientific, and technical consulting services; aerospace product and parts manufacturing; automobile dealers, manufacturers, racers; computer and electronic product manufacturing; psychotherapy; social assistance, except child day care; radio and television broadcasting; motion picture and video industries

Pisces
Chemical manufacturing, except pharmaceuticals and medicine; oil and gas extraction

How To Make Career Choices

Out of the huge list of career possibilities, most of us need a way to narrow the field. Let's look at the job longevity question first. Which careers are expanding and expected to continue to expand? The following list will give you a sense of where the most opportunities are likely to be found. (www.employmentspot.com/features/fastestgrowing.htm, 10-15-05)

Computer and data processing—This field is currently experiencing the most rapid growth and change. In addition, the applications to nearly every industry are nearly infinite.

Health services—Every area of the health services industry is expanding, so the range of job possibilities covers everything from dishwasher to brain surgeon. The income range is just as broad.

Residential care for the elderly—The demand for staffing will increase as the baby boomer generation ages. Unfortunately, pay levels are likely to lag behind other industries. However, the need for trained administrative staff will continue to grow.

Legal assistants—Much of the work formerly done by attorneys is now done by assistants who need less education.

Temporary personnel—Many companies are using temporary personnel to bridge busy seasons and economic booms or slumps.

Social services—There is more demand for social services in our diverse modern world, and less capacity for families to provide the necessary services for themselves.

Museums, botanical and zoological gardens, and veterinary services—Here is a fun surprise! There is a demand for more museums and gardens. The industry is small, but steadily expanding, and there will be a wide range of job possibilities (probably not many at the top salary levels). The demand for veterinary services is growing quickly, with an expected 49 percent expansion. (I added veterinary services to this list; it was not in the original list, but fits here. I found the veterinary information at www.edinformatics.com/careers/fastest_growing.htm and other sites.)

Securities and commodities brokers—This field continues to expand as we enter a global marketplace.

Career Fields within Fields

To examine the multiplicity of opportunities in every field is beyond the scope of this article. I have chosen one example of the interweaving of two broad and flourishing career fields—health services and computer technology.

Health Services

The health services field is vast, and is expected to grow at every level. In the above list, we find at least four broad career fields that can be considered part of health services: psychotherapy, social assistance, health services (!), and pharmaceutical manufacturing. You can see that even the U.S. government is not consistent in describing career fields, so don't worry if you have career ideas that float around on these lists! The following table lists careers in this very broad field, along with the number of positions available and the expected growth. I have added the zodiacal signs that correspond to each category based on the actual work involved for each job.

Table 2. Employment of wage and salary workers in health services by occupation, 2002 and projected change, 2002-12 (Employment in thousands)

Zodiac Sign	Occupation	Jobs in 2002	Prjt. % Inc.
Aries	Optometrists	18	28.6
Aries	Physicians and surgeons	418	28.8
Aries	Emergency medical technicians and paramedics	115	38.6
Taurus	Dentists	87	8.5
Taurus	Management, business, and financial occupations	598	31.2
Gemini	Occupational therapists	58	42.3
Gemini	Physical therapists	117	38.3
Gemini	Respiratory therapists	80	35.1
Gemini	Medical records and health information technicians	123	51.9
Gemini	Medical transcriptionists	83	22.2
Gemini	Office and administrative support	2,251	15.9
Gemini	Billing and posting clerks and machine operators	170	13.7
Gemini	Interviewers, except eligibility and loan	83	27.4
Gemini	Secretaries and administrative assistants	616	13.3
Gemini	Office clerks, general	301	13.0
Cancer	Social workers	146	37.6
Cancer	Registered nurses	1,892	27.9
Cancer	Cooks and food preparation workers	235	8.2
Cancer	Building cleaning workers	367	23.9
Leo	General and operations managers	81	34.1
Leo	Administrative services managers	32	28.4
Leo	Medical and health services managers	171	34.2

Zodiac Sign	Occupation	Jobs in 2002	Prjt. % Inc.
Virgo	Management, business, and financial	598	31.2
Virgo	Social and human service assistants	81	63.7
Virgo	Pharmacists	60	21.1
Virgo	Physicians and surgeons	418	28.8
Virgo	Physician assistants	55	54.1
Virgo	Registered nurses	1,892	27.9
Virgo	Dental hygienists	144	43.5
Virgo	Health diagnosing and treating practitioner support technicians	216	20.9
Virgo	Licensed practical and licensed vocational nurses	577	19.0
Virgo	Service occupations	3,930	33.7
Virgo	Home health aides	407	54.5
Virgo	Nursing aides, orderlies, and attendants	1,163	25.2
Virgo	Occupational and physical therapist assistants and aides	103	46.5
Virgo	Dental assistants	256	43.4
Virgo	Medical assistants	330	63.2
Virgo	Cooks and food preparation workers	235	8.2
Virgo	Personal and home care aides	266	49.1
Virgo	Billing and posting clerks and machine operators	170	13.7
Virgo	Secretaries and administrative assistants	616	13.3
Virgo	Office clerks, general	301	13.0
Libra	Receptionists and information clerks	342	29.9
Scorpio	Dentists	87	8.5
Scorpio	Pharmacists	60	21.1
Scorpio	Physicians and surgeons	418	28.8

Zodiac Sign	Occupation	Jobs in 2002	Prjt. % Inc.
Scorpio	Clinical laboratory technology	250	20.7
Scorpio	Diagnostic related technology	254	25.3
Sagittarius	Clinical, counseling, and school psychologists	37	37.5
Sagittarius	Counselors	134	32.3
Sagittarius	Professional and related occupations	5,453	28.8
Capricorn	Management, business, and financial	598	31.2
Capricorn	Professional and related occupations	5,453	28.8
Capricorn	Chiropractors	19	39.5
Capricorn	Licensed practical and licensed vocational nurses	577	19.0
Aquarius	Clinical, counseling, and school psychologists	37	37.5
Aquarius	Counselors	134	32.3
Aquarius	Social workers	146	37.6
Aquarius	Chiropractors	19	39.5
Aquarius	Receptionists and information clerks	342	29.9
Pisces	Podiatrists	7	24.3
Pisces	Diagnostic related technology	254	25.3

In the first list, we found health service careers associated with Cancer, Virgo, Scorpio, and Pisces. In the second, expanded list, we found jobs for every single sign. I notice that Libra is still somewhat under-represented in the list, so I decided I should explore Libra occupations to see what might be closely (or loosely) associated with health services. Here is what I came up with:

Beauty—There is a growing demand for cosmetic surgery. This may relate to necessary procedures to correct damage from injury, to repairs damage from skin lesions of other kinds, or just to make you look better.

Bedrooms—There is a growing demand for special furniture in the home to accommodate a wide variety of physical needs of the elderly, the injured, and illness in general.

Contracts—Contracts are a Libra-ruled thing. There are medical contracts at various levels, such as the contract to build a hospital, employment contracts, and treatment agreements. Thus contract law has its place in health services.

Elimination of urine through the kidneys—This and other medical specialties (notably the ovaries, lumbar vertebrae, and veins) are related to Libra.

Florists—Many hospitals have a flower shop on the premises.

Litigation—This area of law is expanding in the health field each day.

Twenty-first Century Electronics and Technology

Electronics and technology are two broad career fields that have nearly limitless applications to the medical field. If you consider the medical field, you will inevitably come up against the electronic and technological facts of life. Consider hip-replacement surgery. You could be the surgeon, the surgical nurse, the recovery nurse, the anesthetist, the supply house where the new joint was obtained, the pharmacist who tracks the medications delivered to the patient, the candy striper or intern who delivers meals to the room, the nurse who changes dressings, the physical therapist, etc. This list is anything but exhaustive. Each of these individuals either directly utilizes electronic avenues or technology every day, or is affected by these functions within the medical arena. Each individual has to know a little something about both to do the best possible work.

Suppose that your passion is technology, and not medicine. You might work for a company that manufactures prosthetic devices, including replacement hips. You could have any job in that company, from landscape maintenance, to designer, to shipping clerk.

Suppose your personal passion is computers. You could be the designer of equipment for specific health applications. You could be a programmer, systems analyst, or technical support person for software applications that involve health services.

Suppose all three fields—medicine, technology, and electronics—trip your trigger. You might be the person who tracks all the human resources problems in the hospital, from on-the-job injuries, to payroll, to staffing needs. You might be assigned to investigate recurring physical problems in some area of the office or hospital, and to recommend changes to accommodate the actual demands of the human body in performing job tasks. So you need to understand the human body, know how your tracking and recording software works, develop working relationships with medical suppliers, and know who to ask about designing a special step stool for the nurse on the fourth floor who is too short to reach the top drawer of the filing cabinet. Will a standard library stool that rolls, and then locks down, work for this situation? If not, why not? And where can you buy such a stool?

To do this particular job well, you need a wide range if interests, but you may not need M.D. or Ph.D. educational credentials. You need to be a people-person (there's the Libra touch) to relate to the many levels of staff you see each day. And you probably want to know that your job will still be there next week, next year, and into the next decade.

A New Way to Look at Career

So where do you start when considering a career, or a career change? Let's start with the four items I listed near the beginning, and consider each of them. You may prioritize them differently.

Education—How far will your educational interest and checking account take you? Can you do two years of college and get started working, with the intention of going back later for more education? Can you get started right out of high school and take classes at a community college or online for a while?

Technology—No matter how inept you may feel, you need to consider this one carefully. Even if you only work in your own garden at home, you can benefit from technological advances in tools, electronically controlled sprinkler systems, online resources, etc.

What you really like to do—This is going to be at the top of the list for most readers, especially people who have been doing work that has lost its appeal. I met a lady whose primary consideration was being outdoors. She was attracted to a meter reader position for that reason. You can take some of those aptitude and personality tests to get an objective gauge of your talents and desires. Then you have to look at what initially attracts you to something new. Then you have to examine what sustains your interest.

Job longevity—Even if you change careers at age 55, you still want to know that the job will be there for ten years. The data provided in this article give you lots of information about which career fields are going the fastest. They are new, and many of them (such as elder care) are going to continue to expand for many years to come. Your public library and the Internet provide vast resources to help you figure out what fields are expanding or shrinking. While there may not be a huge demand for candlestick makers in today's market, people will always enjoy the flickering flame of beautiful candles. You just won't find thousands of positions available in this field.

My Favorite Possibilities by Sun Sign

Aries—eyeglass designer; demolitions expert

Taurus—owner of a store called "Comfort First," where there are no thorns on the roses, no sharp edges to furniture, and all the slippers slip on without the need to bend over.

Gemini—magician, especially sleight of hand tricks, but big tricks too; respiratory therapist

Cancer—specialty chef in a hotel or spa; inheritance lawyer

Leo—King or Queen of the world, or failing that, wedding planner for the rich and famous; team leader

Virgo—small animal veterinarian; policeman; computer technician

Libra—candy maker; diplomat

Scorpio—surgeon; vulcanologist

Sagittarius—college professor; travel agent, or better, world traveler

Capricorn—architect or designer of monuments; mathematician; vocational counselor

Aquarius—chiropractor; astrologer; pilot; furniture dealer

Pisces—abbot or abbess; wine maker; mystic; water meter reader

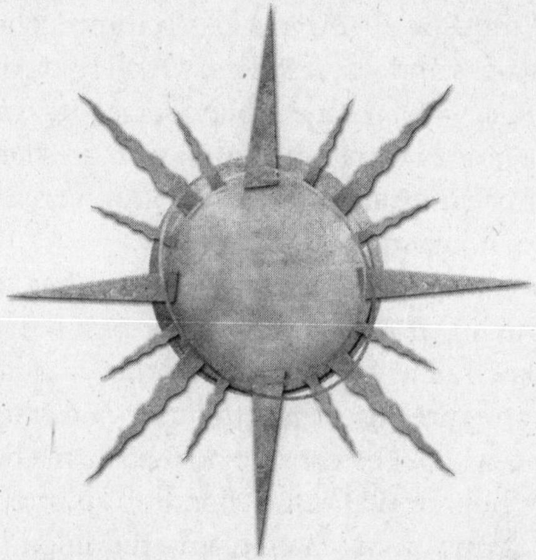

Holidays from Hell

by Sasha Fenton

We have all heard those stories about people whose vacations were ruined by bad weather, theft, or discovering that the dream destination resembles a construction site. Another problem can arise when we discover that our chosen traveling companion has very different ideas about how to spend a holiday. Let us take a brief look at the star signs and see how they like to relax—if that's the word for it.

Bear in mind that not everybody is typical of their star sign as other astrological influences can modify their behavior. Also, this is not a comprehensive list that shows how each sign gets on with the other eleven, it just shows those who might be able to accommodate each star sign type and those who cannot—and why this is so.

Traveling with the Fire Signs – Aries, Leo, Sagittarius

If your idea of holiday heaven is to find a nice beach, marinade yourself with suntan lotion, and emulate a steak lying on a barbeque, don't bother with a fire sign companion. The only way these people can tolerate a beach holiday is if you have a few children they can borrow. Then they direct their energies into gathering up your children—and most of the other kids on the beach—and forming teams for ball games and water sports, which they, of course, direct with all the delicacy of a parade ground sergeant. Another solution is to take lots of money with you, so that your fire sign friend can try out every sport or entertainment venue in the area to prevent the dreaded onset of boredom.

If you prefer your friend's company to his or her absence, be prepared to keep moving from one stimulating pastime to another until it is time to come home—then take another holiday on your own to recover! Of the three fire signs, the only one who can tolerate a little down time is Leo. Leo can sit and read a on a hotel balcony or by a field for an hour or two before standing up, stretching languorously, and wandering off in search of entertainment—and food.

Aries can happily accompany Gemini, Leo, Libra, and Aquarius on a heavy-duty shopping trip, but the stingy signs of Taurus, Cancer, Virgo, Capricorn, and Pisces would be horrified if forced to spend their vacation looking for ways to run up their credit card bill. Scorpio and Sagittarius can spend money with the best of them, but not necessarily in the same shops as an Aries.

One problem that Aries suffers is a lack of sufficient space, or more specifically, the paltry luggage allowance for those who fly. Apart from all the shopping that will need to be carried home, Aries take everything they might possibly need on holiday. I had one Aries friend who booked a holiday in a perfectly nice hotel in Greece and proceeded to pack a tent into his suitcase! My guess is that he was hoping to persuade some unfortunate female to accompany him on a tented trip to horizontal heaven.

All the fire signs love nightlife, but Leo spends more time (and money) on the tiles preparing for an evening than at the event itself. Gemini and Pisces can take their time in the bathroom too—but not while Leo is occupying it! If Aries, Virgo, Scorpio, or Sagittarius have to hang around while all this Leo pampering is going on, they will soon be pacing up and down, looking at their watches, jingling keys, and asking, "How much longer?" This won't get them anywhere at all. While we all know that Leo can't be rushed, this sign gets extremely restive while waiting for others. When traveling with Leo, one really needs to take a stopwatch along to ensure that everything is timed to perfection. The only sign who can cope with this is ruled by a planet that has yet to be discovered.

Sagittarius is a weird sign that is hard to quantify. Some have sunny, outgoing, adaptable natures while others are morose, mean, and penny-pinching—especially when it is you who wants to spend their pennies! If you force them to do something that you like, they will either sulk their way through the experience, or take off and only turn up again in time to go home. One certain way to steer a Sagittarian toward a divorce is to bring your entire family—complete with grandparents and a few distant cousins—along on vacation. Thus, it is a bad idea for Cancerians or Capricorns to travel with Sagittarians. The perfect companion might be an Aquarian, because this sign is as sporty and eccentric as the Sagittarians.

Don't forget that all fire signs expect a lot of sex as part of their vacation since they cannot really relax without it. Don't forget to pack all your sex toys, unless you are going to any country where your case might be searched and you and your lover could end up spending your holiday in the local prison!

Traveling with the Earth Signs – Taurus, Virgo, Capricorn

So you love nothing better than to wander along chatting happily with your loved one about everything you see, hear, and feel. Taurus and Capricorn like to relax, and that includes switching off their brains and their ears. Taurus is a surprisingly sociable sign, but these subjects need time in the morning for silent contemplation—for some, this requirement lasts until sunset. Then they dig out their surprisingly glitzy evening clothes and set off to chat with everyone in the place—apart from you, that is. Those who have an unreasonable desire for real conversation (Aries, Gemini, Cancer, Leo, Virgo, Libra, Scorpio, and Aquarius) should go on a different vacation—with someone else! Remember that Taurus loves comfort and lots of food, so Sagittarians, Aquarians, and Pisceans, whose idea of heaven is exploring the jungles of Borneo with a single change of underwear and some dried beef jerky in a backpack, need not apply.

Virgo will visit every ancient or historical site. Long before leaving home, they will have mugged up on the history of the area so, while visiting every place of boredom, they can happily correct the tour guide and edit those little booklets sold at the information booth. You, of course, will discreetly lose the booklets in the hotel trash bin before leaving. The best traveling companion is another Virgo, although Capricorn and Aquarius can just about cope. Other signs tend to see the larger picture, so they don't really care if the cathedral they are exploring was built in 1247 or 1249. Some signs try gritting their teeth and exclaiming, "Honestly darling, does it really matter!"

The value of having an Aquarian or another Virgo as a traveling companion is that it doubles the size of the medicine chest that these signs deem necessary for the smallest trip. Most other signs have the capacity to come down with an attack of convenient deafness—apart from Gemini, Libra, and Sagittarius, who plead a headache and miss out on the joys of the archeological site altogether. Once Virgo is safely out of sight, these signs leap out of bed and go out in search of fun!

Capricorn is an extremely productive sign, and therefore happiest when achieving something. Capricorns like trips that involve a course on cookery, painting, tennis, ballroom dancing, or creative writing. This means their partner also has to participate. Aquarians can stand learning on holiday because they were once assigned the same planetary ruler as Capricorn—i.e. Saturn, the old misery. Some Capricorns can enjoy a holiday for its own sake, but only when it offers the best possible service for the lowest possible price. Capricorn resents being asked to fork out for extras, so any vacation must be "all inclusive." If traveling with this sign, take plenty of your own money and be prepared to spend it.

The truth is that all the earth signs are reasonably easy company on holiday as long as there is plenty of good food and more than enough good alcohol on hand. A cruise ship is ideal because they will soon find people to do business with and there is enough going on to keep all the other signs happy. Aside from those who get seasick, of course.

Traveling with the Air Signs – Gemini, Libra, and Aquarius

Air signs love to be on the move. Gemini and Libra in particular can be found moving slowly and gracefully between the shops and the quaint local market, the poolside bar and the casino, and the nightclub and the cocktail terrace. These signs will not even wait to unpack before they rush out to that cute little hotel shop to buy new bathing thongs, sun hats, and the dearest little raffia bag to put them in. Of course, they have at least three of each item with them, but they discover within minutes of arrival that their own stuff is "soooo last season!" Once they are suitably equipped, they cover themselves in "Monsieur Moneybags Mango and Beautiful Breadfruit Suntan Crème" and, utterly vanquished by all that shopping, pass out by the poolside for the next three weeks.

Aries and Aquarius can just about cope with the shopping part of this vacation, but the poolside slumber will bore them silly. The worst traveling companion for these two is Scorpio. It isn't that Scorpio can't shop. This sign can do anything in excess, including shopping, but can't take an interest in someone else's shopping. If you want to explore the area, it is best to find a traveling companion who will actually leave the hotel complex from time to time.

Aquarians are very easy traveling companions and they can fit in to just about any situation as long as the accommodations are right for them. They like the idea of a slow boat trip down a river, driving around in an RV or trailer (campervan or caravan for Brits), or pitching a tent in a mountainous area. However, after having fun roughing it or exploring the waterways, they like to return to their five-star hotels. Only there will they find a bed that is long/wide/soft/firm enough for them. The food will be laid out in a lovely buffet or served from a suitably large a la carte menu. All Aquarians (even nondrinkers) know fine wine when they smell it, and that is the only kind they can tolerate on their dining table. They also will not have to encounter spiders (Aquarians loathe spiders), mosquitos, snakes, butterflies, birds, or any other form of wildlife.

Almost anyone can travel with an Aquarian as long as they observe a few simple rules. Aquarians are not good in the mornings, so leave them alone. They like to wander off and talk to other people, so don't expect constant companionship. They enjoy flirting with other merrymakers and they resent this activity being interrupted, so leave them alone when thus engaged. Aquarians are dignified folk who cannot tolerate partners who drink themselves silly and gyrate on the dance floor all night. If you want to go out and have a good time, leave them alone. Having said all this, Aquarians don't like their own company. They are possessive, so they take it badly if their traveling partner chats too much with others—or flirts. They can't cope with children, not even their own (especially not their own). Fortunately, all Aquarians are easy to feed, as their laid-back nature ensures that they love all foodstuffs. Apart, that is, from vegetables, herbs, anything that lived and had to be killed, anything "foreign" or anything hidden under a dollop of sauce. In short, Aquarians are the perfect traveling companion for anyone—as long as the other party is a Libra with a hearing problem.

Traveling with the Water Signs – Cancer, Scorpio, Pisces

The water signs are the true travelers of the zodiac and just the slightest glimpse of a suitcase lurking at the back of their closet sends them searching for a travel agency. These signs especially love the summer sun, but they are equally happy on the ski slopes, in cities, in the desert, up mountains, in the countryside, and, of course, on water. Water signs will try any water sport and even the non-sporty ones love to paddle along the edge of the sea.

My late first husband was a Scorpio and he couldn't resist going up, down, in, through, over, and under anything while on vacation—and not necessarily water-bound places. I learned to overcome my fear of heights, depths, enclosed and open places, and sheer cliff edges during that marriage. I thought life with my second husband would be easier, but I forgot to take into account his Scorpio rising sign. He recently encouraged me to celebrate my sixty-second birthday by walking along a high wire slung between two treetops with nothing but a thin wire handrail to hold onto! There must be something strange lurking in my karma!

Scorpio is a fixed sign, which means that they fixate on one thing to the exclusion of much else. I have a friend who spends all her spare time looking around churches and ashrams in search of the perfect guru. Scorpio is fully aware that life is short, so it doesn't like to waste a moment of it, especially when you want to do something quite unreasonable, such as take a shower or sleep. Like the tides that rule the sign, Scorpio is always in motion!

Cancer and Pisces are far more reasonable. They are both supreme bargain hunters and absolute magicians at finding accommodations free of charge. These signs are intuitive, sympathetic, and good listeners (Cancer especially), which makes them wonderful company. This brings them many friends with whom they keep in touch on a regular basis, thus ensuring an endless supply of places to stay. The urge to travel comes over them whenever the tide goes out. The cell phone was made for them because they are never home long enough to warrant the expense of renting a land line.

The sign of Cancer is said to rule the home and to be supremely attached to domestic life and family, but what Cancer needs is a home base—somewhere with a washing machine and a place to pick up the mail. Like any Crab, this sign feels safe when on the move. Cancerians like to take a family member along for company—as long as the relative is suitably appreciative and able to pay their own way! Any sign of the zodiac can vacation with Cancer as long as it is a relative!

Pisceans are extremely convivial. Teetotaling Pisceans do exist, but they are rare fish. Most Pisceans love to make new friends, especially if they can share a trip, a meal, or a drink with them. Pisces is said to be a flexible sign but will only bend so far. While some are bossy and argumentative, others are sarcastic and opinionated; most can be calmed by liberal doses of local booze. The drinking type of Pisces is best teamed with Aries or Gemini, the only other signs that actually enjoy slugging down strange things like Curaçao, Crème de Menthe, Grappa or Chinese sorghum wine—sometimes all in the same glass. The nonalcoholic Pisces is surprisingly happy to travel with Leo.

Leo will take care of the travel bookings, packing, insurance, shots, and first-aid pack. He will ensure that Pisces bring their drug and spectacle prescriptions along to replace anything that might get lost. Leo, of course, will speak enough Gujarati, Burmese, Serbo-Croatian, and Swahili to get Pisces out of his inevitable scrapes.

By the way, did you know that the word for Lion in Swahili is Simba? What do you think my Sun sign is?

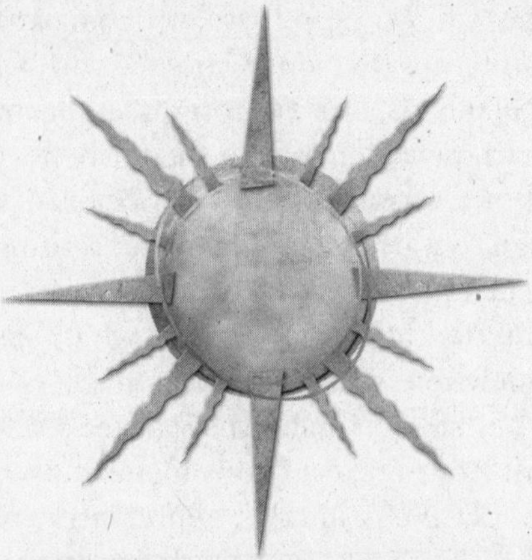

History Repeats
Cycles Get Recycled

by Carole Schwalm

Experts on avian flu do not know what the next pandemic crisis will be. We do know that they occur in thirty-year cycles. One is due. Another one will follow. Millions may die. But then again, they may not. We could create a vaccine. Perhaps we can't or won't produce enough. Possibly there won't be answers in 2035 when the next one comes, and it will. The one sure thing here is the cycle.

Astrologers and those interested in the science know all about cycles because astrology is a study of the cyclic motion of the Sun, Moon, and planets. Since "what goes around, comes around," we are fated to continue repeating events, whether in our personal life or as a member of the planet's population, unless we learn from our mistakes. The cosmos is orderly whether we are or not. Here are a few cycles to ponder.

The Super Flu: "The Micro-killer"

Lest we forget, this isn't the only avian influenza hosted by birds. In 1918, the avian virus known as the Spanish Flu killed up to

50 million people. The seed potential, like that in astrological chart, is latent until stirred to life. How? Perhaps through global warming? Possibly migratory birds, which orient themselves to the Sun, stars, and magnetic fields become upset by the eleven-year sunspot cycle? Maybe, as director Alfred Hitchcock said of his movie, *The Birds*, "We've mistreated animals so much, all that is left is rebellion." The birds have joined the killer bees and created a different spin on "the birds and the bees."

During the Spanish Flu outbreak in 1918, both Saturn and Neptune were in Leo. There was a serious need to create drugs and vaccines to stop what was a world threat. Saturn transited the same degrees in November 2005, when people addressed the need to create drugs and vaccines to stop what could be a world threat.

The United Nations celebrated its sixtieth birthday in 2005. According to U.N. Millennium Developmental Goals, there should be a maintenance of "the highest attainable standard of health" worldwide. Treatment must be made available for the future flu experts knew was coming. At a health conference in New York in November 2005, experts admitted the preplanning was late in coming. Drug companies, said one medical expert when interviewed by Charlie Rose, weren't encouraged because there was no money in this type of research, possibly the reason we are faced with repeating not only the cycle, but the past history. As usual, it is the poor who suffer the most because they can't afford the treatment. Unless the highest standard of health might also include a national health plan in the United States, the people without the medicines and treatment they need spread the disease.

The Bubonic Plague, "a ravaging of mice," didn't disappear either. There are still cycles of flare-ups. The plague exists because fleas found on rats, prairie dogs, chipmunks, and squirrels continue to carry it. We get it when we come in contact with them. The plague wiped out populations in Ethiopia, Egypt, Libya, and Syria in 420 BC and again in the first century AD people suffered during the Black Death. A pandemic plague killed more than 12 million people in China in 1855. If there is order in the cosmos through cycles, there is one here too.

The Monkey Trial

Teaching the Birds & Bees

In current history, the topic of teaching evolution resurfaced. The most famous historically relevant event was a court case in 1925: *The State of Tennessee v. John Thomas Scopes*, in Dayton, Tennessee.

The suit tested a 1925 Tennessee law, The Butler Act, that forbade any state-funded educational establishment in [Tennessee] to teach "any theory that denies the story of the Divine Creation of man as taught in the [Bible], and to teach instead that man has descended from a lower order of animals." John Thomas Scopes taught evolution in his science class.

The ACLU asserted that it was a violation of the constitutional theory of separation of Church and State. People listening to their radios heard Clarence Darrow, an agnostic, on the defense team vs. William Jennings Bryan, a Christian fundamentalist candidate for the Democratic Party, who argued for the prosecution.

During the Scopes trial, Saturn was in Scorpio in the same degree Jupiter transited in November 2005, when people talked again of evolution. Saturn tried to limit teaching to Divine Creation. Perhaps Jupiter, secure in faith, would have no problem teaching other ways of thinking? If we take the cosmic lesson to heart that is. Otherwise, it shall resurface.

Roe v. Wade

"*Supreme Court of the United States: Jane Roe, et al. v. Henry Wade, District Attorney of Dallas County; Texas laws criminalizing abortion violated women's Fourteenth Amendment right to choose whether to continue a pregnancy.*"

—Supreme Court Chief Justice Warren Burger

Vacancies in the Supreme Court via death and retirement resulted in two nominations in 2005. One key question was how the potential justice felt about Roe v. Wade opinion. Might he or she vote to overturn it? To the pro-life camp, the right answer was yes. To the pro-choice camp, the right answer was no.

Roe v. Wade was initially argued December 13, 1971. The decision came down January 22, 1973. This was considered a landmark case about abortion laws violating the U. S. Constitution and a person's right to privacy and the rights guaranteed to pregnant women by the First, Fourth, Fifth, Ninth, and Fourteenth Amendments.

The Fourteenth Amendment, passed in 1868, did not include the unborn and the question arose about when life begins. The Court said they "need not resolve the difficult question of when life begins." The Court noted that if medicine, philosophy, and theology "are unable to arrive at any consensus, the (judiciary), at this point in the development of man's knowledge, is not in a position to speculate the answer."

In the 1970s the U.S. Congress passed the Hyde Amendment, barring federal funding for abortion. The Supreme Court has heard cases from the mid-1970s through the 1980s. President Ronald Reagan, like President George W. Bush, hoped for legislative restrictions on abortion, and that was a prerequisite for judicial appointments. Late Chief Justice William Rehnquist did not want to overrule "Roe." Retiring Justice Sandra Day O'Connor pointedly refused to reconsider "Roe." Recent votes have been running 5-4, so new appointees' opinions are critical. The Reagan-Bush (George H. W. Bush) appointees reaffirmed that the Constitution protects a right of abortion. Until this became a question regarding appointment, justices were just, even if their appointers expected something else.

In 2005 when questions arose, Neptune—the planet of denial and doubt—transited the same degree occupied by Jupiter (appointed judges) during *Roe v. Wade*. The vexing questions: Should we overturn it? How do we get the power needed to do that?

Uranus was in Libra during *Roe v. Wade*, symbolic of changing the laws to overcome restrictions. The planet is indicative of someone (a president) knowing someone so well (Court justices) they think can predict or influence the answer. South Node is a placement where others might be false and deceptive or disagree—and also reaping what we sow.

The idea of "justice for all" means the people's right to justice. There must be accountability and monitoring to ensure laws are implemented. In the U.S. Supreme Court, the highest court, appointees shouldn't vote the way the appointer expects them to.

Flood-Gates: White House Scandals

The Teapot Dome

"When I grow up, I want to be an honest lawyer so things like that can't happen."

—Richard Nixon, as a boy, on the Teapot Dome scandal

The Teapot Dome incident began in 1921 in the administration of President Warren G. Harding, a Republican. The scandal involved oil and the leasing of secret contracts without competitive bidding, with money being paid under the table to Secretary of the Interior Albert B. Fall, and others. News leaked, but people didn't really pay that much attention.

The Senate however, started investigating. Mr. Fall was fined and sentenced to prison, but acquitted on legal technicalities. One accused, Harry F. Sinclair, was imprisoned for contempt of the Senate and attempted jury tampering.

Both Jupiter and Saturn were in Libra during Teapot Dome. Jupiter is the planet of ethics and justice. Saturn is the planet in charge of guilt and the need to carry out the law. Neptune in Leo covered the untruths of people, companies, and corporations dealing with oil. Saturn dealt with guilt and the need to carry out the law.

Similar degrees of Libra were active in 2005, when members of the Bush-Cheney team were under question. And it seems like the question of "oil" was in there somewhere? In 2005, the South Node held the Libra degrees in the sign of justices' scales: the South Node symbolizes affairs that go wrong, as well as dishonorable acts, disgrace, and ruin.

The Watergate Affair

Corruption in the government, according to a United Nations report, is a "breakdown of the rule of law and order."

"Well, when the president does it, that means it is not illegal," said Richard M. Nixon on his interpretation of executive privilege during an interview with David Frost on May 20, 1977. In July 1972, agents of Nixon's reelection committee were arrested in Democratic party headquarters, in the Watergate apartment building in Washington, D.C. Subsequently presidential advisor John Dean revealed that Nixon's Attorney General John Mitchell had known about the burglary: There were tapes.

Special prosecutor Archibald Cox uncovered widespread evidence of political espionage by the Nixon reelection committee, illegal wiretapping, and corporate contributions to the Republican Party in return for political favors. As things progressed, there were indictments and convictions of several high-ranking administration officials, including Mitchell and Dean.

Most political scandals involve cover-ups. Judicially they amount to formal criminal charges of obstruction of justice or perjury. Often the latter crime is more serious than the initial act. In July 1974, the House Judiciary Committee adopted three articles of impeachment against Nixon, the first for obstruction of justice. On August 9, 1974, Nixon became the first U.S. president to resign.

Impeachment doesn't mean removal from office. It is an indictment at the executive level, or a first step toward removal via legislative vote. The causes for same are: treason, bribery, or "other high crimes and misdemeanors." There are two steps. The U.S. House of Representatives has to pass "articles of impeachment" by a simple majority. Upon passage, the defendant has been "impeached." Second, the U.S. Senate conducts a trial. The chief justice of the U.S. Supreme Court or the vice president of the United States presides. However, the vice president can also be impeached.

The Senate can vote to punish the executive by removing him or her from office and prevent them from holding future office. There might not be a punishment, but the impeached is liable to criminal prosecution, even after leaving office, sans pension. The articles of impeachment have been brought forward sixty-two times since 1789. Only sixteen federal officers have been punished.

Libra between 12 and 19 degrees was active in 2005. This is where the South Node resided. South Node symbolizes affairs that go wrong. It represents dishonorable acts, disgrace, and ruin. Libra, the sign of justice, was at the same degree Uranus—the planet of strange, constant turmoil and secret treachery, among other things—was during Watergate. Déjà vu all over again? Or not?

Corruption

"Corruption weakens the financial system while strengthening the underground economy," according to a United Nations report, especially addressing Enron in 2001. The victims, like those in the health care issue, are the poor who lose the basic necessities of life a government could provide instead of lowering the taxes of those who can afford it, or providing favors for campaign contributions that increase corporate purses.

This seems like an apropos topic to address with Jupiter in Sagittarius in 2007. Sagittarius is a symbol of a desire for direct results, not just repeating the same mistakes. However, should the universe want, we can repeat the positive advances! Jupiter in Sagittarius has a keen interest the highest advances for the public. It may be the time, after Scorpio when the power of the few could go awry, for the people to say, "Change!" That is something that falls into the category of cycles too. What goes down, goes up and vice versa.

References

Avian Flu Cycles. November 1, 2005: *The Charlie Rose Show* PBS-TV: Interview with Anthony Fauci, Director, National Institute of Allergy & Infectious Diseases; Irwin Redlener, Director, National Center for Disaster Preparedness; Nils Daulaire, President, Global Health Council; Jeffery Taubenberger, Chief Molecular Pathlogy Department Armed Forces Institute of Pathology.

Diagnostic Tools and Structures for Detecting Suspicious Outbreaks of Infectious Diseases: Submitted by Germany – Meeting of Experts. Geneva, 19-30 July 2004.

Subcommission resolution, 2003/2. Corruption and its impact on the full enjoyment of human rights,in particular, economic, social and cultural rights.

United Nations. Economic, Social and Cultural Rights: Report of the Special Rapporteur, Paul Hunt (12/2003).

Wikipedia. The Concise Columbia Encyclopedia.

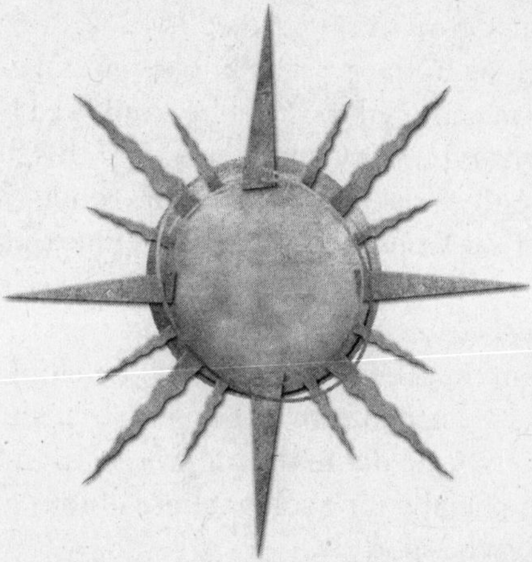

2007 Financial Forecasts
Your Astrological Nest Egg

by Dorothy Kovach

"I will show portents in the sky and on earth,
blood and fire and columns of smoke;
the Sun shall be turned into darkness
and the Moon into blood
before the great and terrible day of the Lord comes."
—Joel 2: 30–31 (Old Testament)

There are few things more awe inspiring than to witness day turn into night, and the stars come twinkling out, at noon. Before eclipses became synonymous with exotic vacation destinations, eclipses could be counted on to send a chill down the spine of our forefathers because, all too often, death and destruction arrived at their heels. While our modern electronic distractions practically prevent us from noticing, great oceanic and geological disturbances still go hand in hand with eclipses. It is no coincidence that an eclipse usually precedes massive earthquakes.

Unlike now, this connection was not lost on our ancestors.

The ancient Chinese saw the eclipse as a fiery dragon who searched the globe in his quest to kill his mortal enemy, the Sun. Once the dragon captured the Sun, he swallowed him whole. The tradition of lighting firecrackers stems from this heavenly battle, and they make the noise to scare the dragon back into heaven. The concept of the celestial dragon is not limited to the Chinese. The British have King George. Eclipses can be especially hard on kings and rulers because the Sun represents rulers everywhere—an eclipse can mean that their star may fall. Therefore, from the dawn of man, they have been known to bring more than a shiver or two to those on high. One ancient king was so frightened when he witnessed an especially long solar eclipse of four minutes that he dropped dead on the spot!

So just what is an eclipse, anyway? Simply put, an eclipse is a darkening of the light. The Sun and the Moon light up our world. Eclipses are shadows that blot out that light. Technically speaking, when the Sun is eclipsed, the Moon has moved into a position where it creates a shadow on the earth that gets in the way of our ability to see the Sun. Solar eclipses can be quite dramatic— they can blot out the Sun entirely at high noon!

Since eclipses are shadows, they can help those who want to get ahead financially because they can clearly pinpoint which sectors are likely to see pitfalls in the coming year. If we want to make money and stay ahead of the competition, we will want to know where the eclipses are and what they represent because, simply put, eclipses represent a reversal of trend. Remember, the trend is always our friend. And with that in mind, we want to stay abreast of shifts in taste and consumption. Being prepared makes the difference between running cheek and jowl with the pack or coming out in front. Those who know where the eclipses are have a leg up on the competition because they know what's going to be hot, and what is not.

Major Influences for 2007

The eclipses have two sides, the Dragon's Head and the Dragon's Tail. The Dragon's Head is lucky. To make money, we might consider investing in sectors symbolized by the sign of the Dragon's

Head. This year, the dragon will have his head in Pisces. With an aging population, drugs will continue to be a hot item, but with the Dragon's Head placed with Uranus, we may witness some remarkable new drugs bring hope where there once was none. Discovery is the key word of the day. Watch for companies working with stem cells to reap the rewards. We may even be on the verge of promising new treatments for cancer. This could spell a boom time for the more experimental in the pharmaceutical industry.

On the other hand, while drugs stocks remain hot, oil prices remain high. Since supply and demand run the market, environmental laws might be overlooked or bypassed to make way for new refineries, which will be built to meet an increased demand for gas. In a free economy, high prices at the pump are the mother of invention. Those with valid methods of extending the life of this valuable commodity open doors to distributing deals for alternate gas products like biodiesel while demand for hybrids will continue to rise. Since corn is a component in ethanol, we can look for corn to find new markets—not just in our stomachs. Hydrogen fuel cells could see new and important innovations that could help wean drivers off of crude oil. New methods of energy production and distribution will increase. While it is no surprise that it is nice to own oil stocks, there may be some surprises coming from the oil companies. For years, there have been rumors that the Earth's oil supply—with no new discoveries since 1981—has peaked. Perhaps this will be addressed now. Look to those suppliers of drilling equipment and oil maintenance companies to do well in the year ahead.

Pisces is one of the more dependent signs and because of this connection, the Dragon's Head here will increase the debt level. Bonds are promises made to pay for debt. With interest rates rising, this may change. Lenders may become disenchanted, so foreclosures on homes, autos, and other major investments may be on the rise, too. However, there are still bargains out there for those who have cash.

Remember in 2007, if it sounds too good to be true, it probably is. When the Dragon's Head is in Pisces, fraud is on the rise. Get-rich-quick" schemes abound. Avoid living beyond your means. With energy costs at record levels, nuclear power doesn't look half bad. This means uranium is a hot commodity. Wise traders will watch the suppliers and all in nuclear industry.

Look for the big screen to take on more viewers, but video games will continue to lead the entertainment market. Hard times call for stiff remedies. Look for alcoholic beverages to continue to do well. It's not only Big Brother who is watching you, everybody is. Camera cell phones will continue to be all the rage, and will probably come down in price. It's a digital world, and the eye in the sky is on you. Look for increased business to all security companies who are known for their sleuthing abilities.

As we have seen, the Dragon's Head will bring growth and boom times. On the other hand, those sectors symbolized by the sign that the Dragon's Tail is in will take on a stench like a fish left in the hot Sun. This year the Dragon's Tail will be in Virgo. This is a double whammy because the planet that rules bear markets everywhere, Saturn, will also be in Virgo. This does not bode well for Virgo-ruled places like car-dependent California, which must adjust to much higher fuel prices, not to mention, live on shaky ground.

High energy prices are a bad sign for the market as a whole because Virgo represents all things small. We may witness stagnation in the smaller corporations, which will stunt the market as a whole. It can't be denied that as interest rates rise, there is less venture capital available for start-up companies, which of course, comprise the cap indexes. As savvy traders know, when the small corporations suffer, the entire market often stagnates. Mergers and acquisitions are on the rise. Get ready to watch as good companies get snapped up by the big boys.

Some kind of trouble may be brewing in the managed health care system. The cost of health care has reached crisis levels. With an aging population, the government may not be able to look the other way as the cost of care goes off the Richter scale. Even with a huge captive audience of baby boomers driving demand, the health industry is ripe for some kind of problem. Look for investigations and probes into some of the more flagrant of its practitioners and administrators of HMOs. With longer hours, more patients and less pay, tired and overworked health care personnel are close to burnout. We will probably be seeing more strikes in the health care industry as workers reach near exhaustion in a system not designed to meet the needs of the ailing, but instead to meet the needs of shareholders. Something is bound to give in this area.

The combination of an aging population and a decreasing ozone layer are problematic for the skin. With the Dragon's Tail in Virgo, we may be realize that injecting noxious poisons to reduce wrinkles perhaps was not the most intelligent idea after all.

The Dragon's Tail in Virgo is hard on little guys. With so much of their hard-earned money going toward expenses, it is frustrating to be a worker right now. Perched at the brink, the housing boom has turned housing bubble. The clock ticks on an industry that has seen property change hands with fewer secured finances than in any time since the late 1920s. Easy times may be coming to an end for construction workers and craftsmen in general as home improvement does not necessarily increase the value of homes that are already overpriced. The housing industry will have more trouble this because there is less disposable money to go around. This discretionary income—usually spent on new computers, gadgets, and other techie toys, unfortunately—will be spent at the fuel pump. With this, business will be sluggish and will not be upgrading as readily.

Fewer goods are made in this country while we buy more abroad, which creates deficits and decreases the buying power of our dollar. We may even see gas rationing in the months ahead. And with copper on the rise, you will be more willing to hang on to your pennies than ever before.

Aries

With your disposable income pretty much disposed of, you might be feeling a bit sluggish financially. When it comes to business, it is important in 2007 to not forget that the devil is in the details. You will need to develop a systematic approach to financial security. That means giving up those impulsive splurges. Now is the time to stop pouring your fiscal future down the drain. Look at the big picture. Where do you want to be in five years, fiscally? To get there, you will need to be brave.

Taurus

Regular as a clock, you have never been one to beat to the tune of a different drummer—until now. As some of your best friends can tell you, getting ahead requires some risk. Just remember, there is a difference between need and desire, and this year you will be forced to choose. Remember, if wishes were horses, then fools would indeed ride. With real estate at gambling levels, don't invest if you cannot afford to lose. A fool and his money are soon parted, so read the fine print. And you already know, neither a borrower nor a lender be.

Gemini

Change is in the air. While movement is always fun, it's not quite as much when it is in your own backyard. Real estate investments could come back to haunt you. For most folks, the home is their biggest investment. Make certain yours is built on a rock-solid foundation. Let go of any unrealistic notions you might still have about money. As P. T. Barnum observed, "a sucker is born every minute"—so make sure you are not one of them. Research all possibilities before investing. This is not the time to network. Keep your own confidence or risk your financial future.

Cancer

Spending your wad because of some misdirected need for security will only make for guilt, not comfort. You need to get more than just your fiscal house in order. If there ever was a year to squirrel away something for a rainy day, this is it! Smart Crabs know that having a secure foundation is the means to succeed. Get your fiscal house in order. Remember, you can't have it all. With energy prices going through the roof, you may watch your future go up in smoke. A penny saved, is indeed a penny earned. Since the United States has a Sun sign of Cancer, this message is really for all of us.

Leo

Are you laughing on the outside but crying inside? Even the youngest of Leo cubs may feel much more weary than usual. The events of the past year have given that mane of yours more than a gray hair or two. You have seen more than your fair share of reality anyway. It would be nice to say that finances were going to pick up, but they are not. You will be working double and triple time to make the same you used to make while all the applause goes elsewhere. Just remember, all that glitters is not gold.

Virgo

If it sounds too good to be true, then it probably is not even close to what it is cracked up to be. Do your financial homework before signing on the dotted line. Make certain that medical health coverage is up to date. Keep your plans close to your vest, and your wallet even closer. Partnerships will be especially tricky in the year ahead. Developing a healthy skepticism is probably warranted now. Face it, you just can't take anybody's word for anything. Check all your facts in a year where agreements are not worth the paper they are written on. In extreme cases, you may be better off going it alone.

Libra

Reality counts. Get the facts before investing. Snake charmers, smooth talkers, and con artists abound. Deals could sound a whole lot better on paper than they really are. Keep those feet planted on terra firma. Arm yourself with all the facts before signing pacts. It is not credit card debt that forces folks into bankruptcy, but medical bills. Health is truly wealth, so take care of yours. Make certain you have ample coverage so you are prepared for the unexpected.

Scorpio

Nobody has to tell you that things are never what they seem. Your instincts can turn to cash when you use them to dig just a bit deeper beneath the surface. With the Dragon's Tail in the 11th House, rewards come to Scorpions who have mastered the art of detachment. While you may not get what you want, you will certainly get what you need—And then some! Remember to seek creative solutions in everything except your financial future. Risk has its rewards, but solid financial futures are built on disciplined choices.

Sagittarius

Have you ever heard that power corrupts? Well in your case, the keys to the kingdom are yours, but there is just one hitch—you will have to be able to keep that pretty mouth of yours zipped up tighter than a nuclear submarine if you are to reap the considerable benefits of Jupiter and Pluto sojourning together. There will be intrigue galore, but how you handle it will spell the difference between you coming out of this year on top of the financial ladder or on the bottom rung of a hellhole to nowhere.

Capricorn

As you stand at the precipice of power, the power that you have dreamed of after years of clawing your way to the top, you realize that all the sacrifice is just about to finally pay off. Yet, oddly enough, all you want to do is crawl in bed in a fetal position. Don't be so addicted to "stuff" for stuff's sake. Rein in unnecessary debts as soon as possible. Emotional spending can hide a serious inferiority complex. Heed your intuition, but remember, there is but a fine line between your inner voice and psychosis. Bottom line: live within your means.

Aquarius

While you are much more evolved than most of the other humanoids out there, you are still down here on earth. And that means you will have to live by the law of supply and demand. Supply does not increase by good intentions alone. Along with those abundant meditations, you will also have to come down off that cloud and rub noses with the competition this year. You may be free as a bird on the inside, but the landlord still wants his rent. Don't be led astray in the coming year. You will have to rely on your own initiative if you want to remain viable in 2007.

Pisces

Now that you have developed all those positive skills and educated yourself, you are full of great ideas and ambitious schemes. With Jupiter and Pluto in your solar tenth, the whole world really is your oyster. There is one hitch, you can't really rely on anybody right now, and there are plenty of pretty unscrupulous types hanging around ready to spend your hard-earned dough. Read all the fine print in anything presented for your signature. Trust only yourself. If you don't want your life to take on the drama of Madame Butterfly, swim upward.

Saturn Sun Shades
Temper That Temper
by Dorothy Oja

If you are fortunate enough to have a strong Sun/Saturn aspect in your birth chart, life will serve to temper you. It will temper your will as well as your ego; it will toughen you for the game of life. At first, you may not think this is fortunate. As a matter of fact, in the early stages of experiencing Saturn shading your light, the Sun, you may be quite resentful. You're likely to go through various stages of unhappiness until you realize that the restriction you are fighting against can actually be a way to shape and train you to move in the direction of your own mastery. This attitude would be taking the high road, yet it is not so easily attainable. Saturn aspects promise rewards from restraint, discipline, and right action.

Some stages associated with a strong Sun/Saturn aspect are the following: you may judge yourself critically or you may feel others are similarly judgmental. Worse yet, you sit excessively in judgment of those very others! The tendency with this aspect is to find what is wrong with a person or situation rather than what is right, due to a strong taste for perfection. There will be times you feel as though you cannot get away with anything and you are likely to feel resentful. However, it is important to be practical with aspects of Saturn and eventually make use of what you have. That is one of Saturn's important lessons. If you continue to focus on your sense of lack or restriction, that is all that will be realized. Another important level of Saturn's experience is fear, which can be debilitating, causing you to delay or procrastinate, or feel unready, insecure, imperfect, unprepared, and unable to participate in your life.

Saturn is also the planet of consequences. When connected to the Sun, it means a consequential and important life in some way—to be defined by you, the native, who holds this aspect pattern. You have all the power in the world to make it work, or not, in your own particular way. That is the challenge of Saturn.

You will have the opportunity to reach mastery in some area of your life—to be competent, to have expertise, and subsequently be respected and acknowledged, but only after you've done the work. Your character will certainly be tested, particularly with the more challenging aspects of Saturn to your Sun. In fact, this aspect is very much about character, integrity, and the ability to stand firm on principles despite sometimes severe challenges and limitations. Sun/Saturn is essentially life lessons. It indicates a lifetime of graduating to a new level of character—but only if you pass the tests!

So remember, having a Sun/Saturn aspect does not have to be bad. Temperance is a fine quality and you might as well get used to it because, after all, there's nothing you can do about it—not in this lifetime at least. Now, let's explore further what it all means by defining the participants—the Sun and Saturn.

The Function of the Sun

The Sun is the brilliant star and center of our solar system. Without its warmth and abundant generosity, we would, quite simply, freeze to death. In an astrological chart, the Sun represents that dynamic and burning solar principle, the heart of what the native is seeking to express. It is the male principle of externalized expression, —the will to be and do—as well as consciousness or awareness and the mysterious life principle itself. We can include the attributes of light, aliveness, vitality, constancy, loyalty, and ego. As the Sun is the center of our solar system, it is also the central planet in the horoscope, the primary energy necessary for the individual to function effectively and to know who they are. Sun is spiritedness, ego, and our understanding of self—the imperative to shine and be recognized for one's unique contributions.

The Function of Saturn

Saturn is the best reality check in the known universe of planets. This planet reminds us of gravity, of what can be measured, of what is prescribed or compartmentalized, of black and white, of right and wrong, of protecting and preserving, and of time and its passage. It is history and ritual, habit and organization. The tempering quality of Saturn can mean that the native is more cautious, circumspect, or controlled than others. Having this signature can mean a life that is somewhat narrower in scope or one that lacks certain kinds of abundant opportunity. In other words, there can be strictures, judgments, and circumstances that restrict, or even deny, a full flowering of the solar principle. It can also mean a dedicated life—one of focus or having a mission, a sense of purpose, and/or a struggle with the definition of the purpose of one's life. Time and appropriate timing—the lessons of life and the consequences of decisions—are all Saturnine interests. Saturn typically places restrictions in the way, but the ultimate task is to rise to the challenge and master the arena that Saturn rules and describes. The overcoming of obstacles will often make Saturnine types persistent and enduring.

Sun/Saturn Aspects

The Sun is hot, providing warmth, and Saturn will cool, filter, or subdue the Sun's heat by "shading" some of its warmth and fire. The Sun can also empower Saturn to create a life of strong will, purpose, and leadership. It's important to recognize both energies and balance them carefully so one does not overpower the other. Together, this is a strong combination meant for a purpose-driven life, providing that liabilities, weaknesses, and other obstacles can be overcome.

It's true that a strong aspect between the Sun and Saturn places a shade on the Sun's light, but it can just as easily focus and channel the power of the Sun. The soul, or the native, often struggles with an understanding of what is important. Am I important? Is life important? Is what I am doing important? How can I make a worthy contribution? Yet, at least initially (or in the formative years of life), Saturn offers certain kinds of restrictions in the life of the native. We can define those restrictions several ways. Individuals may find themselves "older" at a young age because of an early sense of responsibility, which is either sought out or squarely placed upon their shoulders by childhood circumstances.

A Sun/Saturn aspect can also be defined as a testing lifetime, for the personality and the character, and questions of integrity and major turning points will shape the life. The Sun's basic meaning is the overall quality of one's life and Saturn provides form and definition by its natural compressing function. Since Saturn represents time, maturation, and experiencing life's tests and challenges, a Sun/Saturn aspect often means natives get better as they grow older. Sun/Saturn's security comes from knowing what to expect and doing what is expected in the best possible way. The desire and determination for recognition is also typically high. Any aspect with Saturn involves elements of insecurity or fear. In the case of Saturn with the Sun, this may mean fear of authority; fear of making a mistake; or fear of self-expression due to a fear of negative feedback, criticism, or real or perceived restrictions placed on the native. Sun/Saturn recognizes early the importance of timing, sometimes being too early and sometimes too late. With Saturn the issue is always how well can this be done, how well was it done, and the assessment or judgments that follow performance.

The Four Elements—Fire, Earth, Air, and Water

In your birth chart, you will have both the Sun and Saturn placed in one of the four elements—fire, earth, air, or water—which will further define their overall energy expression in your chart and life.

Fire – Aries, Leo, Sagittarius

Fire represents personal expression, one's image, spirit, energy, aliveness, color, speed, action, warmth, heat, impulsiveness, exuberance, brightness, visibility, outreach, and extroversion. Active in its self-expression and wanting to be seen or noticed, fire ignites and stimulates others into action. It has a natural love of life in all its fullness and seeks to experience life fully. Creative and intuitive, fire is related to the Sun, since the Sun rules the fire sign Leo. If you have the Sun in a fire sign, you will be more naturally enthusiastic because the Sun, a natural fire sign ruler, is more comfortable expressing itself in that element. Fire's enthusiasm means that sometimes it can burn itself out or be unable to recognize its limitations. That's where Saturn comes in as the planet that teaches about limitation. Saturn in a fire sign means your main issues will be to temper the willful or temperamental quality of the ego, as well as a tendency toward selfishness or self-absorption. Fire is preoccupied with experiencing life and living it fully, wholly, and completely.

Earth – Taurus, Virgo, Capricorn

Earth represents familiarity, habit, and the world of the tangible, and the kinesthetic,—of what we can measure and define. It is security, stability, constancy, the reality you create, and the money to pay for your basic needs as well as the luxuries you desire. Earth deals with parameters, rules, foundation, and protection. If you have the Sun in an earth sign, you will be focused on practical realities—making enough money to lead a stable life by establishing the basic necessities of food, clothing, shelter—and cash for a few luxuries. Feeling competent in marketing your skills is also important to you. You will do your utmost to make enough money to provide for yourself and your loved ones, and you want to be seen as reliable, responsible, and respected. If you have Saturn in an earth sign, you may struggle with financial matters at times, or you may put far too much emphasis on attaining material things. You will need to examine your early conditioning about money, your sense of security, and your sense of your own worth, the lack of which could make you unreliable or undependable. Earth Saturns have to remind themselves of their intrinsic worth and what they can give and of the unique talents they have that need to be developed.

Air – Gemini, Libra, Aquarius

Air is the realm of the abstract, the conceptual, and information—of ideas and logical communication, and the unemotional, objective interpretation of life's happenings. Air is representative of sociability, social consciousness, and intermingling with others for the purpose of camaraderie and the sharing of ideas and experiences to generate dialogue and the progress that comes from collaboration and the mingling of viewpoints. Air needs a certain amount of space and freedom to gain perspective on life experiences and events. This element is also often considered "distant or cold." If you have the Sun in an air sign, you probably enjoy communicating and sharing ideas with friends, associates, partners, and co-workers—sometimes anyone who will listen, or any venue for the airing of ideas—radio shows, the editorial page, magazine articles, even books. More than the other elements, air learns through experience the importance of the right words at the right time. If you have Saturn in an air sign, some of your challenges come from the area of communications. You may feel that you cannot find the right words or else feel uncomfortable expressing your emotions verbally. Your schooling may have been curtailed due to a variety of circumstances, or you may prefer the world of experience over "book learning." You may hold back your mental processes and your communication until you feel you have it all figured out for yourself.

Water – Cancer, Scorpio, Pisces

Water is the arena of emotions—of tears, feelings, imagination, desire, human passions, sympathy and empathy, naiveté, compassion, and the natural ability to respond to life with all its nuances. Water is what cannot be physically grasped, but merely felt and sensed. Water is instinctive in nature and when channels are clear, emotional intelligence is high. It is often accused of being "too sensitive," but possesses great gut instinct. Of this element it is often said, "Still waters run deep." Water absorbs and reflects back and therefore has a greater understanding of human motives and human nature than the other elements. Because water remembers through the lens of feeling, habits formed with strong emotional impact may be more difficult to change. If you have the Sun in a water sign, your life is preoccupied with the emotional nature of life and the realm of feelings. You excel in getting a sense of a person, a room, or a situation very quickly, and your psychological perceptions are typically very accurate. Since you operate primarily on your instincts, you learn from experience to avoid certain situations and people based on your "sixth sense." You tend to have strong likes and dislikes—again based on what feels right and comfortable to you at the time. Water Sun signs may be easily swayed by the feelings of others and even victimized by strong-willed individuals who seek to dominate and even domineer by arousing feelings of guilt or by eliciting sympathetic responses. If you have Saturn in a water sign, you may also be very good at denying your feelings, submerging them, or even justifying them. Still, because Saturn demands focus, you will be brought into contact with strong emotional situations during your life, so that you are forced to pay attention to and sort out the feelings that disturb, impress, or distress you—and then master them. One of your difficulties could be holding on to hurt feelings or focusing too much on negative emotional experiences to the point that they run your life and deny the experiences you really want.

Your Sun/Saturn Aspect

Conjunction

You have a conjunction aspect if both your Sun and Saturn are in the same sign and within about 6 degrees of each other. A conjunction requires that the two planets merge and forge a blended relationship with each other, a cooperative partnership.

Your Sun/Saturn conjunction will be in one of the above four elements and in either a cardinal, fixed or mutable sign.

The **cardinal** signs are: Aries, Cancer, Libra, and Capricorn.
The **fixed** signs are: Taurus, Leo, Scorpio, and Aquarius.
The **mutable** signs are: Gemini, Virgo, Sagittarius, and Pisces.

If you have the Sun and Saturn conjunct in a cardinal sign, you will be more inclined, even compelled, to take action and make progress in your life than otherwise. A lack of progress, or the perception of its lack, will frustrate you, so patience will be one of your lessons. You may also have learning experiences having to do with applying the right timing in various situations. You will be attuned to learn about the elements of good timing, sometimes being too early but more often being too late when you delay due to overcautiousness or the fear of making a mistake.

If you have the Sun and Saturn conjunct in a fixed sign, you will encounter a certain amount of stubbornness in yourself or in others. Your ego will want recognition, and you may feel frustrated if you don't get what you feel you deserve. You are likely to have more ability to focus, but also be inclined to inflexibility. An important lesson of this fixed conjunction is to know which battles are worth fighting, when to stand your ground, and when to stand down.

If you have the Sun and Saturn conjunct in a mutable sign, you may often feel unstable, as if things are falling apart or you somehow can't keep it all together, even though you want to. You will need to master the art of sorting through details, information, or just the "stuff" of your life in order to separate "the wheat from the chaff." Mastering discrimination is one of the main lessons of this pattern. You are probably good at multitasking, but may carry it to an extreme and need to find appropriate boundaries.

Sextile

You have a sextile aspect if your Sun and Saturn are approximately 60 degrees apart. A sextile is a bridge, an opportunity between elements and energies that operate in a similar fashion. The sextile aspect offers harmonious interaction and compatibility.

Your sextile aspect will be either between a fire and air sign, or a water and earth sign.

A fire and air sextile is generally more extroverted unless there are other strong indicators in the chart to the contrary. The combination is enthusiasm, energy, and the willingness to take action, along with the consciousness and ability to communicate and exchange ideas about something. However, rashness and impetuousness may upset the apple cart.

An earth and water sextile is generally more introverted or cautious unless there are other strong indicators in the chart to the contrary. The ability to form a strong foundation, and to be in touch with what you want from a situation, is one of the hallmarks of this combination. This is also a practical combination and one that can manifest a reality more easily if the desired outcome is known and the energies are focused. On the other hand, the tendency to get bogged down can also occur because of missed opportunities and lack of follow-through.

Square

If you have a square between the Sun and Saturn, you are sure to feel the challenge of some circumstance that will demand much from you. You may have to overcome the limitations of a difficult childhood or a health problem. The Sun and Saturn in this configuration may deny a set of opportunities to the native that others take for granted. The purpose of this denial is to test the native to determine whether they have the core quality to overcome and develop solar potential in spite of these challenges. The extent to which the individual can compensate or overcome hardship, of course, depends on other factors in the horoscope and on the core consciousness, spirit, or soul. There is, in addition to the above factors, a certain criticalness or judgment associated with this aspect. Some people with this aspect may be too sensitive to criticism, and therefore be unable to accept it, while others may carry a "chip on their shoulder" or build a wall around themselves out of protection or fear of being unacceptable or wrong in some way.

Your square between the Sun and Saturn will be in either cardinal, fixed, or mutable signs.

A **Cardinal Square** (between planets in cardinal signs) increases motivation, competitiveness, and the desire to achieve and move toward a specific goal—to make progress. Because of this factor, this aspect also tends to increase impatience and impetuosity. On the other hand, single-mindedness and "forward-desire" to move toward a goal are typical of a cardinal square.

A **Fixed Square** (between planets in fixed signs) increases loyalty and entrenchment. There is a tendency to find a comfortable groove and stay there, which also means developing and staying with what one has chosen. Stubbornness comes with this situation, and any obstacles or challenges are likely to have a stronger or more lasting impact. Another facet of this aspect is persistence, so when the native has chosen well, what is created will have a sense of permanence.

A **Mutable Square** (between planets in mutable signs) increases information gathering and exchange. This is a multidexterous or flexible signature in that many choices are available, yet perhaps not the one(s) you really want. This square impacts making choices among several options and teaches the lesson of not juggling too many balls (projects) at once or "biting off more than you can chew." Follow-through is another major lesson.

Trine

If you have a trine between the Sun and Saturn, you will rise to the challenge a bit more easily, or you may have the necessary mentors early in life to teach you how to organize yourself and succeed in a worldly way—to organize yourself for participation in the "real world." In other words, you will still have your share of Saturnine challenges, but they are unlikely to be as severe, and you may, in fact, enjoy solving problems and meeting those challenges. The extent to which you master problem solving and are dependable (also positive Saturn characteristics) is the extent to which you will be elevated to positions of responsibility and leadership. It is your sense of stability and careful attendance to matters at hand that will win you accolades and the respect of a higher position.

A trine, or 120 degree aspect, is an easy-flowing contact between planets in the same compatible elements—fire to fire, earth to earth, air to air, or water to water.

Your trine between the Sun and Saturn will fall in fire, earth, air or water signs. The elements are explained above and here is more as it applies to the trine aspect.

If you have a Sun/Saturn trine in fire signs, you are likely to be more active in your pursuit of accolades, credentials, credits, honors, and rewards. Saturn is, after all, about externals and what is manifest or visible—what is strong, sturdy, solid and dependable. You are sure to infuse a certain amount of enthusiasm into everything you do and inspire or encourage others to reach their goals or objectives. Others will enjoy your positive spirit.

If you have a Sun/Saturn Trine in earth signs, you exhibit solidity, stamina, and reliability. You will find a way to manifest your dreams, as your natural marketing skills are sure to be better than average. Being respected for keeping your word will be a task you are critically aware of, especially when you fail to meet your own standards. Stability and staying on task is a bit easier for you.

If you have a Sun/Saturn trine in air signs, you are a natural communicator and have social skills when you need them to meet your goal-oriented needs. You will learn through the experience of time the qualities necessary to get along well with others. You may balk at the niceties and subtle consideration required, but you will benefit from learning them. Communication is key in your world.

If you have a Sun/Saturn trine in water signs, you are naturally empathetic and you are likely to keenly feel the emotional tensions that are part of all situations and contacts. This instinctive ability of yours will allow you to "know" what role each person is playing and to maneuver yourself accordingly to best advantage. Your sensitivity and compassion will stand you in good stead.

Opposition

If you have an opposition between the Sun and Saturn in your birth chart, you will need to learn to balance your energies, especially when it comes to relationships and negotiations. You may initially feel as though you have less to offer in a negotiation than the next person, but that is simply the negative aspect of Saturn speaking. You need to come to realistic terms with your value in any partnership and to accurately assess both your strengths and liabilities. With adequate training and experience you will receive the respectful feedback and the necessary credentials you need. There will be times when you will struggle between feeling on top of the world and other times when you feel insecure and less worthy than others. Resist comparing yourself to others' status, experience, or achievements. The more you learn to be conscious of this swing from one pole to the other, the more likely you are to master this seesaw and make the necessary correction to achieve a fair balance, not only for others but also, more importantly, for yourself.

An opposition is an aspect that holds two or more planets in a tension of 180 degrees—one opposed to the other. It subsequently creates a dynamic of opposites, or of opposing forces. The aspect demands balance and negotiation and the careful weighing or assessment of different positions and views.

The opposition between the Sun and Saturn will fall in either fire/air signs or earth/water signs.

Fire/Air Opposition – If you have the Sun/Saturn opposition in fire/air signs (Aries/Libra, Gemini/Sagittarius or Leo/Aquarius), you will be concerned with how things appear to others. You will need to realize that what is advertised about you is accurate and that you are respected. Thinking and reasoning, ideas and their expressive consequences, and a life of fun, independence, and creativity, will be important to you.

Earth/Water Opposition – If you have the Sun/Saturn opposition in earth/water signs (Taurus/Scorpio, Cancer/Capricorn, or Virgo/Pisces), you will be more concerned with security, family, and survival issues. The tangible world will be more relevant and will also be the area that you can master and excel at. You will strive to understand the satisfaction (or not) that comes from getting what you want or what you thought you wanted.

Yes, you will have many obstacles or some difficult circumstances if you have the Sun and Saturn connected, particularly if the combination is one of the more challenging ones. At the same time, if you pause to understand the message of Saturn, you can hone yourself, your skills, and your intentions to such a level that you will be respected, acknowledged, and given the credibility you deserve. Saturn is a harsh taskmaster, but his lessons are integral to your integrity, your standards, and your ultimate success in the world. By the world, I mean what you show that you are capable of, what you are made of, what you stand for, your core and your essence—all this is the message and test of Saturn. You either meet the challenge or you will feel the weight of Saturn until you finally learn the lesson. With Saturn, there is no short cut—you either take up the challenge or not. Saturn can seem cold and cruel, but it is meant to make you aware of a reality that you create (via your habitual patterns), and it teaches you how to survive. Everyone has a contribution to make to the world, and Saturn demands that you find your unique way of contributing to society and civilization. Saturn asks you to leave something behind, a legacy from the gifts and talents that were given to you by your birth into life on Earth.

About the Authors

Nancy Bennett has had her work published in various places including Llewellyn's annuals, *We'moon*, Circle network, and many mainstream publications. Her pet projects include studying history and creating ethnic dinners to test on her family. She lives near a protected salmon stream where the deer and the bears often play.

Stephanie Clement, Ph.D., is a professionally certified astrologer who has been practicing for over thirty years. She has published numerous articles and has written several books, including *Power of the Midheaven*, *Mapping Your Birthchart*, and *Mapping Your Sex Life*.

Alice DeVille is an internationally known astrologer specializing in relationships, real estate, government affairs, and spiritual development. She has conducted more than 150 workshops and seminars with astrological, Feng Shui, metaphysical, and business themes.

Sasha Fenton now has 120 books to her credit, and she is still writing! Her knowledge is based on years of work as a consultant and teacher, but she says that she is an enthusiastic student, as there is still so much for her to learn.

Dorothy J. Kovach is a practicing astrologer, writer, and timing expert based in Northern California. She helps find the best time to start projects for successful outcomes for businesses and individuals worldwide. Dorothy uses the wisdom of the ancients of both Western and Eastern astrology, in all of her work.

Dorothy Oja is an ISAR certified astrological professional and career astrologer offering complete astrological consulting through her practice, MINDWORKS. She specializes in individual and relationship analysis (not just romantic) as well as electional work. Social commentary is part of her weekly e-zine, *Planet Weather*.

Leeda Alleyn Pacotti practices as a naturopathic physician, nutritional counselor, and master herbalist. A former legal analyst in anti-trust and international law, she enjoys poking a finger in political machinations of all sorts.

Carole Schwalm lives in Sante Fe, New Mexico. She has contributed self-help articles and horoscopes for AOL and other websites. She also wrote for Llewellyn's *2006 Astrological Calendar*.

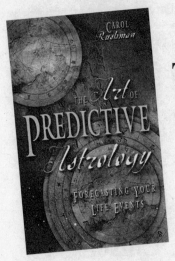

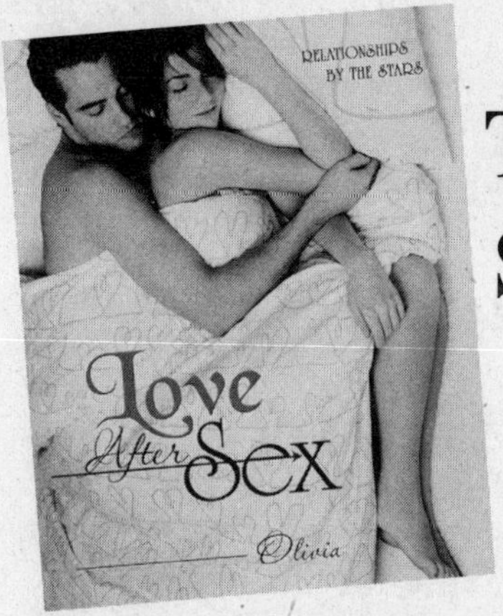

The Lasting Seduction

Seduction is an art, but so is living together! But what happens after the initial infatuation starts to fade and you're confronted with the stubbornness of a Taurus, the impatience of an Aries, or the roving eye of a Gemini? How do you communicate? Can a touch say it all? Olivia, a professional astrologer and author of *Love After Sex*, is here to help you navigate your way through the stormy seas of love.

Love After Sex illustrates how sex, money, and power dynamics play out in relationships based on the Sun sign combinations of the people involved. It also discusses Moon sign characteristics, which indicate how well you are able to emotionally nurture your lover. Real-life scenarios throughout the book illustrate the character traits of each sign, including how you behave in relationships. And once you know what makes you and your partner tick (and what's likely to tick you off!), you're well on the way to making your love last.

LOVE AFTER SEX

Olivia

264 pp. • 7½ x 9⅛

0-7387-0853-4 • U.S. $12.95 Can. $17.50

To order call 1-877-NEW-WRLD

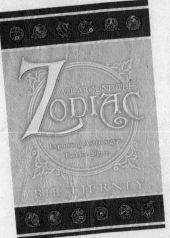